Praise for *Staging Luther*

These Hans Sachs plays led to the Reformation on the ground. There was not only Wittenberg; there were also cities like Nuremberg. There was not only Luther; there were also his admirers: Hans Sachs, a not-so-simple-minded shoemaker, among them. His dialogues breathe fresh impressions of the debates in his time, and they still do so in this excellent and well-annotated English translation.

—Volker Leppin, Horace Tracy Pitkin Professor
for Historical Theology, Yale Divinity School

Not only did the quincentenary of the sixteenth-century Protestant Reformation in 2017 provide ripe occasion for renewed attention to its classic figures and writings; it also granted fresh opportunities to bring into light a lesser-known "cast of characters" like the Lutheran layman Hans Sachs. Shaver and her students' translations of works that appear here for the first time in English, along with the illuminating historical, cultural, and theological introductions to Sachs and his Nuremberg setting (masterfully presented by Robert Kolb), will greatly enrich our grasp of the lay piety and literature that advanced the Reformation movement. An exciting contribution!

—William Marsh, associate professor of theology,
Cedarville University

These delightful translations of Sachs's work bring his plays and poetry into the conversations of sixteenth-century religious literature. Reformation scholars and students of the Renaissance will appreciate the reforming dialogues of the plays paired with insightful historical introductions.

—Jason Lee, professor of theological studies,
Cedarville University; editor of *Matthew* in the
Reformation Commentary on Scripture

This work is an excellent addition to the more overtly theological and social works on Martin Luther and the Lutheran-German Reformation. Being primarily a historian, historical theologian, and political philosopher, I found it outside my "comfort zone" to see these new translations and to be educated that Luther's ideas were transmitted through media apart from prose works. The introductions were also very well written and extremely helpful to those coming to the plays from the arts. These are a welcome and unique addition to Luther studies.

—Marc Clauson, professor of history
and law, Cedarville University

Opening with eminent Reformation scholar Robert Kolb's richly layered exploration of the culture of Nuremberg that produced cobbler, writer, and lay theologian Hans Sachs, *Staging Luther* gives scholars access not only to Sachs's well-known poem "The Wittenberg Nightingale" but also to four of his heretofore untranslated dialogues. In addition to their groundbreaking work of recovering the four dialogues and translating them into modern English, the authors provide meticulously researched footnote references to Sachs's almost-constant biblical allusions in both the poem and the dialogues. Those ubiquitous scriptural allusions evidence Sachs's belief in Luther's teaching of *Sola Scriptura* while also pointing his audience to the absolute authority of God's Word in all matters of faith and practice. Thus, *Staging Luther* establishes Sachs, the self-proclaimed "average man," as a more-than-above-average practitioner and purveyor of Reformation thought whose life and works merit further study.

—Peggy J. Wilfong, professor of English (retired),
Cedarville University

Staging Luther

Staging Luther

FOUR PLAYS BY HANS SACHS

Annis N. Shaver

Ian A. MacPhail-Fausey

Clara G. Hendrickson

Robert Kolb

Authors and Translators

Fortress Press

Minneapolis

STAGING LUTHER
Four Plays by Hans Sachs

Print ISBN: 978-1-5064-8558-4
eBook ISBN: 978-1-5064-8559-1

Contents

Acknowledgments

Our heartfelt thanks go to John S., Teresa, Kristine, and John H. for allowing us to spend long hours on this project. Additionally, we are grateful to our furry friends Hansel, Gretel, Zorro, Zacchaeus, Elsie, Treva, Mira, Sherlock, Lacey, and Günther for their unconditional support.

Introduction

This project began in 2017 as we began to make plans for celebrating the five hundredth anniversary of Luther's posting his Ninety-Five Theses on the door to the Castle Church in Wittenberg. As I began to read and review Luther's writings and investigate the era more closely, I remembered Hans Sachs and the little I knew of him. I had heard of Sachs's poem *Die Wittembergisch Nachtigall* (in English, *The Wittenberg Nightingale*) but had never read it. I knew he was famous for his *Fastnachtspiele* (Fasching/ Shrovetide plays) and *Schwänke* (folksy tales) but quickly learned about his Reformation dialogues, particularly *A Disputation between a Parson and a Shoemaker in Which the Word of God and a Right Christian Character Is Contended*. I realized that such a dialogue would be an ideal way to address the Reformation through the eyes of the populace of sixteenth-century Germany. Knowing that our audience for the celebration would not be familiar with German, whether modern German or late Middle High German, I began to search for an English translation. Finding none and realizing time was growing short, I set about translating *A Disputation . . .* into English. Because the reading of the dialogue was well attended and well received, I began to hatch an idea to translate all four dialogues. When a student started asking about doing a translation for a senior research project, I offered her the opportunity to translate one of the other dialogues. We agreed to finish translating the others. Time did not present itself for finishing that project right away, but another student expressed interest in a similar translation project and agreed to translate the two remaining dialogues. Upon his completion of the project, we three agreed to move forward toward publishing our translation work, adding in a literal translation of *The Wittenberg Nightingale*.

Any translation project can be publishable if there is an audience. We felt then and still feel that the four Reformation dialogues, along with a new translation of *The Wittenberg Nightingale*, written by Hans Sachs, make a worthwhile project that can be of interest to a wide audience. First and foremost, these pieces provide direct insight into the thoughts and opinions of the laity during the time of the Reformation in the German regions. Sachs was an average man yet educated and a member of the middle class in the important market city of Nürnberg. In addition to his business as a shoemaker, he was also a *Meistersinger*, one trained in the art of verse writing, whose *Fastnachtspiele* were well published and widely disseminated because of their catchy rhymes and sarcastic tones. His Reformation poem and four dialogues presented the Reformation message in terminology familiar to the populace of Nürnberg, thereby adding an additional layer of testimony to the discourse. These translations will also be of interest to historians who are interested in sixteenth-century culture as it developed simultaneously with the overpowering cultural upheaval of the Reformation. Finally, English-speaking students of German literature will be interested to engage with Sachs in an easily accessible format in order to get a taste of his prolific career, which spanned over half a century and produced more than six thousand works.

As we have worked closely with these translations, we have come to admire the man who took up the cause of the Reformation, spreading the message to the laity. He took Luther's ideas and spoke them in the language of the common man through the characters of his plays and through his poem. He made clear that the argument of the Reformation was not just a theological discussion among university professors or a political dispute within the alliance that was the Holy Roman Empire but rather a call to make religion a part of one's daily life. In these works, one reads not only the fallacies of the required practices prescribed by the Catholic Church but also the call to make the message of Christ, presented by Scripture alone, an everyday, individual practice. *The Wittenberg Nightingale* allegorically describes how the laity were deceived for centuries and gives the promise of change. *A Disputation . . .* names individual practices required by the church as unscriptural. *A Discussion . . .* addresses specifically the practices of the clergy that serve only the clergy, not the parishioners. *A Dialogue* . . . presents a debate between a rich (Lutheran) citizen and a priest on the topic of greed and unbiblical monetary practices, leaving the reader with the message that greed can affect both Lutheran and Catholic alike. *A Conversation* . . . reminds Lutherans that argumentative words do not win over others to the cause. It is love of one's neighbor that is commanded in the Scripture, not undoing previously prescribed practices. The theme to love one's neighbor is infused into each of these pieces, making it clear that for Sachs, the Reformation was not only a reform of church practices but a reform of the individual.

We can learn from Hans Sachs that doctrine and theological questions do not have to be steeped in dense, academic language. The message of the Scripture is for everyone, even the *gemeiner Mann* (the average man). Sachs was and remains an important voice of the Reformation—a voice that should not be forgotten.

A. N. S.

CHAPTER I

Hans Sachs in Historical Context

The most prominent and productive voices raised to promote Martin
Luther's call to reform in the wake of his Ninety-Five Theses on Indulgences came from theologians at universities or in leadership of the
church in towns and principalities. However, lay voices contributed
significantly to the spreading of Wittenberg reform.

Courtiers on the staffs of the ruler, such as those in Wittenberg—Gregor
von Brück (1485–1557), Christian Beyer (1482–1535), and Matthäus Rat-
zeburger (1501–57)—or Strasbourg, such as Jakob Sturm (1489–1553),[1]
but also a spectrum of those in other social positions broadcast their
delight at Luther's message and their arguments for accepting it. Argula
von Grumbach (ca. 1490–ca. 1564) found the message of Martin Luther
fascinating and liberating, and this noblewoman suffered no little harass-
ment from the dukes of Bavaria because of her published defense
of one of young Luther's followers, Arsatius Seehoffer (1503–45). One of
the most widely read among the lay advocates of Luther's proclamation
was the municipal secretary, the leading civil servant, in Nuremberg,
Lazarus Spengler (1479–1534). From another social situation and with
another genre of communication, the shoemaker and Meistersänger of
Nuremberg, Hans Sachs, used his talents as a public entertainer to help
the common people and their leaders alike see that Luther was calling
them back to the true gospel of Jesus Christ. Like Spengler, Sachs read
Luther and formed his impressions within the milieu of the city to which
their fathers had migrated, Nuremberg.

---

1 Thomas A. Brady Jr., *The Politics of the Reformation in Germany: Jacob Sturm (1489–1553)
of Strasbourg* (Highlands, NJ: Humanities Press, 1997).

Nuremberg as a City of Its Time

In the early sixteenth century Nuremberg lay at the intersection of no less than twelve busy trade routes. That made it a commercial hub. Founded around the castle of a local count in the mid-eleventh century, the town attracted patrician and merchant families engaged in local and distant trade and artisan families engaged in creating the products needed for daily life in the city and beyond. In 1219, it became an imperial city, a "free city," not bound to local princes but answerable only to the emperor of the Germans and his "Holy Roman Empire of the German Nation," precisely so labeled since the late fifteenth century. Burggraf Frederick II constructed the castle of the counts who represented the interests of the empire in 1219. By 1313, the city council had claimed jurisdiction over the counts and in 1427 bought the rights to the castle. Since 1424, Nuremberg had served as the depository of the imperial regalia, and therefore the city remained tightly bound to the imperial throne despite its wide-ranging independence in many matters of governance. In the 1480s, the council had secured local ecclesiastical jurisdiction, and the bishop of Bamberg no longer exercised his power in Nuremberg. This followed a century of increasing control over ecclesiastical institutions within the city. The council assumed administration of foundations set up by families for charitable purposes in the late fourteenth century and increasingly determined policy relating to Nuremberg's monastic institutions. The council began to determine who would be called as priests for the principal congregations, Saint Lorenz and Saint Sebald. Despite its relative autonomy, the city had to tread a fine line between the imperial will and its own best judgment on municipal policies. This became critical as most Nurembergers became convinced by Luther's call for reform.

By 1500, Nuremberg had grown to be among the largest cities of Germany, with some forty thousand to fifty thousand inhabitants, two-thirds the size of Prague, ranked with Cologne, followed by Lübeck and Breslau as the largest cities in the German Empire. Thirty-four patrician families had established their dominance over the municipal government. It consisted of a great council of some two hundred, named by a small council from this patrician group. The patrician families made up about 7 percent of the population, with some 60 percent being merchants in several branches of commerce and artisans of various trades. The coppersmiths, silversmiths, and goldsmiths produced metal work of various kinds. Technicians fashioned astronomical, nautical, and musical instruments. Textiles and weaving continued alongside the new industry of printing. The rest of the inhabitants were journeymen who had not attained the degree of master of their skill set, small gardeners, and the poor and beggars, who worked when jobs were available.[2]

Unlike counterparts in most German towns in the late Middle Ages, Nuremberg's artisans had not organized guilds to regulate their internal standards and conduct and to limit the number of those who became masters in the city. This important social unit was missing in Nuremberg. The absence of guilds accentuated the role of the association of artisans apart from their trades in the singing society of the Meistersänger. The pursuit of this hobby of singing took place within tightly organized choral clubs, for which very specific rules governed the creation of poetry and music in the Meisteränger tradition, going back as much as six hundred years at this point. It provided one means of social interaction and support for some, mostly artisans.[3]

---

2 Details may be found in Gerhard Pfeiffer, ed., *Nürnberg—Geschichte einer europäischen Stadt* (Munich: Beck, 1971), passim; Daniela Kah, *Die wahrhaft königliche Stadt. Das Reich in den Reichsstädten Augsburg, Nürnberg und Lübeck im Späten Mittelalter* (Leiden: Brill, 2018), passim; Berndt Hamm, *Bürgertum und Glaube. Konturen der städtischen Reformation* (Göttingen: V&R, 1996), 15–140; Ronald K. Rittgers, *The Reformation of the Keys* (Cambridge, MA: Harvard University Press, 2004), 9–22; and Harold John Grimm, *Lazarus Spengler: A Lay Leader of the Reformation* (Columbus: Ohio State University Press, 1978), 7–20.

3 Uta Dehnert, *Freiheit, Ordnung und Gemeinwohl. Reformatorische Einflüsse im Meisterlied von Hans Sachs* (Tübingen: Mohr Siebeck, 2017), 63–169.

As a center of urban interests, Nuremberg also established itself as a center of urbane cultivation of the educated within the city. Since the fourteenth century, a spectrum of patrician, merchant, and artisan children received the basic educational program of the time in grammar, rhetoric, logic, arithmetic, geometry, music, and astronomy in four "Latin" schools at the churches of Saints Lorenz, Sebald, and Aegidius and at the hospice of the Holy Spirit. Like other pupils, Sachs learned Greek as well as the language of instruction, Latin. His library shows that he continued to read in both languages as well as German literature.[4] In 1526, Philip Melanchthon came from Wittenberg to help municipal officials establish a new ordinance for the city's formal system of secondary education.[5]

Melanchthon built on a firmly established foundation of the principles of biblical humanism implanted in Nuremberg by the brief periods in which Conrad Celtis (1459–1508) visited the city[6] and by contacts made by Nuremberg merchants as they dealt with colleagues from the Netherlands or Venice, both centers of humanist learning.[7] In addition to their typical accent on the proper rhetorical skills for effective, persuasive communication and their cultivation of the use of ancient sources—whether the Justinian Code, Galen, the Bible and church fathers, or Cicero—these humanists promoted an ethic that combined elements of the late medieval forms of piety with praise of the virtues of the ancients and condemnation of their lists of vices. They turned particularly to the late fourth-century church father Jerome in cultivating rational virtues, and the

4 Dehnert, 68–92; Angelika Wingen-Trennhaus, "Die Quellen des Hans Sachs. Bibliotheksgeschichtliche Forschungen zum Nürnberg des 16. Jahrhunderts," in *Hans Sachs im Schnittpunkt von Antike und Neuzeit*, ed. Stephan Füssel (Nuremberg: Hans Carl, 1995), 109–49.

5 Karl Hartfelder, *Philipp Melanchthon als Praeceptor Germaniae* (1889; Nieuwkoop, Netherlands: De Graaf, 1964), 501–6.

6 Lewis W. Spitz Jr., *Conrad Celtis, the German Arch-Humanist* (Cambridge, MA: Harvard University Press, 1957).

7 Grimm, *Spengler*, 13.

biblical framework for their thinking increased under the influence of preachers in the town's pulpits and also in its cloisters. By 1516, these included Johannes von Staupitz and Martin Luther, both of whom visited Nuremberg occasionally.[8] Such virtues Hans Sachs had learned in school and wrote into his literary works, especially his *Fastnachtspiele* (carnival plays), a popular form of morality play in his time.[9]

The interests of the Nuremberg humanists embraced a wide spectrum of focal points and pursuits. Before Celtis's arrival in Nuremberg in the years around 1500, Johannes Regiomontanus (1436–76) spent the closing years of his life in Nuremberg, there publishing astronomical works and furthering his own research as one of the last of the pre-Copernican Ptolemaists. His disciple Johannes Werner (1468–1522) published works in astronomy, meteorology, geography, and mathematics for use locally and far beyond.

In the years immediately preceding Sachs's birth, the local publisher Hartmut Schedel (1440–1514) was composing his *Chronicle of the World*, a pioneering effort in historiography and cartography. Martin Behaim (1459–1507) left his native Nuremberg but had his globe—the oldest surviving model—produced by colleagues there. Graphic artistic creation flourished in Nuremberg in the early decades of the sixteenth century as Albrecht Dürer (1471–1528), Veit Stoss (1447–1533), Adam Kraft (ca. 1460–1509), Peter Vischer the Elder (1455–1529), Michael Wolgemut

---

8 Berndt Hamm, "Frommer Humanismus und humanistische Frömmigkeit um 1500. Spannungen, Konvergenzen und Synthesen in der Nürenberger Bildungselite," in *Frömmigkeit und Frömmigkeitsformen in Nürnberg um 1500. Pirckheimer Jahrbuch 2018 für Renaissance- und Humanismusforschung*, ed. Franz Fuchs und Gudrun Litz (Wiesbaden: Harrossowitz, 2018), 9–45; Maria E. Müller, "Bürgerliche Emanzipation und protestantische Ethik. Zu den gesellschaftlichen und literarischen Voraussetzungen von Sachs' reformatorischen Engagement," in *Hans Sachs: Studien zur frühbürgerlichen Literatur im 16. Jahrhundert*, ed. Thomas Cramer and Erika Kartschoke (Bern: Peter Lang, 1978), 11–40.

9 Erika Kartschoke and Christiane Reins, "Nächstenliebe—Gattenliebe —Eigenliebe. Bürgerlicher Alltag in den Fastnachspielen des Hans Sachs," in *Hans Sachs: Studien*, 105–38.

(1434–1519), and others practiced their skills and placed their creations across the German-speaking lands and beyond. These efforts formed the context for the intellectual activities promoted by leading citizens of Nuremberg—for instance, Willibald Pirckheimer (1470–1530), whose writings included a defense of Johannes Reuchlin's Hebrew studies and translations or editions of works of Plato, Plutarch, Lucian, Ptolemy, and the church fathers Gregory of Nazianzus and Fulgentius.[10] Christoph Scheurl (1481–1542), who left Nuremberg for a time to serve on the faculty of jurisprudence at the infant University of Wittenberg, shared Pirckheimer's legal interests but published less.[11] The musical life of the city reflected its anchoring in the wider German cultural scene, with the production of liturgical music and hymnbooks[12] alongside the Meistersänger tradition. The origins of this tradition lie hidden in legend and perhaps go back to the tenth century. By the sixteenth century, these bards had established themselves as a prominent form of entertainment for a broad spectrum of the public. The printing press expanded their audience to a new medium.[13]

By the early sixteenth century, the leading minds of Nuremberg had at their disposal a bevy of printers ready to distribute their works. Among the thirty printing operations in the city in the first decades of its involvement in the Reformation, twenty-two published materials from the circle of biblical humanists and advocates of Wittenberg reform.[14] They

---

10 Lewis W. Spitz Jr., *The Religious Renaissance of the German Humanists* (Cambridge, MA: Harvard University Press, 1963), 155–96; Jackson Spielvogel, "Patricians in Dissension: A Caste Study from Sixteenth-Century Nürnberg," in *The Social History of the Reformation*, ed. Lawrence P. Buck and Jonathan W. Zophy (Columbus: Ohio State University Press, 1972), 73–90.

11 Phillip Norton Bebb, "The Lawyers, Dr. Christoph Scheurl, and the Reformation in Nürnberg," in Buck and Zophy, *Social History of the Reformation*, 52–72.

12 Dieter Wölfel, *Nürnberger Gesangbuchgeschichte (1524–1791)* (Erlangen, Germany: Schriftenreihe des Stadtarchivs Nürnberg, 1971), 16–36.

13 Dehnert, *Freiheit*, 103–6.

14 Christoph Reske, *Die Buchdrucker des 16. und 17. Jahrhunderts im deutschen Sprachgebiet* (Wiesbaden: Harrassowitz, 2007), 663–82.

published more treatises by Wittenberg authors than the collective printers of any other town in the German-speaking lands.[15] Although Sachs's early publications appeared from presses in at least seven other towns, Nuremberg printers, including Jobst Gutknecht, Hieronymus Höltzel, Johann Petreius, and Wolfgang Resch, produced his work in print.

Within this cultural context, Hans Sachs emerged, a shoemaker whose command of the language and creative powers propelled him to eminence as a popular entertainer and a serious public voice of Luther's way of thinking.

The Crisis of Pastoral Care at the Time of Hans Sachs

Like Hans Sachs, Martin Luther grew up in a time of intellectual ferment and also rising religiosity, expressed in the fervent pursuit of solutions to the fears and threats of daily life and eternal destiny in the late fifteenth-century German Empire. German society in their time was still emerging from the impact of the bubonic plague at mid-fourteenth century. It had not been the last of the epidemics of its kind; in 1533–34, 1543–44, 1561–63, 1570, and 1573–76, Sachs lived through and in the midst of attacks of the plague on a smaller scale.[16] The specter of death did not cease to hang over German thinking as the population and some measure of prosperity returned during the course of the century and a half following the exhaustion of the Black Death in the early 1350s. The figures of Jesus and Mary along with countless biblical and postbiblical saints attracted devotion from more and more of the populace, but the sense of still falling short of God's demands felt by many created a crisis of pastoral care. New forms of devotion developed to satisfy the longing to please God through sacred ritual and religious activity as well as through proper behavior toward others. Theologians strove to find new religious practices that required less effort to bring some consolation to increasingly restless and anxious believers. Presentations of Christ as

---

15 Andrew Pettegree, *Brand Luther: 1517, Printing, and the Making of the Reformation* (New York: Penguin, 2015), 267.

16 Pfeiffer, *Nürnberg—Geschichte*, 195.

the one who suffers with his people and bears the same burdens they do were coupled with a more intense focus on Mary as the gracious Mother of God, whose mercies flowed to those who loved him and her.[17] These efforts extended to the lowering of the price of indulgences and the expansion of their worth to eternal salvation during the later fifteenth and early sixteenth centuries.[18] Reform was attempted here and there, including within the monastic life in Nuremberg. There the Augustinian Conrad von Zenn (ca. 1375–1460) endeavored to return life in his cloister and others to monastic obedience in strict conformity with the example of Christ and an active life of repentance in the 1410s.[19]

The popular piety of the period centered on human effort, aided by God's grace in Christ, to secure blessings in this life and also life beyond death. This form of Christian living incorporated certain biblical elements that had been set forth by those who initially brought Christianity to the German tribes. But the conversions of most people sprang essentially from the decisions of tribal chiefs or the swords of Frankish conquerors. The preachers and catechists of the earliest years of Christianization were overtaxed by the challenge. Biblical names and ideas penetrated popular concepts of the path of peace with the higher powers, but the structure of the traditional religions framed these names and ideas. Sacrifices had traditionally provided the key to a better life, and the liturgy of the Lord's Supper, representing the sacrifice of Christ, seemed an ideal focus for religious life, especially in view of the insufficient education of most clergy. Most simply were not equal to the demands of preaching and teaching the biblical message, for the Bible's

---

17 Berndt Hamm, *Religiosität im späten Mittelalter. Spannungspole, Neuaufbrüche, Normierungen*, ed. Reinhold Friedrich and Wolfgang Simon (Tübingen: Mohr Siebeck, 2011).

18 Berndt Hamm, *Ablass und Reformation. Erstaunliche Kohärenzen* (Tübingen: Mohr Siebeck, 2016).

19 Hellmut Zschoch, *Klosterreform und monastische Spiritualität. Conrad von Zenn OESA (†1460) und sein Liber de vita monastica* (Tübingen: Mohr Siebeck, 1988). The larger picture of late medieval piety and ecclesiastical life in Nuremberg is sketched by Rittgers, *Reformation of the Keys*, 23–46.

text remained buried for the most part in a Latin beyond the capabilities of a majority of parish priests.[20]

Martin Luther grew up in this religious environment, and its accentuation of the necessity of human performance in conjunction with God's grace found reinforcement in the teaching of his scholastic instructors in theology at the University of Erfurt. They reflected the influence of the stream of thought developed by William of Ockham (1285–1347) and taught to them by Gabriel Biel (ca. 1420–95) and his immediate successors at the University of Tübingen. They taught that God gives his grace to those who do their best. Luther's supersensitive conscience refused to believe that he had ever done his best, so he felt excluded from the process of gaining God's favor through his performance of both sacred and secular good works.

In the midst of his struggles, his superiors in the Augustinian order imposed on him the office of university professor at the infant University of Wittenberg once he had earned his *Doctor in Biblia* degree in 1512. He approached the task with the latest biblical scholarship from biblical humanists, including the Hebraist Johannes Reuchlin (1455–1522) and the Graecist Desiderius Erasmus (1466–1535), with the counsel of his superior in his order, Johannes von Staupitz (1460–1524), ringing in his ears. Staupitz had urged Luther to look to God's predestining will as the only cause of his salvation and to the sacrifice of Christ as the source of complete atonement for his sins. In addition, his own experience as an Augustinian brother aiding priests in the pastoral care of preaching and hearing confessions helped shape his new insights into the biblical message and the Christian life. In the course of lecturing on Psalms, Romans, Galatians, and Hebrews in the years from 1513 to 1518, he came to more and more insights into God's approach to sinners through Jesus

---

20 Keith Thomas, *Religion and the Decline of Magic* (New York: Scribner's, 1971); Robert Kolb, *Martin Luther and the Enduring Word of God: The Wittenberg School and Its Scripture-Centered Proclamation* (Grand Rapids: Baker Academic, 2016), 1–6, 8–10, 17–23, 35–42, 174–79.

Christ for their deliverance from their sinful identity and the restoration of their identity as children of God.

Instead of focusing on his performance of the regulations and rules of the church, Luther came to define what made him a Christian, God's child, as God's initiating and maintaining a parent-child relationship based solely on God's love for him. Being Christian depended on fearing, loving, and trusting in his Creator above all else and hearkening to his word, recorded in Scripture and delivered through oral, written, and sacramental means. For most, that meant through sermons and receiving the Lord's Supper from called pastors within a liturgical setting cleansed of elements that suggested that human performance could contribute to salvation.

Along this path Luther began to bring his new definition of being Christian before the local academic public in Wittenberg. He did so with public university disputations on theses on the boundness of the human will in making decisions about God, which means the sinner's total dependence on God's gift of reconciliation in Christ, and on the bondage of theological thinking to Aristotle's philosophical presuppositions. In late 1517, these insights were overshadowed by the explosion of criticism that resulted from his pastoral protest against abuses in the sale of indulgences. Critics in Rome and in German universities focused on the implied undermining of papal authority and power in these theses. For them, papal authority and power held the church together and guaranteed the ritualistic-hierarchical system that provided the way to salvation. In the wake of the publication of his Ninety-Five Theses on Indulgences and the German explanation of those theses, his *Sermon on Indulgences and Grace*, in late 1517 and early 1518, Luther began to employ the printing press to spread his message beyond Wittenberg—with great success.[21] Printers in Nuremberg and two other printers were responsible for the initial spread of these theses, and the style of printing

---

21 Robert Kolb, *Martin Luther, Confessor of the Faith*, Christian Theology in Context series (Oxford: Oxford University Press, 2009), 72–94.

inaugurated by Lukas Cranach in Wittenberg was "shamelessly copied" by many Nuremberg printers to make their product more attractive.[22]

By 1520, Luther's reconstruction of the popular understanding of being Christian was well underway. His *Open Letter to the Christian Nobility* (August 1520)[23] deconstructed critical practical elements of medieval piety, and his *Prelude on the Babylonian Captivity of the Church* (October 1520) undermined the theoretical reliance on ritual and hierarchy behind those practical elements.[24] His practical guide to Christian living, entitled *On Good Works* (June 1520), was an exposition of the life of following God's commands in the Decalogue and based this life on faith in Christ—on fearing, loving, and trusting in God above all else.[25] The theological framework for understanding the relationship between the Creator and his sinful creatures provided the culmination and climax of the four treatises: *On Christian Freedom* in Latin and *On the Freedom of a Christian* in the author's German translation.[26] Particularly this treatise proceeded from the presupposition of a distinction between the righteousness that God's people enjoyed in the sight of their Creator, "righteousness from outside ourselves" (*iustitia aliena*), and "righteousness that we practice or perform ourselves" (*iustitia propria*).[27] On this view of what it is to be human he built his understanding of the restoration of righteousness in God's sight through his word of promise, the gospel of Jesus Christ. Through

---

22 Pettegree, *Brand Luther*, 75–77, 161.

23 WA 6:404–69; LW 44:123–217.

24 WA 6:497–573; LW 36:3–126. The title provokes the question, To what is this treatise a prelude? Luther does suggest in its preface that "when the most learned papists have disposed of this book, I shall offer more" (WA 6:501, 13–15; LW 36:17). One possibility is that this work of deconstruction of the ritual-hierarchical view of being Christian laid the foundation for the assertion of the evangelical alternative in Luther's view based on God's approach to sinners through his re-creative word of promise, as expressed in *On Christian Freedom*.

25 WA 6:202–76; LW 44:21–114.

26 WA 7:20–38 (German), 42–73 (Latin); LW 31:333–77.

27 Luther developed this "distinction of two kinds of righteousness" in his treatise on that subject (cf. WA 2:145–52; LW 31:297–306).

trust in God's pronouncement of the believer's sharing in Christ's death and resurrection, resulting in the exchange of the identity of sinner for the identity of child of God, freedom is granted to serve God as he designed human beings to serve him.[28] Believers were to hearken to his plan for life, set down in the structure of places in the social grid. These places included the household, including family life and economic activity; society; and the church. In the responsibilities or "offices" given to them in each, they were to obey his law by loving others as they loved themselves and serving those within their reach in self-sacrificial love.[29] This message fit nicely into the world of civic virtues that Sachs had learned in school, and its background in the gospel conformed to the desire for consolation that Sachs shared with the population of the city at this time.

Luther's reputation and his writings commanded almost immediate attention and respect in Nuremberg. The frequent visits of Johannes von Staupitz to the city's Augustinian Eremite cloister had paved the way for Luther to visit there as well. In 1516, Staupitz preached against indulgences in Nuremberg.[30] In the same year, Wenceslaus Linck, who had studied and taught alongside Luther in Wittenberg and lived in the Black Cloister of the Augustinian Eremites there, became prior of the Augustinian cloister in Nuremberg, bringing a strong voice for Wittenberg reform to the city. He participated in a circle of humanist intellectuals there who had dubbed themselves the *Sodalitas Staupitiana*. Later some called it the *Sodalitas Martiniana* in honor of the Wittenberg

---

28 On the formulation of this message in Luther's *On Christian Freedom*, a treatise that influenced Hans Sachs, see Robert Kolb, *Luther's Treatise* On Christian Freedom *and Its Legacy* (Lanham, MD: Fortress Academic / Lexington, 2019).

29 Andreas Stegmann, "The Development and Structure of Luther's Ethics," *Lutheran Quarterly* 33 (2019): 137–52; Gustaf Wingren, *Luther on Vocation*, trans. Carl C. Rasmussen (Philadelphia: Muhlenberg, 1957); Paul Althaus, *The Ethics of Martin Luther*, trans. Robert C. Schultz (Philadelphia: Fortress, 1972).

30 Johann von Staupitz, *Lateinische Schriften 2: Libellus de exsecutione aeternae praedestinationis . . .*, ed. Lothar Graf zu Dohna and Albrecht Endriss (Berlin: de Gruyter, 1979).

visitors. Connections between the electoral Saxon court and Nuremberg had brought Christoph Scheurl to a professorship in law in Wittenberg. Municipal secretary Lazarus Spengler and artist Albrecht Dürer joined many fellow citizens in welcoming the call for reform from Wittenberg.[31] Citizens of Nuremberg sent their sons to Wittenberg; Hieronymus Baumgartner (1498–1565), who returned home because of his parents' opposition to his desire to marry Katherina von Bora, remained in close contact with Melanchthon and other Wittenbergers, as did others of his generation who had studied there. Andreas Osiander came from the University of Ingolstadt to Nuremberg's Augustinian cloister in 1520, accepted the appointment to serve as pastor of Saint Lorenz parish in 1522, and declared himself a follower of Luther.[32] This presence of veterans and sympathizers of the Wittenberg reform brought about a transformation in the population's attitudes toward traditional ways of practicing their faith and a desire for change.[33] Hans Sachs read what was being written in Wittenberg. The spirit of reform, along with the conviction that Luther understood Scripture correctly, guided his creative production as a Meistersinger, a popular entertainer whose verse set to music provided inspiration to many who could read German or could hear it read. During his "dry period" of creative productivity between 1520 and 1523, he undoubtedly received a great deal of positive input regarding the Wittenberg call for reform, and he apparently digested it eagerly. Luther's translation of the New Testament appeared in September 1522, and Sachs must have devoured it.

---

31 Grimm, *Spengler*, 26–27.

32 Gottfried Seebass, *Das reformatorische werk des Andreas Osiander* (Nuremberg: Veren für Bayerische Kirchengeschichte, 1967). On Osiander's later tensions with the council and others in the ministerium over confession and absolution, cf. Rittgers, *Reformation of the Keys*, 98–214. On his disputes over the doctrine of justification that erupted after he left Nuremberg in 1548, cf. Martin Stupperich, *Osiander in Preussen, 1549–1552* (Berlin: de Gruyter, 1973); and Timothy J. Wengert, *Defending Faith. Lutheran Responses to Andreas Osiander's Doctrine of Justification, 1551–1559* (Tübingen: Mohr Siebeck, 2012).

33 Rittgers, *Reformation of the Keys*, 47–79.

Nuremberg's Early Involvement in Wittenberg Reform

Municipal secretary Lazarus Spengler composed a defense of Luther that appeared in print against the author's will in 1519; this tract earned him a place alongside Luther in John Eck's bull of excommunication issued by Pope Leo X shortly before the Diet of Worms. In this treatise he had praised Luther for his Scripture-based teaching and for showing the proper way to true Christian freedom on the basis of sound reasoning. Luther, Spengler argued, focused on freeing the conscience and on practicing the Christian life. His teaching addressed the issues at hand in the church. He stated, "No teaching or preaching has seemed more straightforwardly reasonable, and I also cannot conceive of anything that would more closely match my understanding of Christian order as Luther's and his followers' teaching."[34] Although the municipal government had not yet committed itself to Wittenberg reform, it did not suppress this public servant, who went on to publish a presentation of "the chief articles of the Christian faith," with a preface by Luther's close friend and colleague in Wittenberg, Nikolaus von Amsdorf, in 1523,[35] about the time that Sachs's *The Wittenberg Nightingale* reached the book stands in marketplaces.

As a leading imperial city, Nuremberg had a natural place at imperial diets even if the imperial cities did not have rights equal to those of princes at them. At the imperial diet in Worms in 1521, Lazarus Spengler attended as one of the city's representatives, and Luther's personal statement before the diet reinforced his commitment to the cause of Wittenberg reform. In his report to colleagues in the municipal government, Spengler commented that participants in the diet could be divided into

---

34 Spengler, *Schützred vnd christenliche antwurt ains erbarn liebhabers götlicher warhait der hailigen geschrifft/ auff etlicher widersprechen/ mit antzaigunge warüber Doctor Martini Luthers leer nitt samt vnchristnlich verworffen/sonder mehr als Christenlich gehalten werden soll . . . Apologia* (Augsburg: Sylvan Otmar, 1519). This citation is the translation of Pettegree, *Brand Luther*, 214.

35 Spengler, *Die haubtartickel durch welche gemeyne Christenheyt bysshere verfuret worden ist* (Wittenberg, 1522, and in two subsequent editions).

two groups: those who favored the pope over the truth and those who had the good of God's kingdom and the Holy Roman Empire at heart.[36] In the following three years, Emperor Charles V summoned the diet to Nuremberg three times, where the papal legates representing the Roman court's opposition to Luther encountered open contempt on the streets of the city.[37] Spengler practiced impressive diplomatic skills in guiding municipal policy between, on the one hand, thoroughgoing adoption of Luther's and Melanchthon's views and, on the other, avoidance of unseemly offenses against imperial policies that aimed at the eradication of Wittenberg reform and the execution of its leadership. Hans Sachs did run afoul of council censors with one sharp attack on the papacy, but for the most part, the municipal government permitted the city's most prominent popular propagandist for Luther's cause to publish his powerful presentation of Luther's thought at home and in other towns. For in so doing, Sachs also promoted the civic virtues and solidarity that the council recognized as essential to the welfare of Nuremberg.[38]

In the wake of Sachs's *The Wittenberg Nightingale*, Spengler's *Chief Articles*, the proclamation of the preachers, and maneuvering in the city council, reform measures took on momentum as Nuremberg became firmly committed to Wittenberg reform and to the leadership of principalities and towns with similar policies.[39] Over the years of its existence, Nuremberg had had a sometimes cordial, sometimes tension-filled or hostile, relationship with the family Hohenzollern, members of which served as local counts in early times and as rulers of the neighboring principalities of Franconian Brandenburg. By 1523, Margrave Georg of Brandenburg-Ansbach had committed himself personally to Luther's theology and sought to introduce Wittenberg preachers into the parishes

---

36 Grimm, *Spengler*, 35–47.

37 Armin Kohnle, *Reichstag und Reformation. Kaiserliche und Ständische Religionspolitik von den Anfängen der causa Lutheri bis zum Nürnberger Religionsfrieden* (Gütersloh, Germany: Gütersloher Verlagshaus, 2001), 105–247; Grimm, *Spengler*, 60–65.

38 Dehnert, *Freiheit*, 12–15.

39 Rittgers, *Reformation of the Keys*, 80–97.

of his lands, opposed to some extent by his brother Casimir but supported by the powerful imperial city at the northeastern border of the county. The city council under Spengler's leadership began to work closely with representatives of the court of Margrave Georg to reinforce mutually the advance of Wittenberg thought and practice throughout the region.[40]

Throughout Sachs's lifetime, Nuremberg continued to have a prominent voice in the circle of evangelical princes and towns, and his writing reflects his continued interest in the course of the Reformation.

---

40 Martin Gernot Meier, *Systembruch und Neuordnung. Reformation und Konfessionsbildung in den Markgraftümern Brandenburg-Ansbach-Kulmbach 1529–1594. Religionspolitik—Kirche—Gesellschaft* (Frankfurt: Peter Lang, 1999), esp. 25–29, 48–56, 104–27.

CHAPTER 2

The Life and Works of Hans Sachs

Of the preachers, craftsmen, and artists who contributed to the Reformation movement in the early 1500s, Hans Sachs stands out as an exemplary spokesman—conscientious, reflective, and committed to his ideals. His down-to-earth yet highly knowledgeable writings served to spread the knowledge of Reformation theology throughout the working classes in a clear and captivating way. Like many men of his time, there is not much written about Sachs by his countrymen. The primary source for what we know about Sachs and his life comes in fact from his own autobiographical statements scattered throughout his numerous works. Altogether, these and his other writings give a clear picture of who Sachs was, what he believed in, and those things of most importance to him.

Pre-Reformation Years

Sachs was welcomed into the world in Nürnberg on November 4, 1494, the only child of Jörg Sachs, a respected tailor. Though a craftsman himself, Jörg prioritized his son's education and, in doing so, laid a strong foundation for Hans's future contributions to society. At seven years old, Sachs began attending *Lateinschule* (grammar school), where, according to his later recollections, he learned grammar, geography, singing, astronomy, and Latin, among other things.[1] Here he showed a clear comprehension and craving for learning consistent with his scholarly future. After eight years of study, at fifteen years old, he began a two-year apprenticeship to a shoemaker. During his subsequent years as a

---

1 In this poem from 1568, Hans Sachs reminisces about his childhood experiences.

Als ich in meiner Kindesjugend	When I in my youth
Erzogen ward zu Sitt' und Tugend,	Was raised to customs and virtue
Von meinen Ältern zu Zucht und Ehre	By my elders for breeding and honor
Dergleich hernach auch durch die Lehre	The same afterward also through lessons
Der Präceptoren auf hoher Schule,	By the preceptor of the higher school
So saßen auf der Künste Stuhle,	Sitting in the arts chair
Der Grammatika, Rhetorika,	Grammar, rhetoric
Der Logika und Musika,	Logic and music
Arithmetika, Astronomia	Arithmetic, astronomy
Poeterei, Philosophia—	Poetry, philosophy—
Ward meinem sinnigen Verstand,	My sensical understanding
Die Lehr' durch hohen Fleiß bekannt	Was known through diligence in the lessons
Ich lernt' da Griechisch und Latein	I learned Greek and Latin
Wol reden artig, wahr und rein;	Well enough to speak true and pure
Auch Rechnen lernt; ich mit Verstand,	Also calculations I learned to comprehend
Die Ausmessung von mancherlei Land;	The measuring of various lands
Ich lernt' die Kunst auch der Gestirn',	I learned the art of the stars
Die Geburt der Menschen judizir'n,	To justify the birth of mankind
Auch die Erkenntniß der Natur . . .	Also the awareness of nature

wandering journeyman, he spent time in many towns across modern-day Germany and Austria, including Regensburg, Passau, Salzburg, Hall im Inntal, Braunau, and München, to name a few. For a time, he stayed at the court of Maximilian I in Innsbruck, where he was first introduced to *Meistersingen* (master singing) and resolved to cultivate the art of poetry alongside his work as a shoemaker. The first principles he learned from Leinhard Nunnenbeck, a linen weaver, and he published his earliest poem in 1513. During his year in München, he helped lead a school for *Meistersingen* and went on to found his own in Frankfurt am Main.

The art of *Meistersingen* was an honorable pursuit for men of Sachs's artisan class, allowing all types of craftsmen to try their hand at beautiful works of poetry and song. It differentiated itself from the looser patterns of *Volkslieder* (folk songs) as well as the *Minnesang* (poetry) of the high courts from which it originally developed by being constructed around a very strict set of rules and forms called the *Tabulatur*. As Richard Zoozmann describes, aspiring poets had to follow thirty-two rules, such as the number of syllables, the rhythm of the syllables, and the line rhyme.[2] Whether spoken or sung, a pleasant sound was the goal, often utilizing modifications of correct word form and sentence structure to reach this. One result of this exhaustive set of rules was sometimes a tendency toward simplicity and banality of content in an effort to comply. The truly successful poets managed to create beauty and originality within the established structure. Adherence to these rules was judged at the *Schule* (school) meetings on Sundays, as a panel of critics mercilessly counted each mistake in a performance against the standards. Meeting all requirements would result in the bestowal of official masterhood, signified by a costly wreath placed on the fortunate performer. Originality itself was, however, not a requirement. Poets mainly set their own words to the *Ton* (meter and melody) of prior artists, as Sachs did in his first-ever written piece. Due to a push from Hans Folz in the school at Nürnberg toward more freedom, some of the restrictions on allowable melodies

---

2 Richard Zoozmann, *Hans Sachs und die Reformation: In Gedichten und Prosastücke* (1904; Hamburg, Germany: SEVERUS Verlag, 2017), 7–8.

and subjects were loosened there. This gave Hans Sachs more room to experiment and write some of his own melodies, thus displaying his talent for and mastery of the art. He went on to be an important influence on the Nürnberger school, helping lead it to its larger popularity and membership in comparison to other schools of the time. Over the course of his life, he eventually strayed more and more from the regulations of *Meistersingen* in his numerous works as a free, creative poet.

Sachs utilized 272 different *Töne* (plural of *Ton*) across his numerous *Meistergesänge* (songs in the *Meistergesang* format). Of these 272, 13 were his own compositions, including "der gülden Ton" (the golden tone), "die morgenweis zu Nürenberg" (the morning melody at Nürnberg), and others. As other *Meistersingers*, he wrote his poetry mainly in *Bar* form, using an AAB melodic verse (not to be confused with rhyme scheme) with three or more stanzas. These would follow the pattern of two *Stollen* (stanzas) using the same exact melody (an *Aufgesang*, or up-song), followed by a different *Stollen* with a similar melody (the *Abgesang*, or down-song). In his poem *The Wittenberg Nightingale* we see Sachs utilize rhyming couplets of eight or nine syllables throughout, as exemplified in the first few lines of the poem.[3]

In 1516, Sachs returned to Nürnberg from his journeys as a man more knowledgeable of the world and the people he would go on to write for. His choice to return home also put him in a very good position for influence due to the situation of the city itself. At this point in German history, Nürnberg had reached its highest point, having attained an influential position in the stream of trade. It was also home to a school

---

3 The number of syllables in the following section of *The Wittenberg Nightingale* proceed as eight, eight, nine, and eight. "Tag" and "Hag" rhyme, as do "Nachtigall" and "Tal."

Wacht auf, es nahent gen dem Tag!	Wake up, the day is drawing nigh!
Ich hör singen im grünen Hag	I hear singing in the green hedges
Eine wunnikliche Nachtigall;	A winsome nightingale;
Ihr Stimm durchklinget Berg und Tal.	Her voice rings through mountain and valley.

for *Meistersingen* that would become quite influential. Upon his return, Sachs built his cobbler's trade and pursued mastery, soon becoming known as one of the most skillful and successful shoemakers in the area. At the time, however, one could only be considered a master workman after being honorably married. Thus, in September 1519, Sachs married Kunigunde Kreuzer, a seventeen-year-old young woman from a neighboring town. The newlywed pair received the house that Sachs had grown up in as a wedding gift and began what would be a happy marriage of more than forty years together.

Reformation Times

The defining circumstance of Sachs's lifetime was without a doubt the Reformation movement, begun by Martin Luther in 1517. This crucial time in the history of Germany and the Christian church allowed Sachs to have a far more prominent life than he otherwise would have had. At the point where he stepped into the picture of the Reformation, the movement had already experienced several key points. Luther's ideas had spread through Germany like wildfire in the late 1510s, largely due to intense interest in his Ninety-Five Theses. Key ideas included in Luther's works included justification by faith as the only path to salvation, challenges of a Christian's dependency on the Catholic Church, and total supremacy of the Scripture as the source of truth. The movement continued despite Luther's excommunication from the church in 1521 and his designation as an outlaw later the same year.

At the beginning of the Reformation, Sachs had returned from his journeyman years just a year prior, perfectly poised through his status, education, poetic skill, and experiences to lend an influential voice to the discussion. However, Sachs was clearly not hasty to jump into the brewing drama. As the Reformation ramped up in the three years following its birth, he focused on the masterhood of his trade and his new marriage to Kunigunde. In the years from 1520 to 1523, we find a distinct and irregular gap in poetic writings broadly assumed to be a time when Sachs poured himself into the study of Scripture and Luther's writings, of which he had collected at least forty by 1522. Luther had also published his own translation of the New Testament in 1522, which would have greatly aided Sachs's studies. Just as Luther put a primary emphasis on "sola Scriptura," Sachs continued this theme in his writings, almost exclusively using Scripture to back up his characters' viewpoints. The immense number of verses used throughout *The Wittenberg Nightingale* and the four Reformation dialogues points to an author who was thoroughly knowledgeable and reflective regarding the Holy Bible—and Luther's translation specifically.

In 1523, Sachs finally broke his silence with *The Wittenberg Nightingale*, clearly announcing his position on the side of Luther and the evangelical movement. The poem became instantly popular, with six editions printed the same year. As well as declaring his religious and political viewpoints, this poem fulfilled the purpose of explaining to the common, uninstructed man the current religious disputes and dramatizing Luther's struggles. As it praised Luther, it also effectively delivered his message. The very next year, Sachs published four Reformation dialogues, marking his first and only departure from poetic form into the world of prose. The first two continue Sachs's critique of the Catholic Church, while the second two also tackle internal issues within evangelical circles. Although this order is widely accepted among scholars, the actual publication order is not definitely known. There is also a record of the number of dialogues being seven, though the contents of the remaining three have not been passed down through history. The four dialogues and the *Nightingale* were published in pamphlet form, with all but the fourth dialogue accompanied by an illustration. Among the designers of the woodcut illustrations were Sebald Beham, who was later accused of radical involvement and expelled from Nürnberg, and Erhard Schön, who went on to collaborate extensively with Sachs over the following years.[4] During the peak of the Reformation controversy, pamphlets like these were an important medium for the dissemination of

---

4 Rosemarie Bergmann, "Hans Sachs Illustrated: Pamphlets and Broadsheets in the Service of the Reformation," *RACAR: Revue d'art canadienne / Canadian Art Review* 17, no. 1 (1990): 12.

information. They were relatively simple and quick to print, inexpensive, and easy to conceal from authorities. Works like those of Sachs, written in language understandable and relevant to a common person, were vital to the growth and spread of Reformation ideas.

Although a strong supporter of Luther and contributor to the Reformation movement, Hans Sachs was by no means a passive follower. As aforementioned, he undoubtedly devoted a great deal of time to studying Luther's works and comparing them to the Scripture before publishing any stance in either direction. This commitment to keeping himself theologically active and accountable to the Bible amid the strong opinions and voices of the time speaks volumes of his integrity and conscientious nature. Though *The Wittenberg Nightingale* granted him a receptive audience, he did not stay entrenched in publishing more of the same to continue his success. After his firmly antipapal viewpoints were expressed, he was certainly not a one-dimensional copy of Luther in every view. Instead, he acted as both a spokesperson and critic of the Reformation in the years following. His early Reformation works can accurately be described as strongly anti-Catholic and pro-Luther, but this transitioned in the following years to a focus on the person of Christ instead. According to Sachs, the only way to Reformation was in the peaceful spreading of God's word and the working of the Holy Spirit, not in rabble-rousing sensationalism. Ironically, he was accused and reprimanded by the Nürnberg city council a few years later in connection with religious radicalism due to a collaboration with the preacher Andreas Osiander. They ordered him to stick to his primary trade of shoemaking, though later evidence suggests that he did not heed that warning.

In many ways, Sachs focuses on similar issues to Luther and the majority of the Reformers, including the sufficiency of Scripture, the centrality of grace, and justification through faith. His very high opinion of Luther and his work to further these concepts throughout Germany is exemplified in the flattering portrayal found in *The Wittenberg Nightingale*. Over time, however, Sachs differentiated himself in several ways. He focused on social issues such as the treatment of the poor lower classes, the civic responsibilities of clergy and religious leaders to contribute to the common good, and fairness in financial transactions. To Sachs, social reform and good works toward others were a necessity for successful theological reformation and evangelical faith.

Sachs's writings and ideas were well timed in his home city of Nürnberg, adding another persuasive voice to the mix of opinions. In 1523, when Sachs first spoke in favor of Lutheran ideas, tensions and uncertainty were growing as the general populace increasingly leaned toward the new teachings and some into even more radical thoughts. Other artists and writers of the town aired their views through their own various types of works, including other pamphleteers, artists, and preachers. The dissension reached a boiling point in 1524, as Sachs was writing and publishing his four Reformation dialogues. Finally, in March 1525, the Nürnberg city council spent eleven days discussing and deciding on an official stance toward this new movement, becoming one of the first imperial cities to formally recognize and cooperate with the Reformation. Throughout the conflict, the city council had been involved in its growth and direction, choosing to tolerate, encourage, protect, or hinder the movement's various activities, with the overall goal of maintaining civic peace throughout.[5] This highly involved but flexible stance, as well as the early official decision made by the city council, served to protect the city from greater violence and turmoil that other cities of the time experienced while still allowing some space for growth and consideration of alternate ideas.

Sachs after the Reformation

After the crucial years of the Reformation movement had passed, Sachs showed greater consistency and steadfastness than his counterparts by continuing to publish on spiritual-related matters, though he did not again take the same explicitly pro-Reformation stance as in his early works. Among his later religious works are adaptations of Catholic hymns

---

5 Guenther Vogler, "Imperial City Nuremberg, 1524–1525: The Reform Movement in Transition," in *The German People and the Reformation*, ed. and trans. R. Po-chia Hsia (Ithaca: Cornell University Press, 1988), 46–49.

into evangelical theology—for example, changing the name of saints or Mary to Jesus instead. In the 1530s, he began to transcribe large portions of the Old and New Testaments into verse, resulting in a large body of compositions designed for the public performance of Scripture. These works generally began with verse transcription, which used close approximations of the original wording of Luther's translation. Sachs would conclude with an explanation and interpretation of the text and its significance to the listener, including an emphasis on the most important points.[6] This format would have made it easier for a broad audience to understand the sometimes difficult concepts handled in Scripture. Sachs also continued his pattern of independent thought, publishing poems in 1539 and 1540 critiquing what he viewed as the decline of the Reformation. In these he grieved the lack of change in people's lives as a result of the evangelical faith they had supposedly accepted.[7] As mentioned before, Sachs was especially preoccupied with the functional outworkings of faith rather than just the intellectual or inward acceptance of it.

The rest of Sachs's personal life progressed with both joy and sorrow. He spent forty years in a happy marriage to Kunigunde, in which they had five daughters and two sons. Throughout this time, he penned several verses about marriage, some joyful, some in a jesting nature about the peculiarities of women. While conveying both light and dark sides of married life, all these poems carry an underpinning of love for his dear wife. In 1560, she passed away, leaving her devoted husband alone in grief, as all seven children had previously died. Except for writing a touching, sorrowful poem in Kunigunde's memory, Sachs's generally prolific output was very subdued during the years of 1560 and 1561. He did not spend much time in widowerhood, however, as per the custom of the time. In late 1561, he married Barbara Harscher, a young widow

---

6 Philip Broadhead, "The Biblical Verse of Hans Sachs: The Popularization of Scripture in the Lutheran Reformation," in *The Church and Literature*, ed. Peter Clarke and Charlotte Methuen (Suffolk: Boydell Press, 2012), 125.

7 N. Walling Clark, "Hans Sachs, the Poet of the Reformation," *Methodist Review (1885–1931)* 11, no. 5 (1895): 706–7.

with several children. The joy that she brought back into Sachs's life is exemplified by the complimentary and loving poem he penned about her a year after their marriage, in which he goes into great detail about her physical and personal virtues, a topic so far not found among his works.

Over the course of his life, Sachs was a singularly prolific poet and writer, with the total of his works coming to at least six thousand by his own account. A large number of these would never have been published, being written specifically for public performance. Although historical counts differ, one source numbers his output as 4,275 *Meisterlieder* (songs in the *Meistersingen* format), 73 folk songs, 1,700 rhyming couplets (of which 208 are plays), and 7 prose dialogues.[8] He also persevered diligently at his primary craft, working at his shoemaker's bench even until sixty-three years old. This indefatigable, faithful man finally passed away at eighty-two years old on the evening of January 29, 1576. He was buried in the Cemetery of St. John along with Albrecht Dürer and other important Nürnbergers, though the knowledge of the specific gravesite has been lost over the years.

The following selection of Sachs's works includes some of his most influential and exemplary published pieces. In them the reader can see Sachs's talent for imaginative and image-filled poetry as well as the clarity and directness of his critiques. He showcases his extensive knowledge and deep understanding of Scripture, which he used to earnestly seek truth and measure his society against it. They rightfully deserve a place among the most skillful and effective products of the pro-Reformation movement. Through these English translations of Sachs's Reformation writing, we hope to allow English-speaking Reformation scholars an opportunity to experience and appreciate Sachs's impact on the growth of the movement among the laity.

---

8 Karl Pannier, *Hans Sachs' Ausgewählte Poetische Werke* (Leipzig: Verlag von Philipp Reclam, 1879), Projekt Gutenberg, https://www.projekt-gutenberg.org/sachs/poetwerk/poetw00.html.

CHAPTER 3

The Translation Process

A common conception of the work of translation is that it is a direct, one-to-one task, where the translator takes a given message in the language of origin, called the source text, and relays an equivalent message in the target language, into the target text. Thus, translators are sometimes seen as having a functionally simple job, as they may be viewed as simply "saying something again." However, this is a misconception of the complexity of translation and loses sight of the creative work of the translator, whose function is that of an artist who interprets and expresses the ideas of a source text in the medium of a separate language. Translation is generally seen as creating what is known as equivalence. Anthony Pym states that equivalence means there is equal value word to word or phrase to phrase.[1] In addition to equivalence, scholars have proposed translation theories that shift the focus from the text itself to the target audience. One of the principal and most revolutionary translation theories is Skopos theory. *Skopos* is the Greek word for goal, aim, or purpose. Skopos theory is defined by Pym as the idea that a text should be translated to express the communicative purpose of a translation.[2]

The two theories, Skopos and equivalence, can function simultaneously in the case that the *skopos* of the translation includes maintaining a certain level of equivalence—that is, the purpose of the translation includes "loyalty" to the source text. According to Clara G. Hendrickson, however, Skopos theory is not commonly applied to literature-based

---

1 Anthony Pym, *Exploring Translation Theories* (New York: Routledge, 2010), 7.
2 Pym, 44.

translations, such as the translations in this book.[3] Additional theories of translation are domestication and foreignization theories, which concern themselves with the effect that the translated text has on the intended audience. Foreignization as described by Xuxiang Suo is translating a text in a manner that leads the reader to recognize that the source text is foreign.[4] This means retaining the source text's cultural features rather than transforming them to be easier to understand for the target audience. Domestication is the transformation of the cultural features and what makes a text "feel" foreign to suit the cultural setting of the target audience. The audience for whom we translated *The Wittenberg Nightingale* and the four Reformation dialogues is made up of Reformation scholars, those interested in church history or Reformation literature who are not able to read Middle High German.

Obstacles to Translation

These texts were written approximately 350 years prior to the first spelling reforms of modern German at the First Orthographic Conference of 1876. Due to the lack of a unified writing system, German was written to phonetically reflect the dialect of the author. Sachs was no exception to this, spelling words differently even among his own works. One of the most apparent and classic examples of this is the way that Sachs spells *ein* in the title of each work, with the variations *ain*, *eyn*, and *ein*. These variations in particular may be due to the use of the printing press and the limited number of available letters that were needed to print one page with the press. Some examples of the unique spelling put forth by Sachs include the spelling of *Brot* as *Prot*, *sie kommt* as *sie kumbt*, and *sieht* as *sicht*. Though unique, Sachs's spelling did have fairly predictable patterns that were important for the translation team to differentiate in ambiguous

3 Clara G. Hendrickson, "The Translation Process in Interaction between Purpose and Context," *Linguistics Senior Research Projects* 22 (May 2019): 3, https://digitalcommons.cedarville.edu/linguistics_senior_projects/22/.

4 Xuxiang Suo, "A New Perspective on Literary Translation Strategies Based on Skopos Theory," *Theory and Practice in Language Studies* 5 (2015): 176–83.

situations. One such ambiguous situation is Sachs's spelling of both *geben* and *gehen* as *gen*. This particular example with *gen* further complicates the translation, as he may have used *gen* to preserve his poetic form and rhyming scheme in *The Wittenberg Nightingale*. Recognizing Sachs's spelling conventions was both necessary to the translation of the text and a useful tool for ridding troublesome portions of the source texts of ambiguity. Additionally, Sachs's pattern of either omitting or changing noun endings complicated the process of identifying the case markings, which could show the difference between whether a noun was possessive or instead a direct or an indirect object in the phrase.

While the spelling of words was a tricky first obstacle, the lexical items in the text were also quite different from modern German terms and often required research into their range of meaning according to Middle High German. Not only were many of the lexical items in the text different from modern German words, but some also either no longer existed in modern German or were used in an entirely different sense in the modern variety. A good example of this is found in the first dialogue with the word *nasweis*, which in modern German would mean "nosy" but in Middle High German meant being wise as a dog with his nose to the ground; thus, we chose to translate it as "astute."

Another challenge while translating Sachs's texts was the decision of which meaning a word had in its context and which English words to choose to best convey that meaning. Certain words are difficult to translate because either they refer to a very wide range of meanings or they are more or less abstract and can also refer to an emotion or idea or imply a change of intensity. In the text, one example that we encountered was the intensifier *in voller Schwank*, which would literally translate to "in full tale." At some points we translated this as "in full swing" and at others as "in full power."

Sentence structure was yet another difficult part of translating Sachs's works; Sachs was indeed a fan of relative clauses and was generous with them. It does not take a long look at his works to see that Sachs painted these works with sequences of relative clauses, often even embedding them into one another. While this did not pose a problem for Sachs's intended audience in his time, it certainly created an obstacle to translation where the information that was carried or implied across relative clauses needed to be joined or separated differently in English in order for the target text to reflect the meaning of the source text. An example of a sentence constructed of many relative clauses, which we divided into multiple sentences, is the following:

> Weiter regiert der Geiz gewaltiglich unter den Kaufherren und Verlegern, die da drucken ire Arbeiter und Stueckwerker; wenn sie inen ir Arbeit und Pfenwert bringen oder heim tragen, da tadeln sie in ir Arbeit aufs hinderst, dann stet der Arbeiter zitrend bei der Tuer mit geschlossnen Henden, stilschweigend, auf dass er des Kaufherren Huld nit verlier, hat etwann vor Gelt auf die Arbeit entlehent, alsdann rechent der Kaufherr mit im wie er wil.

> *Translation:* In addition, greed violently reigns among the merchants and distributors who employ these methods to oppress their employees and workers. Whenever workers take up the fruits of their labor or carry home their penny's worth, their work is rebuked to the extreme, and then the poor worker stands trembling at the door with folded hands, frozen in silence, so that he does not lose the favor of his boss, the merchant, having borrowed some money from his work. Consequently, the merchant deals with him as he wants.

Yet another difficulty in the translation process was translating idiomatic phrases, as there were multiple considerations of how to properly convey them. Idiomatic phrases could be substituted for an English equivalent, though this would lose the cultural value of the original. They could also be translated literally to a word-for-word equivalent of the source text, but in doing so they would lose their idiomatic application and could be confusing and feel foreign to the reader. We resolved this dichotomy by translating the idiomatic phrases literally and providing their contextual meaning in the footnotes. This method seemed to be the most applicable to our purpose to minimize the total loss of meaning as a result of the translation. A clear example is found in the third dialogue with the phrase "sagt mirs . . . under der Rosen"—literally, "tell it to me . . . under the roses"—which we translated as "tell it to me . . . in confidence."

Cultural differences also posed a challenge to translation, as they demanded consideration for the words used for group titles/identifiers. For example, the word *evangelisch* appears many times throughout these texts, yet it does not refer to the same group of people or to their religious beliefs as the word "evangelical" in modern English does. This word might more closely align with the English word *Protestant*, though still having different social and cultural implications about the people who are being referred to. Another such example would be the term *Romanisten*, which was used to refer to the members of the Catholic Church in the mid-sixteenth century. Due to the large time gap, the beliefs and practices of Catholic Church members have changed drastically since the Reformation age, and thus the designation of "Catholics" does not imply the same social and cultural connotations as today.

Verse references also created an obstacle to translation for four major reasons. First, the Bible that Sachs would have quoted did not yet contain verse numbers, which were not added until 1551 in the Geneva Bible. This meant that for every reference Sachs made, he only used the chapter in reference to Scripture, which complicated the process of finding the exact verse being referenced. Second, a few of these Scripture references were inaccurate or printed incorrectly, which meant searching through multiple chapters to find a verse that was referred to in the source text. One example of this is found in the first dialogue, where Sachs references Exodus 22 but in the original writes "Exodi xij," which in English would be "Exodus 12." Third, the verse references were from the Latin Vulgate Bible, which meant that the references to the books of the Bible were written in Latin and named according to the Vulgata. For instance, the book of 1 Samuel became "3 Regum." Also, the books of the Apocrypha were included, which meant that "Ecclesiasticus" was not Ecclesiastes but the book of Sirach. Fourth, the characters in Sachs's texts did not quote the verses word for word but rather paraphrased the verses that they referenced, sometimes paraphrasing a larger portion of text than just a single verse. Thus, finding which verses were being referenced became a challenge, as it meant looking for similarities and imagining what the referenced verse(s) might sound like when not paraphrased. One example is a reference in *A Disputation . . .* where Sachs named a verse in Job 5 and gave the meaning "A man is born to work as a bird is born to fly." We chose Job 5:7, which says, "Man is born to trouble as the sparks fly upward."

Despite these issues, contextual clues in Sachs's works allowed for discernment in most cases of ambiguity, and an analysis of the continuing themes of the text made it easier to settle any uncertainty in problematic portions of the text. Many word choices throughout the translation of the text were made based on the idea of discourse analysis, the examination of linguistic patterns that occur across stretches of spoken and written texts.[5]

Translation of *The Wittenberg Nightingale*

Translation of poetry is always a complicated task. There are many considerations about which features to maintain from the original and which features are acceptable to lose. For this reason, we chose to adopt Skopos theory, focusing on the purpose and audience of the translation to decide our priorities. Examples of previous English translations of *The Wittenberg Nightingale* include one in 1883 by C. W. Schaeffer and another published in 1917 by Charles Harvey Genung. Genung translated to preserve the rhyming features of the original—namely, an AABB rhyming pattern that was characteristic of Sachs's poetry. However, in preserving the rhyme of the original, the said translation allowed for a loss in the accuracy to

---

5 Brian Paltridge and Wei Wang, "Researching Discourse," in *Continuum Companion to Research Methods in Applied Linguistics*, ed. Brian Paltridge and Aek Phakiti (New York: Continuum International, 2010), 256–73.

the original meaning,[6] and as a consequence of this loss, it was our goal to provide a translation that was accurate to the meaning of the original despite not maintaining the original rhyming scheme, thus establishing our *skopos*. For example, in Genung's translation of *The Wittenberg Nightingale*, he translates "den Holzweg ein"—literally, "in the wooded path"—as "to the break." Another example is his translation of the line "Mit Scheren, Melken, Schinden, Fressen," which he translates as "They prowled, and greedy watch did keep." We translated this line as "Sheering, milking, skinning, devouring" and noted that these verbs symbolize a purposeful, systematic dismantling of the sheep for the wolves' own benefit. The perception that there is an incurred loss in the meaning of the original by maintaining the rhyming scheme can also be seen from Randall W. Listerman's comment that he "came to see that while the results [of maintaining Sachs's form] might amuse scholars, the general reader would find them alien and the actor impossible to recite with conviction."[7] Generally, the reader of Genung's translation would find the poetic style pleasant, but a large amount of creative license is required to maintain the rhyming scheme.

While using language that feels natural to the intended audience is important, of greater importance to the purpose of this translation of *The Wittenberg Nightingale* is its accuracy to the meaning conveyed by the original text. A translated portion of a source text may be deemed accurate when the function that the original portion serves, its meaning, and any details are also found in the target text, even if the word order is rearranged or the length, punctuation, syntactical features, or rhetorical devices are different in the target text.

A major difficulty when translating poetry is the challenge of poetic license. Poetry is by nature one of the most liberal and creative writing forms, and as such, it often follows that poets adapt words in a creative

---

6 Sándor Hervey, Michael Loughridge, and Ian Higgins, *Thinking German Translation*, 2nd ed. (London: Routledge, 2006), 25.

7 Randall W. Listerman, *Nine Carnival Plays by Hans Sachs* (Ottawa: Dovehouse Editions, 1990), 24.

manner to portray the image that they would like while continuing rhyming schemes, meter, or other poetic devices. The employment of poetic
license takes many forms previously mentioned, including shortening
words by removing vowels, changing vowels to fit a rhyming scheme,
leaving off inflected endings, and other forms as well. The inflected
endings that denote grammatical gender in German serve the purpose
of informing the reader of what or who is written about and what the role
in the sentence is for that noun. The absence of these endings became a
challenge with the translation of *The Wittenberg Nightingale* because the
poetic license that Sachs used, coupled with the pre-reform spelling of
his writing, created ambiguity, especially found at the end of a line of the
poem. A strong example of this is when Sachs rhymes *verbieten* with *Güte* by
changing the latter to *Gieten*.

The Importance of These Translations

We chose to translate these dialogues into modern English because there
seem to be none in existence (except for the 1548 translation of the first
dialogue by Anthony Scolocker, titled "A goodly dysputacion between a
cristen shomaker, and a popysshe parson with two other persones more,
done within the famous citie of Norembourgh. Translated out of [the]
Germayne tongue into Englysshe"). Despite previous translations of
The Wittenberg Nightingale, we found it useful to provide a literal translation
designed for our target audience. It is important to note that there are
many ways that a translator can translate one text and that each translation serves a function or gives a new perspective of the source text. Thus,
our purpose for translating those texts that had already been translated is
deeply rooted in bringing the reader to a more intimate understanding
of the message and cultural context of Sachs's writings about the Reformation. For those translations that had not yet been translated, we felt
it was important for the modern English reader to have access to these
influential works of the Reformation age. In a similar way to how Sachs
felt it important to write more than only one dialogue and *The Wittenberg
Nightingale*, it is important that if a reader has access to one dialogue,
they should be able to read the accompanying three dialogues as well.

Through loyalty to the original text, maintenance of cultural features of the original text, and a focus on the target audience, our translations address the modern reader so as to remove them temporarily from the current cultural moment and allow them to understand and experience the period in which Sachs wrote while the message of the translated text remains precise to its source.

Translation Aides

It is rare that any translation can be made without the use of dictionaries, glossaries, and other aids. The translations included here are no exception. We made use of multiple dictionaries in order to provide the best translation possible. After spending much time with these "friends," it seems right to give them credit here. The *Deutsches Wörterbuch von Jacob Grimm und Wilhelm Grimm* was invaluable as a comprehensive source for word usage dating back to the Middle Ages.[8] *LEO German-English Dictionary* is a reliable source for modern German usage.[9] Finally, the work of Walter Tauber, *Der Wortschatz des Hans Sachs. Band 1, Untersuchungen* and *Band 2, Wörterbuch*, provided not only translation assistance but also insight into Sachs's writing style.[10]

---

8 Jacob and Wilhelm Grimm, *Deutsches Wörterbuch von Jacob Grimm und Wilhelm Grimm*, Trier Center for Digital Humanities, Wörterbuchnetz, continually updated at https://www.woerterbuchnetz.de/DWB.

9 *LEO German-English Dictionary* (Sauerlach, Germany: LEO GmbH), continually updated at https://dict.leo.org/german-english/.

10 Walter Tauber, *Der Wortschatz des Hans Sachs. Band 1, Untersuchungen* (Berlin: Walter de Gruyter, 1983); Walter Tauber, *Der Wortschatz des Hans Sachs. Band 2, Wörterbuch* (Berlin: Walter de Gruyter, 1983).

CHAPTER 4

The Wittenberg Nightingale

Die Wittenbergisch Nachtigall
Die man yetz höret vberall.

Ich sage euch/wa dise schweygē/so werden die stein schreyē Luce.19.

Introduction

The Wittenberg Nightingale was Sachs's first text written in support of Luther and the movement to reform the church. It is the best known of all the texts included in this book. Published in 1523, it is the result of Sachs's hiatus from writing his well-known *Fastnachtspiele*[1] and his intense study of the newly translated Bible.

---

1 Sachs's stock-in-trade was the plethora of *Fastnachtspiele*: plays/dialogues written to be performed during the *Fasching* season, the season before Lent. His plays

Sachs's support for the Reformation movement is evident through his use of Scripture to support his arguments within this poem as well as in the four subsequent dialogues. Quotes from Scripture support Luther and argue against the teachings of the pope and those of the Catholic Church. It is remarkable how well Sachs knew the Scripture only a year after the publication of Luther's translation of the New Testament.

Sachs wrote *The Wittenberg Nightingale* in verse form using an AABB rhyme scheme for the full seven hundred verses of the poem. He also made use of strict rhythm, both according to an original *Bar* format. As can be expected with poetry, he took poetic license with his word usage and grammatical forms. Word endings that denote tense, subject-verb agreement, or grammatical case (noun function) are often dropped. Sachs's use of poetic license made translating this poem doubly difficult because in the German language, inflectional morphemes (word endings) are more important than word order. Thus, a missing morpheme can easily cause a thought to be misinterpreted.

Historians and theologians recognize parts of the poem: the evils of the church (particularly as they affected the common man), a summary of Luther's theology, the reaction of the pope, and the plan of salvation.[2] The poem makes heavy use of animal allegories, such as sheep to represent the laity of the church; the serpent and his offspring to represent the pope and the clergy (also represented by the lion and the wolf); a goat to represent Hieronymous Emser; the cat, Thomas Murner; a donkey, the barefoot Franciscan monks; the snail, Johannes Cochlaeus; and of course the nightingale, Martin Luther. The poem contains no markings to indicate a new topic or direction within the poem. There are no

---

were satirical, tongue-in-cheek dialogues that poked fun at well-known people and situations.

2 Harold John Grimm, *Lazarus Spengler: A Lay Leader of the Reformation* (Columbus: Ohio State University Press, 1978), 63; Guenther Vogler, *Nuremberg 1524/25 Studien zur Geschichte der reformatorischen und sozialen Bewegung in der Reichsstadt* (Berlin: VEB Deutscher Verlag der Wissenschaften, 1982), 77.

stanzas. In this translation, a shift in topic or focus has been indicated with a footnote.

This poem, as well as three of the four dialogues translated here, was published along with illustrations, which added a visual element to entice the illiterate. The illustration accompanying *The Wittenberg Nightingale* pictures all of the animals noted. The nightingale is high in a treetop, out of the reach of the animals who would prey on the sheep.

The poem has been translated here using Skopos theory—translation targeting a particular purpose or audience. The audience for this text includes Reformation scholars as well as literati interested in German literature of the Middle Ages. This translation, although at times laborious, seeks to remain as close to the original meanings and ideas as possible.[3] Trying to match Sachs's form in rhythm and rhyme would result in a loss and modification from the original direct meaning of his poem and would too often veer from the ability to express the meaning of the content in today's English.[4] This translation follows the lead of Randall W. Listerman, who noted he "came to see that while the results [of maintaining Sachs's form] might amuse scholars, the general reader would find them alien and the actor impossible to recite with conviction."[5] Of interest to the reader would be the 1917 rhymed translation by Charles Harvey Genung[6] or the 1883 translation by C. W. Schaeffer.[7]

---

3 Robert Pinsky mentions facing the same challenge when translating Dante's *Inferno* from the Italian. He chose to retain the sense of the original, not the form. Robert Pinsky, *The Inferno of Dante: A New Verse Translation*, bilingual ed. (New York: Farrar, Straus and Giroux, 1994), 20.

4 Randall W. Listerman, *Nine Carnival Plays by Hans Sachs* (Ottawa: Dovehouse Editions, 1990), 25.

5 Listerman, 24.

6 Charles Harvey Genung, "The Nightingale of Wittenberg," in *The Library of the World's Best Literature: An Anthology in Thirty Volumes*, ed. C. D. Warner et al. (New York: Warner Library, 1917).

7 C. W. Schaeffer, *The Wittenberg Nightingale* (Allentown: Brobst, Diehl, 1883).

Sachs relies solely on Scripture to support the claims of the evangelical against the Catholic. As an aid to the reader, each verse reference has been noted. Sachs cited by chapter only, whereas we have provided specific verse references (verse numbers were not added to Scripture until 1551). Footnotes have been used to identify specific German or Latin words or phrases that have been translated other than literally or to add contextual information for the reader.

The Wittenberg Nightingale

which one now hears everywhere

I tell you, if these are silent, then the rocks will cry out. Luke 19[8]

Wake up, the day is drawing nigh!
I hear singing in the green hedges
A winsome nightingale;
Her[9] voice rings through mountain and valley.
The night is declining in the Occident,
The day is dawning in the Orient,
The red-glowing morning sky
Shines through the gray clouds.
The bright sun peeks through,
The moonlight is dying away;
He[10] has become pale and dark,
Who earlier with his false brilliance
Had blinded the whole herd of sheep,[11]
So that they turned away
From their shepherd[12] and the meadow
And abandoned them both,[13]
Left to follow the light of the moon
Going into the wilderness along the path

---

8 Luke 19:40: He answered, "I tell you, if these were silent, the very stones would cry out."

9 A nightingale in the German language is grammatically feminine; thus, the feminine pronoun is used to refer to the nightingale.

10 The moon in the German language is grammatically masculine; thus, the masculine pronoun is used, and this ties the darkness of moonlight to Pope Leo X, referred to hence as a lion leading the sheep (believers) astray.

11 As in Scripture, followers of Jesus are often referred to as sheep.

12 Jesus Christ is the shepherd of this flock.

13 Both the shepherd and the meadow.

They heard the voice of the lion[14]
And followed after him
Who led them with a ruse
Far away deep into the wasteland.[15]
For that reason they lost their sweet meadow,
Having to eat weeds, thistles, and thorns;
The lion lay a hidden snare for them
The sheep fell into it with anguish.
Where the lion found them ensnared,
He tore them apart, then swallowed them up.
Such provision helped
A whole pack of destructive[16] wolves
To possess the miserable herd[17]
With shearing, milking, skinning, devouring;[18]
Also many snakes lay in the grass,
Suckling the sheep relentlessly
Through all suffering down to the marrow.
Because of this the sheep became scrawny and gaunt
Throughout the very long night,[19]
And they have just now awakened,
Because the nightingale sings so clearly,
And insistently sings of the brightness of the day,
Which calls their attention to the lion,
To the wolf, and also to their false meadow.

---

14 Pope Leo X.

15 *Wüste*: Desert, used in comparison to the beauty and bounty of the meadow.

16 *reißender*: More than destructive, ripping and tearing.

17 The sheep.

18 These verbs express a purposeful, systematic dismantling of the sheep by the
    wolves for their own benefit.

19 The night refers to the time under the control of the lion (the pope). Sachs
    has mixed multiple metaphors for this time under the pope's influence (means
    of torture, night, desert, cold and ice, the presence of wolves and snakes) in
    order to make clear the desolation of this time.

Because of that the furious lion is awakened,
He rages and is not deterred
By the song of the nightingale
As she announces the rising sun,
From which his kingdom has been taken.
Because of that the furious lion is angry,
Stalking the nightingale for her life
Cunningly in front of, behind, and next to her;
But he can't grab her.
In the hedges she can sleep well[20]
And sings merrily forever.[21]
Now the lion has many wild animals,
That snarl at the nightingale,
Wild donkeys, pigs, bucks,[22] cats, and snails;[23]
But their howling is for naught.
The nightingale sings much too clearly
And lays them all low,
Also the snake's offspring stirs itself,[24]
It rustles strongly and fights[25] against
And greatly fears the light of day.
The wretched herd will evade him[26]
From whom they [previously] nourished themselves
[in] the long and well-measured night,
Praising the lion as still the best,

---

20 Luther was well protected.

21 *für und für*: Forever, on and on.

22 *Böck*: Perhaps a *Ziegenbock* (male goat). This would align with his later reference to these animals.

23 Sachs identifies such animals at the end of the poem with the names of Luther's foes.

24 The snake here is in reference to Satan appearing in Genesis in the form of a snake.

25 *widerficht*: Fencing against; swordplay.

26 Referring to the good shepherd.

His meadow is sweet and good,
Wishing to burn the nightingale at the stake.
In a similar manner the frogs croak
Back and forth in their lakes
Over the nightingale's racket,
For their water wants to avoid him;[27]
The wild goose also cries honk-honk
Against the bright light of day,
And they all cry out together:
What does the nightingale sing that is new?
She announces to us the delights of the day.
As if the sun alone is fruitful,
Disdaining the shine of the moon.
She remains silent and still in her nest,
Making no commotion among the sheep.
She should be punished with fire,
But this call to death is futile;[28]
The dawn of the day is shining here,
And the nightingale sings so clearly,
And very many sheep in this flock
Return again from this wilderness
To their meadow and mild shepherd.
Some of them resoundingly announce the day
In the same manner as the nightingale.
Against them the teeth of the wolves do shine,
Chasing them[29] into the thorny hedges
And martyring them to the blood[30]
And threatening them with a blaze of fire;
[So that] they should remain silent about the day;

---

27 Implying that the water is unsettled.
28 The call of the lion for the death of the nightingale.
29 The sheep.
30 Killing them.

So they show them the sunshine.

The shine that no one can hide.

Now[31] that you do more clearly understand

Who the dear nightingale is,

Who declares to us the bright day:

It is Doctor Martin Luther,

Of the Wittenberg Augustinian order,

Who awakens us from the night,

Into which the moonlight brought us;

The moonlight refers to the human message[32]

Of the Sophists[33] back and forth

Within the past four hundred years[34]

Who have been driven according to their reason

And have led us far astray

From the evangelical message

Of our shepherd Jesus Christ

To the lion in the desert.

The lion is the pope,

The desert the spiritual practices

With which he greatly seduced us

To human schemes,[35] as we now recognize them.

That with which he had pastured us,

Interpreted as serving God, which now goes

In full power around the whole earth

With[36] becoming monks, nuns, pastors,

With wearing cowls, shaving heads,

---

31 At this point, Sachs's focus changes to an exposition about the meaning of the
first part of the poem.

32 The message of the pope.

33 Referring to the followers of Sophocles.

34 Since Gregor VII—1076.

35 In contrast to scriptural teaching.

36 Here begins a list of the human schemes, traditions of the church.

Day and night praying in church,
Midnight Mass, prime-time prayers, third prayers,
    evening prayers, Compline,[37]
With waking, fasting, long prayers.
With hoeing in the garden, lying in the shape of a
    cross,[38]
With kneeling, leaning, bowing, bending,
With bell ringing, and organ playing,
With holiness, candles, carrying banners,
With smoke[39] and blessing bells,
With keeping lamps lit, selling grace,
With the blessing of churches, wax, salt, water;
And the same for the laity
With sacrifices and burning little candles,[40]
With pilgrimages to serve the holy ones,
The evening fasts, celebrating the day,
And penance according to the old practices;[41]
With brotherhood and wreaths of roses,
With reading indulgences, church attendance,[42]
With kisses of peace, observing holiness,
With monastic [financial] support and church building,
With great cost to decorate the altar,
Practicing Communion in the manner of the Welsh,[43]
[With] silk Mass garments, golden vessels

---

37 Referring to the eight daily prayer periods practiced in monastic orders.
38 Lying in a prone position, facedown.
39 Incense.
40 *Liechtlein*: Little lights.
41 *. . . nach der alten Leiren*: According to the old lyres (old ways or old practices).
42 The implication is attending church for the purpose of being seen or recognized.
43 References any people group other than Germanic.

With monstrances[44] and embossed silver,[45]
Created in abbeys with income and interest.
This is all called worship by the pope.
He says: one earns heaven with it
And absolves the shadow of sin.
It is of course unfounded in the Bible,
Vain poetry and human sin
In which God takes no pleasure.
Matthew 15[46] says:
They serve me in vain
In their human laws;
So also this type of plant is
Tilled and torn out completely,
That my Father did not plant.[47]
Listen, you entire holy state,
Where are you with your earthly works?
Now let us notice the noose:
This means to us the pope's net,
His decrees, commands, laws,
With which he coerces the sheep of Christ;
With [the threat of] banishment[48] he forces us
     to penance,
All year long to go to the Sacrament,

---

44 A receptacle used in the Catholic celebration of Communion, often ornate.

45 Silver melted and poured into forms for artistic purposes.

46 Matthew 15:3: He answered them, "And why do you break the commandment of God for the sake of your tradition?"

47 Matthew 15:13: He answered, "Every plant that my heavenly Father has not planted will be rooted up."

48 *Ban*: Excommunication, which prohibits the excommunicated from taking the Eucharist and participating in the litany; the *Ban* was for a limited time.

In banishment [they are] forbidden from the blood of
    Christ,[49]
Due to banishment mandated, every year
To fast for forty days in truth.[50]
Otherwise many days and the quarterly fast[51]
Also to avoid meat and eggs;
Many days he commands celebrations,
Other days forbids weddings,
Fatherhood,[52] and various plans;
He forbade to marry
Monks and priests with banishment;
But of course, they like to have prostitutes,
Pious people injure their children,
And replace wives with strangers[53]
The pope has innumerable commands such as this,
Which of course God did not command;
[He] chases the people to the abyss of hell,
To the devil with body and soul.
Paul pointed out to him
In Timothy 4[54]
And speaks: the Spirit says clearly,
That in the last times,
Many will leave the faith

---

49 Participating in the sacrament of Communion.

50 The forty days of Lent.

51 *Quatemer*: Referring to a quarterly fast; in other texts Sachs uses *Quatember*.

52 Accepting and celebrating the responsibility of being a godparent at a christening.

53 Divorce.

54 1 Timothy 4:1–3: Now the Spirit expressly says that in later times some will depart from the faith by devoting themselves to deceitful spirits and teachings of demons, through the insincerity of liars whose consciences are seared, who forbid marriage and require abstinence from foods that God created to be received with thanksgiving by those who believe and know the truth.

And cling to the devil's salvation.

People will forbid marriage

And some food, which God through goodness

Created with thanksgiving.

I think that is clear enough.

Now let us look to the wolves,

Who helped the pope in this situation,

To lead such tyranny:

Bishops, provosts, priests, and abbots,

All prelates and ministers,

Who suggested to us the human teachings

And suppressed the word of God,

Taken with warnings,

And when one looks at it with the light,

It is as if it is judged by money.

One has to give money at the baptism,

One has to buy the confirmation from him,[55]

One has to give money as penance,

One gives money at Mass,

The sacrament has to be paid,

If there is a wedding, one gives everything,

If one dies, they[56] sing for money,

If one would not do it, one will be forced,

Even if one has to sell a cloak.

Therefore, they pluck the wool out of us;[57]

And what they require [from us] through simony,[58]

They deposit [for themselves] as extortion.

From twenty gulden[59] [comes only] a malt grain.

---

55 The pope.

56 The church, the mourners.

57 Pull the stuffing out of us.

58 The selling of religious objects for profit.

59 Currency.

In my opinion that means the sheep are shorn;
Also the way they strongly bind the mouths of the
    people,
Dragging them to the country.
As one bans them because of their guilt
Since one plays God with them,
And they drive them out with torches.
The poor farmers miss serving the Lord,
Which the slave drivers celebrate,
Half of the time sitting around in the pub.
Four sacrifices one has to give to him,
And the same thing for the Mass money.
And in addition to that on the holidays,
They carried around the little board;[60]
Always at church dedications[61] they write about money,
They set up the annual market as a holy time
At which they have indulgence declarations.[62]
They allow coins to be buried in the church;[63]
Therefore, the poor folk have had enough;
That means the sheep of Jesus have been milked!
The stationers[64] also come around,

---

60 A board for tallying up the money each person had given to the church for various requirements.

61 *Kirchweih, Kerwe*: The dedication of the church (the founding of the church) is celebrated annually, even to this day.

62 Bulls.

63 This most likely refers to the practice of burying coins along with the dead as a way of paying a fee for the burial. Burial fees, which were originally considered unacceptable by the church, were becoming more and more prevalent.

64 Various individuals and groups who solicited for various causes.

Antonians,[65] Valentinians,[66]
They tell many lies
About what has happened here and there,
Applying to women and men
With a gold-plated donkey tooth[67]
And also extort the power of money,
Enrolling people in their brotherhood
They get the interest year-round.
Then a single regiment comes;
One calls them in German the Romanists.[68]
With great boxes of indulgence bulls,[69]
They erect red crosses on flags
And call out to women and men:
Put your money in, give your help and taxes,
And save the soul from purgatory.
As soon as the money rings in the boxes,
The soul flies up to heaven.[70]
Whoever has unworthy[71] goods in his power,
They help them to get rid of them.
There are also letters for guilt and anguish;
One puts in gulden for that too.
The joker's rope is so varied.
That means Roman oppression to me.
Further notice the bishops,

---

65 The Antonians sold relics of Saint Anthony as a means of curing *Antoniusfeuer*, an illness caused by fungus on grain. The term *Antoniusfeuer* was also used to name distemper, even lupus, and other diseases.

66 The Valentinians sold remedies for *Saint Veltins Krankheit*, or epilepsy.

67 In the Middle Ages, it was believed that kissing a donkey would cure a toothache.

68 Referring to Catholics. This term was also used in the four dialogues.

69 Certificates.

70 The slogan used by Johann Tetzel, best known as a seller of indulgences in Luther's time.

71 Extra, unnecessary.

How it continues in their courts,
With notaries, officials,
With secretaries and beadles[72]
And their fallacious holy rights,
As one mistreats both mighty and lowly,
Also how one shreds marriage
And takes money and other things,
And they necessarily pledge together;
Also how they rant with the people,
Who are chased to him[73] in penance,
Who somehow have gone perhaps
To meat or eggs during the fast;
They question them sharply,
As if they had committed a murder,
Also how they avoid banishment,
How they summon it and renew it,
Also how they tax the poor folk.
Also with the wild and the hunted
Do they damage him in his fields,[74]
Stopping robbers in their locations,
Who rob, murder, are put into stocks, snarl.
Also the bishops wage war with resistance,
Pouring out much Christian blood,
Making wretched widows and orphans,
Burning villages and ripe fields,
Rotting, tricking, squeezing the people;
I mean they eat up the sheep.
Christ got rid of such wolves.

---

72 *Pedellen*: In modern German, *Hausmeister*: a caretaker of a school or business
who usually lives on the premises, much like a "super" in a large apartment
building in the United States.

73 The pope.

74 *am Getreit*: On the grain, meaning planted fields.

Matthew 7[75] states:

Beware of false prophets,

Who roam around in sheep's clothing,

Who, inwardly he says, are ravenous wolves;

You'll know them by their fruit.

In Mark 12,[76] he explains.

Speak: Beware of the Pharisees,

Who like to go around in long robes

And like to be greeted by everyone

In the markets and streets, where they stand,

And like to sit in high places

In school and also at dinners.

They devour the widows' houses

And go about praying long prayers;

For that reason, they will, you understand,

Fall into greater damnation.

O, how does Christ portray

The godless character of our spiritual ones,

As if he [Christ] had been with them [the spiritless]
    just now!

Thereby they are recognized with seeing eyes.

The snakes who swallow up the little sheep

Are monks, nuns, the lazy bunch,

Who sell their good works

For money, cheese, eggs, candles,[77] and fat,

For hens, meat, wine, grain,[78] salt

---

75 Matthew 7:15: Beware of false prophets, who come to you in sheep's clothing but inwardly are ravenous wolves.

76 Mark 12:38–39: And in his teaching he said, "Beware of the scribes, who like to walk around in long robes and like greetings in the marketplaces and have the best seats in the synagogues and the places of honor at feasts."

77 *licht*: Light, but most likely candles, another valuable commodity.

78 *Koren*: Corn or grain.

So that they live in richness
And collect also great treasure besides.
Instead, they fictionalize;[79]
They construct many prayers and communities,
Many dreams, stories, and childish beings
That he the pope then confirms,
Taking money, and getting indulgences in addition,
Who cries out then late and early.
With such fables and foolishness
They have led us onto the ice,
That we have left the word of God
And only did what they told us to do,
Many works that God hasn't required;
They never told us of faith
In Christ, which makes us holy.
This lack means the night,
Into which we have all gone confused.
Therefore, the wolf and snakes have
In the four and a half hundred years[80]
Held us in their abode unfortunately[81]
And plagued [us] with the pope's power
Until Doctor Martin wrote
Against the abuse of holy power
And also uncovered
The word of God, the Holy Scripture
He orally and in writing completed
In four years by a hundred portions
In the German language and had them printed.
So that one understands what he teaches,

---

79 *Vil neuer Fünt sie stets erdichten*: Instead they tell many new opinions.
80 Since Gregor VII—1076.
81 *Fürwar*: Forsooth.

I want to briefly explain a little.[82]

God's law and the prophets

Mean to us the morning salvation;

In that Luther shows that we all

Are heirs to Adam's fall

In bad desire and bias.

For that reason, no person can follow the law enough.

We appear to hold it already in memory.

But of course our heart is unclean

And is prone to all sins,

That Moses very clearly pointed out.

Now since the heart then is flawed,

And God judges according to the heart.[83]

So are we all children of wrath,

Condemned, damned, and lost;

Whoever feels this in his heart,

The gnawing and biting of his sin

With sorrow, fear, dread, horror, pain

And recognizes his weakness;

Then the human becomes totally submissive,

So insists the brilliance of the day,

That means the gospel

That shows Christ to mankind,

The only begotten Son of God,

He has done all things for us,

Fulfilled the law[84] with his own power,

Destroyed the condemnation, paid for our sin,

And conquered the eternal death,

Destroyed hell, bound the devil,

---

82 Here begins an explanation of the significance of Luther's translation of the Bible.

83 The heart of man—what is truly in one's heart.

84 The commandments from Scripture.

And bought for us the grace of God,

As John showed

And announced Christ, the Lamb of God,

Who takes away the sin of the world.[85]

Also Christ says, he did not come

To earth for the righteous and pious

But rather for the sinners; he also said

The healthy do not need a doctor.[86]

Also John 3 reports

God so loved the world,

That he gave his only Son;

All who believe in him,

These ones should never perish,

Nor die the eternal death,

But rather have eternal life.[87]

Also Christ speaks in 11[88] even:

Whoever believes in me,

He will not die eternally.

So now the man hears such comforting words

Said by Jesus Christ,

And he can believe it and build on it

And trust the words in his heart,

Which Christ has said to him

And rely without doubt on it.

---

85 John 1:29: The next day he saw Jesus coming toward him, and said, "Behold, the Lamb of God, who takes away the sin of the world!"

86 Mark 2:17: And when Jesus heard it, he said to them, "Those who are well have no need of a physician, but those who are sick. I came not to call the righteous, but sinners."

87 John 3:16: For God so loved the world, that he gave his only Son, that whoever believes in him should not perish but have eternal life.

88 John 11:25–26: Jesus said to her, "I am the resurrection and the life. Whoever believes in me, though he die, yet shall he live, and everyone who lives and believes in me shall never die. Do you believe this?"

The same man is named newborn
From the fire and Holy Ghost
And becomes clean from all sins,
Living solely in the word of God,
From which nothing can tear him away,
Neither hell, devil, death, nor sin.
Whoever then is renewed in the spirit,
He serves God in spirit and in truth;
That is: that he loves God from his heart
And gives himself completely to him [God].
He considers him a God of grace;
In adversity, sorrow, in fear and need,
He surrenders himself to him as property;
God gives, God takes, and whatever happens,
He is willing and full of comfort
And does not doubt God would want him completely
Through Jesus Christ his Son,
Who is his peace, solace, joy, and delight
And remains also his only comfort.
With whom such faith is associated,
The same person is already holy;
All his works are pleasing to God,
Whether he sleeps, drinks, or works;
Such faith spreads widely
To the neighbor with true love,
That he disturbs no one, [but]
Rather practices at all times
In works of compassion,
Gives to everyone from the heart as alms
Freely given love, looking for no gain,
With advice, help, giving, loaning,
With teaching, punishment, guilt forgiven,
Does to others as he himself wants,
As that which should happen to him[self].

The Holy Spirit would do such work in him;
Therefore, the law is fulfilled
According to Christ in Matthew 7.[89]
Notice here that these alone are
The true Christian good works;
Here one must diligently notice
That they don't earn blessedness.[90]
The blessedness that one has
Is through the belief in Christ.
That is the lesson in short summation,
Which Luther has presently brought to light.[91]
This has awakened Leo, the pope
Who has tasted right away this roast,[92]
Fearing that the annates[93] have escaped him
And would reduce[94] for him the pope's income,
Which supports his life[95] in Rome.
Also one would no longer buy indulgences,
Also no one would make a pilgrimage to Rome,
[He, the pope,] would never be able to store up money,
Would also never more be the Lord of the World.[96]
One would never more keep his commands,
His spiritual practices would leave and die
If one knows the right truth;
For that reason he needs a fading ruse,

---

89 Matthew 7:12, "The Golden Rule": "So whatever you wish that others would do to you, do also to them, for this is the Law and the Prophets."

90 *Seligkeit*: Blessedness, or salvation.

91 *... an Tag gebracht*: Brought to the day; revealed.

92 Here begins a litany of consequences to the pope and the Catholic Church, when people read the Scripture and turn to Luther's teachings.

93 The half of the income paid by a Roman Catholic Church to the pope.

94 *... und würt im das Bapstmonet lom*: And would make the pope's income lame.

95 *Pfründt*: Easy living.

96 The pope.

Would gladly suppress[97] the truth
He sent quickly to Prince Friedrich,
That he burned the books with the name
And sent Luther to him to Rome.[98]
Yet his elector[99] grace
Held him [Luther] in Christian regard,
To protect the word of God
That he then noticed, reviewed, and stored up.
Because this measure failed,[100] the pope
He sent him to Augsburg quickly.
The cardinal commanded him [Luther] to be silent,
Yet could not show him in the Scripture
Clearly that Luther had been mistaken;
Because with this the pope also did not succeed,[101]
He declared Luther to be banished[102]
As well as all who followed him [Luther],
Without questioning [before a judge], writing and
    interrogation.
Rather, Luther wrote only more and more[103]
And did not allow the bull[104] to confuse.
First the kaiser[105] cited him
At the parliament meeting in Worms;
There Luther started a storm.
In short, he was now supposed to recant,

---

97 verdricket: Squeezed.
98 Prince Friedrich saved Luther from being sent to prison (and worse) in Rome.
99 Elector of the Holy Roman Empire (Prince Friedrich).
100 The pope failed in his attack on Luther.
101 . . . auch nit gieng firt: (entgehen) to avoid.
102 Excommunicated from the church.
103 für und für.
104 Papal edict.
105 Emperor Karl V of the Holy Roman Empire.

But no one wanted to dispute
With him and make him a heretic;
Therefore, he stayed firm in his causes
And renounced not a single word,
For all his writing was
Evangelical, apostolical.
Therefore, he took his leave happy and fresh
And let no mandate scare him.
The wild pig represents[106] Doctor Eck,[107]
Who fought against him in Leipzig
And brought from it a much rougher mess.[108]
The goat means Emser,[109]
Who is the comfort of all nuns;
So the cat means Murner,[110]
The pope's bird of prey,[111] guard, carpenter;[112]
The wild donkey [means] the barefooter[113]
In Leipzig, the rough lecturer;
So the snail means Cochlaeus.[114]

---

106 *deut*: Means, points out.

107 Johann Eck disputed Luther in Leipzig in 1519.

108 *Seu*: Sow (pig).

109 Hieronymus Emser, a priest who initially favored Luther but eventually attacked him. Emser's own translation of the Bible heavily borrowed from Luther's translation.

110 Thomas Murner was a Franciscan monk who was also in favor of reforming the church but criticized Luther's teaching.

111 *Mauser*: A cat that hunts mice.

112 *Turner*: Wood turner (carpenter).

113 The discalced Carmelites, a monastic order who wore no shoes. This reference may be to Johann Eberlin, who may have left the Franciscans to become a *Barfüsser*.

114 Johannes Cochlaeus assisted with negotiations with Luther in Worms. He was very vocal in attacking Luther and participated in the Diet at Augsburg.

These five[115] and otherwise much in total

Have long written against Luther;

Those he has driven away from him,

For their writing has no basis,

Only stood from long habit,

And could try nothing with Scripture,

So Luther does try to introduce Scripture

So that it causes a farmer to notice

That Luther's lesson is good and righteous.

Therefore, became unsuccessful and nonsensical

Now the snakes, nuns and monks,

Wanting to defend their human inventions[116]

And crying loudly in their preaching:

Luther speaks the gospel;

He also has letters and seals on it;

Is the gospel true?

Luther points to new heresy:[117]

O dear people, don't let yourselves be lead astray;

The Roman church cannot make a mistake;

Do good works, keep the papal commands,

Give alms and sacrifice, it pleases God;

Have Mass read, it comes to taxes;

The poor souls in Purgatory;

Earn the salvation and call them up;

Diligently go to vespers[118] and go to all the prayers.

The time is short, a single notice,

You partly do our work;

---

115 Referred to earlier in the poem.

116 *Fünt.*

117 The following lines outline the church's condemnation of Luther and his
followers, speaking from the point of view of the church officials to the
parishioners.

118 Evening prayers.

We sing, cry out often with strength,
So you at home lie down and sleep.
You remain silent about the true service to God;
Dance to your old violin
And act flatteringly among the laity.
Your wine cellar will run dry,
Your grain floor will be empty,
One never wants to tolerate him.
Have of course willingly praised poverty,[119]
Now one sees how their group rants
In such a way he is dispatched into their kitchen [into
    their homes]
As they vilify Luther, curse
An arch [of the highest order] heretic, rogue, and villain.
No one of course goes to the light
But hides it under the little hat,[120]
Crying, as if they want to break in two
Where they sit next to their nuns
And so also that they boil [in anger]
Against the gospel,
As one now notices around here.
The frogs croaking in their holes
Mean some higher schools,
Which also plead against Luther,
And that without validating all of the Bible.
The gospel hurts him,
Their heathen art doesn't count as before;
With it all doctors are taught
Who have twisted the Scripture for us[121]

---

119 Even if one's wine cellar and grain floor become empty due to the requirements
     of the church, one is expected to accept it because poverty is a virtue.
120 *under den Hütlein stechen*: Keeps it secret.
121 Followers of Luther.

With their heathen art,
Also carry disfavor to Luther.
The wild goose shows to us the laity,
Who curse him [Luther] and taunt him;
What does the monk[122] want to teach new
And turn around the whole of Christendom;
Our good works he does deride,
Because one should not earn salvation,
To God alone should we ask for help,
No creature wants to help us;
Our pilgrimage he also sets aside,
He doesn't think much of fasting, celebrations
As we have long had in our tradition,
Likewise for the support of the churches also;
The monastic orders he calls human inventions.[123]
Also Luther writes that there is no sin
Other than what God has forbidden us;
Spurn the pope's commands with that,
Spurn also the Roman indulgence,
Speak, Christ has made us holy,
Whoever believes that has enough.
I think that the monk[124] is not clever;
He does not think there have been people before
Who also have read the Scripture.
Our parents, who were before us,
Have also not been fools,
Who have taught us such things,
Have lasted[125] a few hundred years;
Should they all have been mistaken

---

122 Luther, the monk.
123 *Menschenfünt.*
124 Luther.
125 *gewert*: Granted. If it has been tradition for hundreds of years, it must be correct.

And us together with him been led astray.

God wouldn't want that; I want to drive that away

And stay in my old belief.

Luther writes unusual adventures,[126]

One should throw him in the fire,

Drive him away and all his retinue.

This [is what] one hears a lot from old women,

From nuns[127] and old men,

Who snarl at the gospel,

Scorning it in a wonderful sense,

And our salvation stands in that!

Of course it doesn't help to speak against it;

The truth is coming to light.[128]

For that reason the Christians are returning

To the evangelical teaching

Of our shepherd Jesus Christ,

Who is for us all a redeemer;

Faith in him alone makes us holy.

From that all human sins are scorned

And the pope's command destroyed

As lies and human stories

And hang only on the word of God

That one now hears in many places

From many Christian men.

Now [it is[129]] taken up by the bishops,[130]

Along with all the worldly princes,

Who also would thirst for the blood of Christians,

---

126 The gospel is considered adventures or fiction by the church hierarchy.

127 *Zopfnunnen*: The ones who even then adhered to old practices and beliefs.

128 Here the poem moves from the call of the Roman Church to the call to follow Luther.

129 "The attitude of the antichrist" (explained in the next 18 lines).

130 The desire for revenge against the evangelicals.

Allowing such preachers to be caught

In prison and be beaten with iron

And pressing them to recant,

Also singing to them a song from the fire

That they would like to give up hope in God;

That means to chase the sheep into the hedge.

This causes one to lose much secretly

If they even test their teachings;

One part remains bound in iron,

One part is chased out of the land.

One also burns Luther's writings

And forbids them in many locations;

By body and goods and by the head

Whom one grabs, he leaves a tuft (of hair)

Or chases him from wife and child;

That is the main attitude of the antichrist.

Christ announced that

Matthew 10 says:[131]

Take it as true, I send you like sheep

Into the middle of a pack of wolves;

Therefore, be as clever as snakes

131　Matthew 10:16–23: "Behold, I am sending you out as sheep in the midst of
wolves, so be wise as serpents and innocent as doves. Beware of men, for they
will deliver you over to courts and flog you in their synagogues, and you will
be dragged before governors and kings for my sake, to bear witness before
them and the Gentiles. When they deliver you over, do not be anxious how
you are to speak or what you are to say, for what you are to say will be given
to you in that hour. For it is not you who speak, but the Spirit of your Father
speaking through you. Brother will deliver brother over to death, and the
father his child, and children will rise against parents and have them put
to death, and you will be hated by all for my name's sake. But the one who
endures to the end will be saved. When they persecute you in one town, flee
to the next, for truly, I say to you, you will not have gone through all the towns
of Israel before the Son of Man comes."

And like doves without deception,
And protect yourselves before men, they
Warn you to give yourselves over
For their city halls and those
Capture you in their schools
And will before princes, kings
For my sake bring you captured.
Don't worry about what to say;
It [the Holy Spirit] will give you what you should
Speak through the spirit of your Father [God],
A friend like others will be asked for
And then death will help him.
You will be hated by every man
And be holy for my name's sake.
Whoever persists to the end will be holy;
When you are chased out of one city,
Then move to another quickly.[132]
Also comes the time, and who kills you
Will think he is serving God through it.
Don't fear those who kill your body;
They cannot hurt the soul.[133]
You Christians, notice the comforting word;
If one chases you here or there,
Don't let tyranny drive you out;
Stay with the word of God,
Abandon body and goods.
Abel's blood will call out
About Cain in the early days.[134]

---

132 End of the Matthew reference.

133 Matthew 10:28: And do not fear those who kill the body but cannot kill the soul. Rather fear him who can destroy both soul and body in hell.

134 Genesis 4:10: And the Lord said, "What have you done? The voice of your brother's blood is crying to me from the ground."

Let murder those who can only murder,

It will come at the end,

The true spiritual practices of the antichrist.

In Revelation it is stated clearly,

In the eighteenth chapter;[135]

The angel calls with loud sounds

Twice: Babylon has fallen,

She[136] was a home for the devil

When from the wine of the horrible rage

All heathens drank her fornication

All have sunk into her fornication

Kings and princes of this earth;

Also her merchants become very rich,

Dealing with the souls of mankind.

Afterward he[137] tells further:

---

135 Revelation 18:1–8: After this I saw another angel coming down from heaven, having great authority, and the earth was made bright with his glory. And he called out with a mighty voice, "Fallen, fallen is Babylon the great! She has become a dwelling place for demons, a haunt for every unclean spirit, a haunt for every unclean bird, a haunt for every unclean and detestable beast. For all nations have drunk the wine of the passion of her sexual immorality, and the kings of the earth have committed immorality with her, and the merchants of the earth have grown rich from the power of her luxurious living." Then I heard another voice from heaven saying, "Come out of her, my people, lest you take part in her sins, lest you share in her plagues; for her sins are heaped high as heaven, and God has remembered her iniquities. Pay her back as she herself has paid back others, and repay her double for her deeds; mix a double portion for her in the cup she mixed. As she glorified herself and lived in luxury, so give her a like measure of torment and mourning, since in her heart she says, 'I sit as a queen, I am no widow, and mourning I shall never see.' For this reason her plagues will come in a single day, death and mourning and famine, and she will be burned up with fire; for mighty is the Lord God who has judged her."

136 Referring to Babylon as "she."

137 The angel (Revelation 18).

And another voice I hear cry:

My dear people, get away from her.

For her sin arose toward God;

He saw her sacrileges as true,

Paid them, as they paid you,

And counted against her twofold;

When she speaks in her heart:

I sit as a queen without pain,

And is secure in her thinking

And drank completely of the holy blood

For that reason so will her plague

Come together on that day,

The death, suffering hunger, all manner of suffering

And with fire she will be burned.

Then truly strong is the Lord God,

Who will judge her?[138] Now hear more:

Daniel chapter 9[139] records

And explains all symbols[140]

So that one may understand very clearly

---

138 The end of the Revelation passage.

139 Actually referring to Daniel 8:15–26 (following Daniel's vision in verses 1–14).

140 Daniel 8:15–17: When I, Daniel, had seen the vision, I sought to understand it. And behold, there stood before me one having the appearance of a man. And I heard a man's voice between the banks of the Ulai, and it called, "Gabriel, make this man understand the vision." So he came near where I stood. And when he came, I was frightened and fell on my face. But he said to me, "Understand, O son of man, that the vision is for the time of the end."

Verses 17–23 interpret Daniel's vision. Verses 24–25 speak to Sachs's purpose: "His power shall be great—but not by his own power; and he shall cause fearful destruction and shall succeed in what he does, and destroy mighty men and the people who are the saints. By his cunning he shall make deceit prosper under his hand, and in his own mind he shall become great. Without warning he shall destroy many. And he shall even rise up against the Prince of princes, and he shall be broken—but by no human hand" (Daniel 8:24–25).

The papacy is clearly Babylon,
Of which John has seen.
For that reason, you Christians, wherever you are,
Turn again from the pope's desert
To our shepherd Jesus Christ;
He himself is a good shepherd,
Has tested his love with death,
Through which[141] we all have been redeemed.
He is our only comfort
And our only hope,
Righteousness and holiness
To all who believe in his name;
Whoever desires that, he may say Amen.

The year of salvation[142] 1523, on the 8th day of July.

---

141 His "testing."
142 Latin: *Anno salutis.*

CHAPTER 5

A Disputation between a Parson and a Shoemaker in Which the Word of God and a Right Christian Character Is Contended

Difputacion zwifchen ainem Chor herzenn vnnd Schüchmacher darin bas wort gottes vnd ein recht Crift lich wefen verfochtten wirtt. **Hanns** **Sachs.** M D XXiiij.

Jch fag euch / wa difefchweige / fo werbe die ftein fchrefe.lu.19

Introduction

A Disputation between a Parson and a Shoemaker in Which the Word of God and a Right Christian Character Is Contended is the first of four Reformation plays (often referred to as dialogues) written by Hans Sachs in 1524. In these plays, Sachs departs from his customary verse for which he was known and which he used for *The Wittenberg Nightingale*, published in 1523. Richard

Zoozmann notes that from the time Martin Luther burned the papal decree that excommunicated him from the Catholic Church in 1521, Sachs turned his attention to Luther's propositions, studying his treatises and his translation of the Bible.[1]

This first play is based on Luther's text *The Freedom of a Christian*, published in 1520, which Luther sent to Pope Leo X in hopes of persuading the pope to consider the reforms Luther had proposed. Within this disputation, Sachs examines the multitude of practices required by the church of its parishioners and declares them unscriptural. As he had done in *The Wittenberg Nightingale*, he calls attention to the practices of vows of celibacy, the sale of indulgences, requirements for monetary support, the building of large churches furnished with expensive articles used for Mass, and the wearing of expensive robes by the clergy.

In this play, when a shoemaker (Sachs himself) delivers a pair of slippers to a parson, the conversation quickly turns to spiritual matters. The parson mentions the nightingale he keeps in his garden house, and the shoemaker, who has newly freed himself from the restrictive practices of the Catholic Church, takes the opportunity to make a connection to *The Wittenberg Nightingale* (a metaphor for Martin Luther). So begins a sometimes heated discussion about the illegitimacy of common church practices. As Philip Broadhead[2] contends, Sachs was of the opinion that no one should be compelled to participate in practices that were not outlined in Scripture. At the same time, it should be incumbent on the laity to be familiar with Scripture so that they can make their own decisions about worship. This dialogue also includes the thoughts of the parson's cook and his calefactor,[3] who has also recently become an

---

1 Richard Zoozmann, *Hans Sachs und die Reformation: In Gedichten und Prosastücke* (Hamburg, Germany: SEVERUS Verlag, 2017), 18.

2 Philip Broadhead, "The Biblical Verse of Hans Sachs: The Popularization of Scripture in the Lutheran Reformation," in *The Church and Literature*, ed. Peter Clarke and Charlotte Methuen, 124–33 (Suffolk: Boydell Press, 2012), 129.

3 The calefactory was the employee of the parish responsible for keeping the church and the associated living quarters heated.

"evangelical," providing further evidence that the common man was involved in the Reformation.

Throughout the dialogue, the two men "duel" with Scripture. It is interesting to see the use of Scripture to support the claims of both participants, especially since Luther's New Testament translation had only been published in 1522. To see Sachs's familiarity with the Scripture, in both the Old and New Testaments and the Apocrypha, is impressive. The dispute could be considered swordplay if we consider Scripture to be the "sword of the spirit,"[4] to which the shoemaker refers in this dialogue. It is interesting to note how the evangelical, Sachs the shoemaker, cites the Scripture with fervor and accuracy, while his Catholic conversant, the parson, regularly misquotes the Scripture or takes verses out of context.

It should be noted that Sachs focuses strongly on Luther's statement that salvation comes through faith alone. Additionally, Sachs goes on to describe Christian works (charitable works) and how those should be manifested in a person's life as opposed to the works commanded by the Catholic Church (works that related to serving the church and not serving one another). This focus exemplifies Sachs's own faith and understanding of the Scriptures and Luther's teaching.[5]

Translation and historical notes are found in the footnotes, as are Scripture references. As a reminder to the reader, verse numbers were not added to Scripture until 1551. Sachs cited by chapter only, while we have provided specific verse references.

An interesting note is that this play was previously translated into English in 1548 by Anthony Scolocker: "A goodly dysputacion between a cristen shomaker, and a popysshe parson with two other persones more, done within the famous citie of Norembourgh. Translated out of [the] Germayne tongue into Englysshe."

---

4 Ephesians 6:17.

5 Broadhead, "Biblical Verse of Hans Sachs," 124.

A Disputation between a Parson[6] and a Shoemaker
in Which the Word of God and a Right
Christian Character Is Contended

Hans Sachs (1494–1576)

1524

I tell you, if these are silent, then the rocks will cry out. Luke 19[7]

Shoemaker:[8] Good day,[9] good fellow.

Cook:[10] Peace to you.[11] You are welcome here, Master Hans.

Shoemaker: I thank you with all my heart.[12] Where is your master?

Cook: He is in the garden house. I will go and call him. Master, master! The shoemaker is here.

Parson:[13] Welcome,[14] Master Hans.

Shoemaker: Thank you.[15]

Parson: What brings you here? Did you bring my slippers?

Shoemaker: Yes, I thought you had already gone to the church.

---

6 A *Chorherr* was a role or rank in the Catholic Church used by different religious orders, such as the Augustinians. The *Chorherr* would have been responsible for the liturgy and the daily prayers. Thus, he was a man very familiar with the Scripture. The word *parson* is used because it is clear the person is a church servant, a priest, a parson, or a pastor, with a home provided by the church.

7 Luke 10:40: He answered, "I tell you, if these were silent, the very stones would cry out."

8 The shoemaker coming to the parson's house, speaks to the parson's servant.

9 Original in Latin: *Bonus dies*, Latin being the language of the Catholic Church at this time.

10 *Koechin*: A female cook.

11 Original in Latin: *Semper quies!*

12 Literally "God thank you."

13 The parson enters. The cook exits.

14 Original in Latin: *Beneveneritis.*

15 Original in Latin: *Deo gratias!*

Parson:	No. I was out there[16] in the garden house saying my litany.[17]
Shoemaker:	What? You were praying?
Parson:	Yes. I was saying the hourly prayers and feeding my nightingale at the same time.
Shoemaker:	Sir,[18] what kind of nightingale do you have? Does it still sing?
Parson:	Oh no, it's too late in the year.
Shoemaker:	I know a shoemaker who has a nightingale[19] that has just begun to sing.
Parson:	The devil should take the shoemaker with such a nightingale. How he chastised the Holy Father, the pope, the holy fathers, and us worthy gentlemen like boys with their hands in the cookie jar.[20]
Shoemaker:	Oh sir, just leave it![21] He only revealed your worship practices, your teaching, commandments, and income to the average man and how terrible it all is at that. Are your practices the same as a boy stealing cookies?
Parson:	What do our practices matter to the great shoemaker?
Shoemaker:	It is written in Exodus 23, "If you see your enemy's donkey fallen under its yoke, do not leave it, but rather help it."[22]

---

16 *Hinden*: Yonder.

17 *Horas*: The word implies prayers said mechanically (memorized and repeated often).

18 By using "sir" (Herr literally means "Lord"), the Shoemaker shows respect to his conversant. This is in contrast to the condescending phrase used by the priest, "dear one."

19 Reference is to Martin Luther, referred to in Sachs's allegorical poem as *The Wittenberg Nightingale*.

20 *aussgeholhipt, wie ein Holhipbub*: Literally, a shame-bringing action, such as a boy running away with the baked goods. Using the English turn of phrase, boys with their hands in the cookie jar.

21 *fart schon*: Literally, drive already; in other words, leave this line of thought.

22 Exodus 23:5: If you see the donkey of one who hates you lying down under its burden, you shall refrain from leaving him with it; you shall rescue it with him.

	Shouldn't a baptized Christian help his brother if he sees him lying under the burden of his conscience?
Parson:	He shouldn't lump the spiritual and the weak ones together,[23] the donkey![24] The spiritual ones certainly know what sin is.
Shoemaker:	If they are sinners, as it says in Ezekiel 33, "If you see your brother sin, then punish him, or I will demand his blood on your hands."[25] For that reason, a baptized one should and must reprimand his sinful brother, whether he is weak or not.
Parson:	Are you an evangelical?[26]
Shoemaker:	Yes.
Parson:	Haven't you read in the Gospel of Matthew 7, "Judge not lest you be judged"?[27] But you Lutherans don't take such sayings to heart; you don't notice them when they speak against what you are doing.
Shoemaker:	Reprimanding and judging are two different things. We understand not to judge, which alone belongs to God; like Paul says to the Romans in chapter 14, "No one should judge the servant of another,"[28] and so on but rather admonish and reprimand, as God speaks to the prophet in Isaiah 58: "Cry out, don't stop, raise your voice like

---

23 Weak here refers to those who are not as spiritual or as spiritually trained as the parson.

24 *Eselskopf*: Donkey head.

25 Ezekiel 33:8: If I say to the wicked, O wicked one, you shall surely die, and you do not speak to warn the wicked to turn from his way, that wicked person shall die in his iniquity, but his blood I will require at your hand.

26 Evangelical refers to the emerging Lutheran church.

27 Matthew 7:1: "Judge not, that you be not judged."

28 Romans 14:4: Who are you to pass judgment on the servant of another? It is before his own master that he stands or falls. And he will be upheld, for the Lord is able to make him stand.

a trumpet to announce to my people their misdeeds," and so on.[29]

Parson: It is also written in Exodus 12,[30] "You should not shame the leader in front of his people."[31]

Shoemaker: Who then is the leader of the people? Is it not the kaiser, followed by princes, and dukes together with the knights and worldly leaders?

Parson: No, the pope is the vicar of Christ, then the cardinals, bishops together with all of the spiritual leaders from whom come canonical law, to Christ alone the most subjection and obedience:[32] They represent the sun, and the worldly powers represent the moon; for that reason, the pope is much more powerful than the kaiser, who must kiss the pope's feet.

Shoemaker: Even if the pope is a powerful lord, he is certainly no governor of Christ, as Christ says in John 18, "My kingdom is not of this world,"[33] and in John 6, Christ fled when the crowds wanted to make him king.[34] Also, Christ spoke to his disciples in Luke 22, "The worldly kings rule and the powerful are called gracious Lord, but not you. The greatest among you should be like the lowest and the highest ranking

---

29 Isaiah 58:1: "Cry aloud; do not hold back; lift up your voice like a trumpet; declare to my people their transgression, to the house of Jacob their sins."

30 The verse is actually in Exodus 22.

31 Exodus 22:28: "You shall not revile God, nor curse a ruler of your people."

32 Latin: *C. solite de majoritate et obedientia*, from "Corpos Iuris Canonici liber i. titulum xxxiii. Decretals de Gregorius Augustus Anglorum Episcopo."

33 John 18:36: Jesus answered, "My kingdom is not of this world. If my kingdom were of this world, my servants would have been fighting, that I might not be delivered over to the Jews. But my kingdom is not from the world."

34 John 6:15: Perceiving then that they were about to come and take him by force to make him king, Jesus withdrew again to the mountain by himself.

	like the servant."[35] For that reason, the pope and you spiritual ones are only servants of the Christian community. You should be reprimanded where you differ from God.
Parson:	Oh, the pope and his people are not obliged to attend to God's commandments, as it is stated in the canonical law "to Christ alone the most obedience."[36] From that can be inferred that the pope is not a sinner but rather the most holy; for that reason, he does not need to be reprimanded.[37]
Shoemaker:	First John 1 says, "Whoever says he is not a sinner, lies."[38] For that reason, the pope is a sinner or a liar and not the mightiest but rather to be reprimanded.
Parson:	Oh dear one,[39] and if the pope were so bad that he were to lead a great number of people to the devil, even then no one would be allowed to reprimand him. It is written in our canonical law, disputation 40 of the pope. How do you like that?
Shoemaker:	Oh, it is written in Matthew 18, "If your brother sins against you, go and reprimand him between the two of you; if he hears you, you have won his soul."[40] Does the pope abstain from such holy work?

---

35 Luke 22:25–26: And he said to them, "The kings of the Gentiles exercise lordship over them, and those in authority over them are called benefactors. But not so with you. Rather, let the greatest among you become as the youngest, and the leader as one who serves."

36 Latin: *C. solite de majoritate et obedientia.*

37 Or he is above reproach.

38 1 John 1:8: If we say we have no sin, we deceive ourselves, and the truth is not in us.

39 The priest speaks here and throughout in a condescending manner to the Shoemaker by often referring to him as "dear one."

40 Matthew 18:15: "If your brother sins against you, go and tell him his fault, between you and him alone. If he listens to you, you have gained your brother."

Parson:	Should then such a brother be reprimanded openly?[41]
Shoemaker:	Oh, it continues in the text, "If your brother doesn't hear, so take one or two with you, if he still doesn't hear, say to the congregation, if he doesn't hear the congregation, treat him like a heathen."[42] What do you say to that sir?
Parson:	Oh dear one, what good is it when you cry against us for so long, like a child with his hand in the cookie jar?[43] We don't turn toward that; we stick to the papal decrees.
Shoemaker:	Christ says in Matthew 10, "If one doesn't hear you, then shake the dust from your feet as a witness that the kingdom of God has been there. For it will be more tolerable for Sodom and Gomorrah at the day of judgment than for such people."[44] How will it go with you if you take no reprimand?
Parson:	I'll agree where learned men are reprimanding, but not where the laity are reprimanding.
Shoemaker:	Doesn't a donkey punish the prophet Balaam in Numbers 22?[45] Why shouldn't then a layperson reprimand a holy man?

---

41 *Am Tag*: In the daylight, as opposed to secretly or in the dark.

42 Matthew 18:16–17: "But if he does not listen, take one or two others along with you, that every charge may be established by the evidence of two or three witnesses. If he refuses to listen to them, tell it to the church. And if he refuses to listen even to the church, let him be to you as a Gentile and a tax collector."

43 Returning the previous insult.

44 Matthew 10:14–15: And if anyone will not receive you or listen to your words, shake off the dust from your feet when you leave that house or town. Truly, I say to you, it will be more bearable on the day of judgment for the land of Sodom and Gomorrah than for that town.

45 Numbers 22:22–35: But God's anger was kindled because he went, and the angel of the Lord took his stand in the way as his adversary. Now he was riding on the donkey, and his two servants were with him. And the donkey saw the angel of the Lord standing in the road, with a drawn sword in his hand. And the donkey turned aside out of the road and went into the field. And Balaam

Parson: A shoemaker works with leather and dye and not with the Holy Scriptures.

Shoemaker: With which Holy Scripture do you want to teach a baptized Christian not to research, read, and write? For Christ says in John 5, "Search the Scriptures, they give testimony of me."[46] So speaks the psalmist in Psalm 1, "Holy is the man who practices day and night the law of the Lord."[47]

---

struck the donkey, to turn her into the road. Then the angel of the Lord stood in a narrow path between the vineyards, with a wall on either side. And when the donkey saw the angel of the Lord, she pushed against the wall and pressed Balaam's foot against the wall. So he struck her again. Then the angel of the Lord went ahead and stood in a narrow place, where there was no way to turn either to the right or to the left. When the donkey saw the angel of the Lord, she lay down under Balaam. And Balaam's anger was kindled, and he struck the donkey with his staff. Then the Lord opened the mouth of the donkey, and she said to Balaam, "What have I done to you, that you have struck me these three times?" And Balaam said to the donkey, "Because you have made a fool of me. I wish I had a sword in my hand, for then I would kill you." And the donkey said to Balaam, "Am I not your donkey, on which you have ridden all your life long to this day? Is it my habit to treat you this way?" And he said, "No."

Then the Lord opened the eyes of Balaam, and he saw the angel of the Lord standing in the way, with his drawn sword in his hand. And he bowed down and fell on his face. And the angel of the Lord said to him, "Why have you struck your donkey these three times? Behold, I have come out to oppose you because your way is perverse before me. The donkey saw me and turned aside before me these three times. If she had not turned aside from me, surely just now I would have killed you and let her live." Then Balaam said to the angel of the Lord, "I have sinned, for I did not know that you stood in the road against me. Now therefore, if it is evil in your sight, I will turn back." And the angel of the Lord said to Balaam, "Go with the men, but speak only the word that I tell you." So Balaam went on with the princes of Balak.

46 John 5:46–47: "For if you believed Moses, you would believe me; for he wrote of me. But if you do not believe his writings, how will you believe my words?"

47 Psalm 1:1–2: Blessed is the man who walks not in the counsel of the wicked, nor stands in the way of sinners, nor sits in the seat of scoffers; but his delight

So writes Peter in his first letter, chapter 3, "Appear at all times reverent, ready to answer every man the reason for hope that is in you."[48] So Paul teaches the Ephesians in chapter 6, fighting against the advances of the devil with the word of God, which he calls a sword.[49] Sir, how would we survive if we are not vested in the Scriptures?

Parson: Like a goose in the water.[50]

Shoemaker: You must be joking. The Jews know their law and prophets by heart; should then we Christians not also know the gospel of Jesus Christ, which is the power of God alone, which should make us holy, as Paul says in 1 Corinthians 1?[51]

Parson: Yes, you should know it, but how? As Christ called you in Matthew chapter 23, "On Moses's throne you have put the scribes and the Pharisees, now do all that they say."[52] That means the daily sermon; don't the laity have enough of that?

---

is in the law of the Lord, and on his law he meditates day and night.

48 1 Peter 3:15–16: But in your hearts honor Christ the Lord as holy, always being prepared to make a defense to anyone who asks you for a reason for the hope that is in you; yet do it with gentleness and respect, having a good conscience, so that, when you are slandered, those who revile your good behavior in Christ may be put to shame.

49 Ephesians 6:16–17: In all circumstances take up the shield of faith, with which you can extinguish all the flaming darts of the evil one; and take the helmet of salvation, and the sword of the Spirit, which is the word of God.

50 The implication is that laypeople do not need the Scripture; they survive without it as a goose survives in the water.

51 1 Corinthians 1:24: But to those who are called, both Jews and Greeks, Christ the power of God and the wisdom of God.

52 Matthew 23:2–3: "The scribes and the Pharisees sit on Moses' seat, so do and observe whatever they tell you, but not the works they do. For they preach, but do not practice."

Shoemaker: Oh, it says in the same place in Matthew 23, "They bind heavy burdens and lay them on men's shoulders."[53] Such burdens certainly and without doubt refer to the traditions and commandments of men, by which you exasperate us laypeople and bring us to bad thoughts. Why should we then follow you?

Parson: How do you prove that by the Scriptures?

Shoemaker: Christ spoke in the same chapter, "Like you Pharisees and hypocrites that close up the kingdom of heaven for the people, you will not enter and will not allow anyone else to enter."[54]

Parson: Oh, Christ said that to the priests of the Jews; it is a different thing for us priests.

Shoemaker: Oh sir, you assumed first the Pharisees, who sit on Moses's throne, and so on. Although it was spoken of the priests of the Jews, even so also it was spoken to you. For your works bear witness, you devour the widows' houses as the text does further declare,[55] for sir, you have presumed too much.

---

53 Matthew 23:4: They tie up heavy burdens, hard to bear, and lay them on people's shoulders, but they themselves are not willing to move them with their finger.

54 Matthew 23:13: But woe to you, scribes and Pharisees, hypocrites! For you shut the kingdom of heaven in people's faces. For you neither enter yourselves nor allow those who would enter to go in.

55 Reference actually found in Mark 12:38-40: And in his teaching he said, "Beware of the scribes, who like to walk around in long robes and like greetings in the marketplaces and have the best seats in the synagogues and the places of honor at feasts, who devour widows' houses and for a pretense make long prayers. They will receive the greater condemnation."

Parson: Pshaw,[56] you Lutherans are so astute;[57] you can hear the grass grow. If one of you knows one saying or two from the Gospels, you vex others with it.

Shoemaker: Oh sir, don't be angry. I mean well.

Parson: I'm not angry, but I have to tell you, it isn't becoming for the laity to meddle with the Scripture.[58]

Shoemaker: Christ says in Matthew 7, "Beware of false prophets,"[59] and Paul says to the Philippians in chapter 3, "Beware of dogs."[60] If we are not allowed to read the Scriptures, how can we recognize these things?

Parson: Such belongs to the bishops, as Paul said in Titus 1: "He should exhort and punish those who lead others astray."[61]

Shoemaker: Yes, but they don't do that but rather do the opposite daily.

Parson: Let them take care of that.[62]

Shoemaker: No, not us. If they don't want to, then we must take heed that we don't follow them, for no one should bear another's burden.[63]

Parson: Oh dear one, say what you want; it behooves the laity not to meddle[64] with the Scripture, as Paul says in 1 Corinthians 7:

---

56 *Pi Pu Pa!*

57 *Nasweis:* In modern German, the word is used to mean "curious" or "nosy"; however, in Sachs's time, the word was used to describe the wisdom of a dog sniffing with his nose to the ground, hence the choice of "astute" here.

58 Or to use the Scripture so freely.

59 Matthew 7:15: Beware of false prophets, who come to you in sheep's clothing but inwardly are ravenous wolves.

60 Philippians 3:2: Look out for the dogs, look out for the evildoers, look out for those who mutilate the flesh.

61 Titus 1:13: Therefore rebuke them [Cretins] sharply.

62 It is their responsibility.

63 Follow another's mistake.

64 Another option would be "to interact." "To meddle with," however, gives a better sense of the tone ascribed to the *Chorherr*/parson.

"Let every man walk according to the Lord's calling."[65]
Do you hear? You have coveted the Scripture.

Shoemaker: Yes, Paul spoke of outward conditions and actions, of slaves and free persons, as it is clearly specified in the same place and chapter, but here the word of God is not forbidden to be handled by the average man.

Parson: Oh, don't you hear? You have to be called through the holy sanctification[66] and after that be chosen by the higher authorities; otherwise it is not becoming for the laity to meddle with the Scriptures.

Shoemaker: Christ spoke in Luke chapter 10, "The harvest is great, but the workers are few. Pray to the lord of the harvest to send workers to the field."[67] For that reason, the calling must be not outwardly but rather inwardly from God. All preachers are called outwardly, the false as well as the righteous.

Parson: Your speech is the work of a fool.

Shoemaker: It is the same with you as it is with the disciples. It says in Luke 9, they were annoyed that another also drove out spirits in the name of Christ. But Christ said, "Forbid them not, for whoever is not against you is for you."[68] And if you were true Christians, you should rejoice in your heart that laity can be found who would take on the burden as enemies of the world for the sake of the word of God.

---

65 1 Corinthians 7:20: Each one should remain in the condition in which he was called.

66 A recognized practice for the installation of clergy.

67 Luke 10:2: And he said to them, "The harvest is plentiful, but the laborers are few. Therefore pray earnestly to the Lord of the harvest to send out laborers into his harvest."

68 Luke 9:50: But Jesus said to him, "Do not stop him, for the one who is not against you is for you."

Parson: Why does this need to concern you?

Shoemaker: Because in our baptism, we have renounced the devil and his empire; it is our duty to fight his empire with the word of God and also to risk our bodies, honor, and goods.

Parson: You laity should be concerned with feeding your wives and children.

Shoemaker: Christ forbade in Matthew 6, "Don't worry about what you should eat or drink or put on, the heathens worry about such things, seek ye first the kingdom of God and his righteousness, and all the things will be added to you."[69] And in 1 Peter 4, "Cast all your cares on him for he cares for you."[70] Also, Christ says in Matthew 4,[71] "Man does not live by bread alone, but rather from every word that proceeds out of the mouth of God."[72]

Parson: Satisfy and content yourself with that. Don't grumble.

Shoemaker: We should work as Adam was commanded in Genesis 3[73] and as in Job 5: "Man is born to work, as the bird is born to fly."[74] We should not worry but rather trust God so that

---

69 Matthew 6:25: "Therefore I tell you, do not be anxious about your life, what you will eat or what you will drink, nor about your body, what you will put on. Is not life more than food, and the body more than clothing?"

70 This reference is actually to 1 Peter 5:7: . . . casting all your anxieties on him, because he cares for you.

71 This verse refers to Christ's response to Satan when Christ was being tempted following his baptism and before the beginning of his ministry. The words of Christ come from Deuteronomy 8:3. "Every word" can be translated as "inspiration," and "God" can be translated as "Jehovah."

72 Matthew 4:4: But he answered, "It is written, 'Man shall not live by bread alone, but by every word that comes from the mouth of God.'"

73 Genesis 3:19: By the sweat of your face you shall eat bread, till you return to the ground, for out of it you were taken; for you are dust, and to dust you shall return.

74 Job 5:7: Man is born to trouble as the sparks fly upward.

we would want to hang on the word of God, which is the best part—Luke 10.[75]

Parson: Where should you laity have learned? Many of you can't even spell.

Shoemaker: Christ spoke in John 6, "You will learn everything from God."[76]

Parson: There also has to be art; is that not what the universities are for?

Shoemaker: At which university did John study, who wrote so well? (In the beginning was the word and the word was with God, etc., John 1).[77] He was only a fisher, as Mark 1 says.[78]

Parson: Dear one, he had the Holy Spirit, as noted in Acts 2.[79]

Shoemaker: It says in Joel 2, "And it shall pass in the last days, says the Lord, I will pour out my spirit on all mankind,"[80] and so on, as if it were said of us.

Parson: No, that was said of the apostles, as Peter witnessed in Acts 2.[81] Therefore, hold your peace and speak no more of the Spirit.[82]

---

75 Luke 10:41–42: But the Lord answered her, "Martha, Martha, you are anxious and troubled about many things, but one thing is necessary. Mary has chosen the good portion, which will not be taken away from her."

76 John 6:45: "It is written in the Prophets, 'And they will all be taught by God.' Everyone who has heard and learned from the Father comes to me."

77 John 1:1: In the beginning was the Word, and the Word was with God, and the Word was God.

78 Mark 1:19: And going on a little farther, he saw James the son of Zebedee and John his brother, who were in their boat mending the nets.

79 Acts 2:4: And they were all filled with the Holy Spirit and began to speak in other tongues as the Spirit gave them utterance.

80 Joel 2:28: And it shall come to pass afterward, that I will pour out my Spirit on all flesh; your sons and your daughters shall prophesy, your old men shall dream dreams, and your young men shall see visions.

81 Peter's sermon at Pentecost, found in Acts 2:14–41.

82 Literally, pack up your talk of the Holy Spirit.

Shoemaker: Christ spoke in John 7, "He who believes on me (as it is written), from his body will flow a river of living water."[83] That, according to the evangelist, is spoken about the Holy Spirit, who is received by those who believe on him.

Parson: In my opinion, you stink like Mantuano, the heretic[84] with the Holy Ghost.

Shoemaker: Paul says in 1 Corinthians 3, "Don't you know that you are the temple of God and the spirit of God lives in you?"[85] And in Galatians 4, "Because you are children, God sent the spirit into your hearts, which cries Abba, Father."[86] And in Titus 3 we read, "According to his compassion, he sanctifies us through the baptism of the rebirth and renewal of the Holy Spirit, which he richly poured out on us."[87] And in Romans 8, "So now the spirit of this, which raised Jesus from the dead lives in you."[88]

---

83 John 7:38: "Whoever believes in me, as the Scripture has said, 'Out of his heart will flow rivers of living water.'"

84 Montanus, labeled a heretic by the Catholic Church in the second or third century, is accused of leading Tertullian astray. Montanus was the leader of a sect that claimed direct access to the Holy Spirit. He himself claimed the Holy Spirit spoke directly to him. "Five Heretics That Every Catholic Should Know and Why They Matter Today," Catholicism Pure and Simple, October 31, 2012, https://catholicismpure.wordpress.com/2012/10/31/five-heretics-that-every-catholic-should-know-and-why-they-matter-today/.

85 1 Corinthians 3:16: Do you not know that you are God's temple and that God's Spirit dwells in you?

86 Galatians 4:6: And because you are sons, God has sent the Spirit of his Son into our hearts, crying, "Abba! Father!"

87 Titus 3:5–6: He saved us, not because of works done by us in righteousness, but according to his own mercy, by the washing of regeneration and renewal of the Holy Spirit, whom he poured out on us richly through Jesus Christ our Savior.

88 Romans 8:11: If the Spirit of him who raised Jesus from the dead dwells in you, he who raised Christ Jesus from the dead will also give life to your mortal bodies through his Spirit who dwells in you.

Parson: I find no Holy Spirit in me; you and I are not worthy of it.

Shoemaker: Why then are you called the holy ones[89] if you don't have the spirit of God? You should be called the spiritless ones.

Parson: It is other people, neither you nor I, who have the Holy Spirit.

Shoemaker: You shouldn't be looking for islands[90] or for a red cap and gown.[91] God is no respecter of persons—Acts 10.[92] Isaiah 66 says, "The spirit of God will rest on a contrite heart."[93]

Parson: Prove it![94]

Shoemaker: Paul speaks openly to the Romans in chapter 8, "Whoever doesn't have Christ's spirit, is not his."[95]

Parson: Oh the poor in spirit, the spirit that you Lutherans have; I believe he is as black as coal. Dear one, what is your Holy Ghost doing with you? I believe he sleeps day and night. He is nowhere to be found.[96]

---

89 *Geistlichen*: The spiritual ones.

90 *Insel*: Here a figurative island describing a perception of self-contained uniqueness.

91 Those with special recognitions.

92 Acts 10:34: So Peter opened his mouth and said: "Truly I understand that God shows no partiality . . ."

93 Isaiah 66:2: All these things my hand has made, and so all these things came to be, declares the Lord. But this is the one to whom I will look: he who is humble and contrite in spirit and trembles at my word.

94 *Zeigt mir ein*: Show me!

95 Does not belong to Christ. Romans 8:9: You, however, are not in the flesh but in the Spirit, if in fact the Spirit of God dwells in you. Anyone who does not have the Spirit of Christ does not belong to him.

96 *Man spurt ih ie nindert*: No evidence of him is to be found.

Shoemaker: Christ speaks in Matthew 7, "Don't give what is holy to the dogs, neither cast your pearls before swine, lest they trample them under their feet."[97]

Parson: Dear one, aren't you ashamed to speak such rude and uncomely words to me?

Shoemaker: Oh dear sir, don't be mad. It is the Holy Scripture.

Parson: Yes, yes, yes, you Lutherans speak much of God's word, and the longer you speak, the worse it gets. I see no improvement.

Shoemaker: Christ says in Luke 17, "The kingdom of God came not outwardly or with notice, that one might say: here or there, but rather it is inward in you."[98] That is so because it is not in outward works.

Parson: That is evident in your worship service; you don't pray, and you pay attention to neither the church nor the scheduled prayer time[99] or anything anymore. Is such a kingdom of God in you Lutherans?[100] I believe it is the devil's kingdom.

Shoemaker: Oh, Christ says in John 4, "A time is coming and is already present, that one will worship the Father neither on this mountain nor in Jerusalem, but rather those who truly worship will worship the Father in spirit and in truth, for the Father wants to have those who worship Him in this way; God is a spirit and those who worship must

---

97 Matthew 7:6: "Do not give dogs what is holy, and do not throw your pearls before pigs, lest they trample them underfoot and turn to attack you."

98 Luke 17:20–21: Being asked by the Pharisees when the kingdom of God would come, he answered them, "The kingdom of God is not coming in ways that can be observed, nor will they say, 'Look, here it is!' or 'There!' for behold, the kingdom of God is in the midst of you."

99 *Tagzeit*: One of the seven canonical hours dedicated to prayer.

100 *Ist dann ein solches Reich Gottes in euch Lutherischen?*: Is that the kind of kingdom of God you Lutherans recognize?

worship to him in spirit and in truth."[101] Therefore, lay down all churchgoing, regularly scheduled prayers, and your counting of daily prayers, which are said not in spirit and truth but rather much more according to the legal requirements and the counting of prayers, outwardly required and sleepily murmured, about which Christ complains, in Matthew 15: "This folk honors me with lips, and their heart is far from mine."[102]

Parson: Christ says, though, in Luke 18, "You should pray without ceasing."[103]

Shoemaker: Yes, prayer in the spirit can occur without ceasing, but your many prayers are rejected by Christ in Matthew 6: "You should not babble."[104]

Parson: Dear one, what is then a prayer or worship service in spirit and truth? Teach me so that I will never be required to pray at midnight Mass or the scheduled hourly prayers.

Shoemaker: Read the little book by Martin Luther on Christian freedom,[105] which he sent to Pope Leo X; there you will find a short description.

Parson: I wish that Luther and all his books would be burned. I have never read one of them and don't want to read them.

---

101 John 4:21–24: Jesus said to her, "Woman, believe me, the hour is coming when neither on this mountain nor in Jerusalem will you worship the Father. You worship what you do not know; we worship what we know, for salvation is from the Jews. But the hour is coming, and is now here, when the true worshipers will worship the Father in spirit and truth, for the Father is seeking such people to worship him. God is spirit, and those who worship him must worship in spirit and truth."

102 Matthew 15:8: "'This people honors me with their lips, but their heart is far from me" [Christ quoting Isaiah].

103 The actual reference is found in 1 Thessalonians 5:17: Pray without ceasing.

104 Matthew 6:7: "And when you pray, do not heap up empty phrases as the Gentiles do, for they think that they will be heard for their many words."

105 Martin Luther, *Von der Freiheit eines Christenmenschen* (1520).

Shoemaker:	Well,[106] then what are you judging?
Parson:	What? You never worship the saints.
Shoemaker:	Christ says in Matthew 4, "You should serve the Lord your God and serve him alone."[107]
Parson:	Yes, we have to have intercessors with God, though.
Shoemaker:	First John 1 says, "And if one sins, so too do we have an intercessor with God, Jesus Christ, who is righteous, and the same is the reconciliation for our sin."[108]
Parson:	Yes, dear one, yes, necessity breaks iron. If your hand were broken, you would call Saint Wolfgang.[109]
Shoemaker:	No, Christ says in Matthew 11, "Come to me, all you who are tired and burdened, and I will refresh you."[110] Where would you seek better help? You have made false gods out of the saints and are being led away from Christ.
Parson:	Yes, you have misinterpreted it. How is it that you Lutherans never fast; does the Lutheran spirit teach you that?
Shoemaker:	Fasting is not commanded of us but rather left to choice. Christ says in Matthew 6, "Whenever you fast, anoint your head";[111] don't say, "You should or must fast" as the stepfathers in Rome do.

---

106 *Ei*: An interjection that can be translated in multiple ways.

107 Matthew 4:10: "You shall worship the Lord your God and him only shall you serve."

108 1 John 2:1–2: My little children, I am writing these things to you so that you may not sin. But if anyone does sin, we have an advocate with the Father, Jesus Christ the righteous. He is the propitiation for our sins, and not for ours only but also for the sins of the whole world.

109 Saint Wolfgang: One of the fourteen holy helpers, particularly an intercessor for healing.

110 Matthew 11:28: Come to me, all who labor and are heavy laden, and I will give you rest.

111 Matthew 6:17–18: But when you fast, anoint your head and wash your face, that your fasting may not be seen by others but by your Father who is in secret. And your Father who sees in secret will reward you.

Parson: Yes, but you never fast.

Shoemaker: I believe the handworkers[112] fast the true fast more if they eat four times a day than all the monks and nuns and priests in the whole German lands. The day is almost gone. I don't want to speak of it anymore.[113]

Parson: So be quiet, but I want to talk. Fasting is the least of it. You Lutherans stuff yourselves with meat on Fridays that the devil blesses for you.

Shoemaker: Also, eating meat is not forbidden by God; therefore, it is not a sin, as one troubles the unknowing weak with this. Christ says in Matthew 15, "What goes into the mouth does not make a man unclean, but rather what comes out of the mouth makes man unclean, such as unclean thoughts, murder, adultery, fornication, theft, false witness, profane language."[114] And Paul says in 1 Corinthians 10, "Whatever is sold at the meat market may be eaten."[115]

Parson: Say what you want, but don't have what you want. One should not set aside good old customs that have had value for four or five hundred years.

Shoemaker: Christ says in John 14, "I am the way, the truth, and the life."[116] He doesn't say, "I am the custom."[117] Therefore, you must follow the truth, which the word of God and

---

112 Craftsmen or tradesmen, such as shoemakers.

113 We need to move on.

114 Matthew 15:11: "It is not what goes into the mouth that defiles a person, but what comes out of the mouth; this defiles a person."

115 1 Corinthians 10:18–20: Consider the people of Israel: are not those who eat the sacrifices participants in the altar? What do I imply then? That food offered to idols is anything, or that an idol is anything? No, I imply that what pagans sacrifice they offer to demons and not to God. I do not want you to be participants with demons.

116 John 14:6: Jesus said to him, "I am the way, and the truth, and the life. No one comes to the Father except through me."

117 *Gewonheit*: Could be translated as custom, practice, or habit.

God himself is, that remains eternally, as it says in Matthew 24,[118] but customs come from mankind, who are all liars, according to Psalm 115;[119] therefore, customs are short lived.

Parson: Dear one, tell me one thing. Why do you Lutherans never go to confession? That is much more heretical.

Shoemaker: That is also not commanded by God, neither in the Old nor in the New Testament.

Parson: But Christ says in Luke 17, "Go and show yourselves to the priest, and so on."[120]

Shoemaker: If showing[121] is called confession, that is unusual German to me; you have to prove it to me with more Scripture. Should such a necessary and healing thing be confession for the ears, as you say, then it must be clearly stated in the Scripture.

Parson: So don't you want to do what is commanded by God and written in the Scripture? That is a woeful thing.

Shoemaker: I can't fulfill such a thing, like in Acts 15.[122] Why should I add to my burden?

Parson: Such things have been ordered by the holy fathers in their councils.

Shoemaker: From whom do they have the power?

Parson: Christ says in John 16, "I have much to say to you, but you can't bear it yet, but when the true spirit comes, he will

---

118 Matthew 24:35: Heaven and earth will pass away, but my words will not pass away.

119 Actually, Psalm 116:11: I said in my alarm, "All mankind are liars."

120 Luke 17:14: When he saw them [ten lepers] he said to them, "Go and show yourselves to the priests." And as they went they were cleansed.

121 Showing oneself to the priest after a miracle.

122 Acts 15:10: Now, therefore, why are you putting God to the test by placing a yoke on the neck of the disciples that neither our fathers nor we have been able to bear?

guide you in all truth."[123] Hear, this is how the councils of Christ were appointed.

Shoemaker: Oh, Christ says before that in John 15, "The comforter, the Holy Spirit which my Father will send in my name, the same will teach you all and remind you of everything that I have said."[124] Hear, sir, he doesn't say he will teach you new things that I have not told you but rather that which I have already said. He will remind you and explain it so that you can understand it correctly as I have meant it. He means therefore when he says, "He will guide you in the truth."

Parson: Do you Lutherans hold no councils?

Shoemaker: Yes, we recognize the council of the apostles in Jerusalem.

Parson: Did the apostles hold a council?

Shoemaker: Yes, don't you have a Bible?

Parson: Cook, bring me the big old book.

Cook:[125] Lord,[126] is this it?

Parson: No, that is the decrees; don't confuse me.

Cook: Lord, is this it?

Parson: Yes, brush off the dust and cobwebs.[127] Now, Master Hans, where is it written?

Shoemaker: Find the Acts of the Apostles 15.[128]

---

123 John 16:13: When the Spirit of truth comes, he will guide you into all the truth, for he will not speak on his own authority, but whatever he hears he will speak, and he will declare to you the things that are to come.

124 John 15:26: "But when the Helper comes, whom I will send to you from the Father, the Spirit of truth, who proceeds from the Father, he will bear witness about me."

125 The cook, who has not been present, enters.

126 *Herr* is translated here as "lord" instead of "sir" so as to demonstrate the greater deference shown to the parson by the cook than by the shoemaker.

127 Literally, the old dirt and curses.

128 Acts 15:4–11: When they came to Jerusalem, they were welcomed by the church and the apostles and the elders, and they declared all that God had done with

Parson: Find it yourself; I'm not acquainted with it. I know more useful things to read.

Shoemaker: Here it is, sir.

Parson: Cook, mark Acts 15. I would like to read about the good deeds of the old fellows.

Shoemaker: Yes, read. You'll find that one may not lay the burdens of the Old Testament upon the Christians, not to mention the much newer commandments and sins that have been conceived[129] and with which the Christians are burdened. Therefore, we are not required to hear you.

Parson: Christ says, though, in Luke 10, "Whoever hears you hears me, whoever spurns you, spurns me."[130] Is that not clear enough?

Shoemaker: Yes, when you proclaim the gospel and the word of God, we will hear you as Christ himself, but where you proclaim your own ideas and imaginations, we shouldn't listen to you at all, when Christ says in Matthew 15, "You serve me

---

them. But some believers who belonged to the party of the Pharisees rose up and said, "It is necessary to circumcise them and to order them to keep the law of Moses." . . . The apostles and the elders were gathered together to consider this matter. And after there had been much debate, Peter stood up and said to them, "Brothers, you know that in the early days God made a choice among you, that by my mouth the Gentiles should hear the word of the gospel and believe. And God, who knows the heart, bore witness to them, by giving them the Holy Spirit just as he did to us, and he made no distinction between us and them, having cleansed their hearts by faith. Now, therefore, why are you putting God to the test by placing a yoke on the neck of the disciples that neither our fathers nor we have been able to bear? But we believe that we will be saved through the grace of the Lord Jesus, just as they will."

129 A newer, clearer explanation of sin.

130 Luke 10:16: "The one who hears you hears me, and the one who rejects you rejects me, and the one who rejects me rejects him who sent me."

in vain, when you teach the doctrines of men,"[131] and further, "Whatever plant my heavenly Father has not planted will be ripped out by the roots."[132]

Parson: Are the councils the doctrines of men?

Shoemaker: To be perfectly honest, the councils have done harm to Christianity.

Parson: Which? Show me.

Shoemaker: First of all, the commandments, which are innumerable, as you know, are much worse that have to do with excommunication and mostly not grounded in the Scripture. Such laws are extremely inflated and restrict and convolute the human conscience so that they have been regarded as equal to and even preferred to the true commandments of God and so that God's true laws are disrespected by the people. Such people are the ones to whom Paul refers in 1 Timothy 4: "In the end times some will be driven from faith and give heed to seducing spirits and doctrines of devils, speaking lies in hypocrisy and having their consciences seared with a hot iron, forbidding to marry and commanding to abstain from meats which God created to be received with thanksgiving of them which believe and know the truth."[133]

Parson: Where has that happened? With which commandment?

---

131 Matthew 15:6: So for the sake of your tradition you have made void the word of God.

132 Matthew 15:13: He answered, "Every plant that my heavenly Father has not planted will be rooted up."

133 1 Timothy 4:1–5: Now the Spirit expressly says that in later times some will depart from the faith by devoting themselves to deceitful spirits and teachings of demons, through the insincerity of liars whose consciences are seared, who forbid marriage and require abstinence from foods that God created to be received with thanksgiving by those who believe and know the truth. For everything created by God is good, and nothing is to be rejected if it is received with thanksgiving, for it is made holy by the word of God and prayer.

Shoemaker:	Eating meat on Fridays has been declared a greater sin than adultery, and similarly when a priest is truly married, he has committed a bigger sin than if he cavorted with prostitutes.
Parson:	I understand you very well.[134] What is another harm?
Shoemaker:	Another is the establishment of the new worship [order] and good works, which have to do mostly with monks, nuns, and priests, and are certainly (if you want to speak about this strongly) vain outward masquerades, which God has not named,[135] and through these orders you have abandoned true Christian good works, which God did command.
Parson:	What are the true Christian good works?
Shoemaker:	Christ taught us in Matthew 7, "Do unto others as you would have others do unto you. That is the whole law and prophets."[136] And in Matthew 25, he teaches us to feed the hungry, to give drink to the thirsty, to shelter the poor, to clothe the naked, to heal the sick, and to give comfort to the enslaved.[137]
Parson:	Are only Christian works all that make up a Christian life?

---

134 *Spricht der Walch*: A saying meaning "says the Welshman."

135 Commanded.

136 Matthew 7:12: "So whatever you wish that others would do to you, do also to them, for this is the Law and the Prophets."

137 Matthew 25:34–40: "Then the King will say to those on his right, 'Come, you who are blessed by my Father, inherit the kingdom prepared for you from the foundation of the world. For I was hungry and you gave me food, I was thirsty and you gave me drink, I was a stranger and you welcomed me, I was naked and you clothed me, I was sick and you visited me, I was in prison and you came to me.' Then the righteous will answer him, saying, 'Lord, when did we see you hungry and feed you, or thirsty and give you drink? And when did we see you a stranger and welcome you, or naked and clothe you? And when did we see you sick or in prison and visit you?' And the King will answer them, 'Truly, I say to you, as you did it to one of the least of these my brothers, you did it to me.'"

Shoemaker: Yes, a true believer who is reborn is from water and spirit [and], as it says in John 3,[138] serves God alone in spirit and in truth and your neighbor with works of Christian charity. That is the sum of the Christian being. But these works happen in secret,[139] because one hangs up neither a sign, a helmet, nor a coat of arms, which is expected of the saints who tout works. Such Christians do nothing more, so they go around with their masquerade.

Parson: Are you saying that our singing and reading don't matter?

Shoemaker: Christ commands nothing of us other than the works of compassion in the last commandment, Matthew 25.[140] Then you monks and priests will survive like the wife of the ring maker,[141] who lost her ears at the priory.[142]

Parson: You have ideas! Go to the oven and warm yourself.[143] Does Luther teach you such absurdities?

---

138 John 3:5–6: Jesus answered, "Truly, truly, I say to you, unless one is born of water and the Spirit, he cannot enter the kingdom of God. That which is born of the flesh is flesh, and that which is born of the Spirit is spirit."

139 He provides no identification, does not advertise himself.

140 Matthew 25:41–46: "Then he will say to those on his left, 'Depart from me, you cursed, into the eternal fire prepared for the devil and his angels. For I was hungry and you gave me no food, I was thirsty and you gave me no drink, I was a stranger and you did not welcome me, naked and you did not clothe me, sick and in prison and you did not visit me.' Then they also will answer, saying, 'Lord, when did we see you hungry or thirsty or a stranger or naked or sick or in prison, and did not minister to you?' Then he will answer them, saying, 'Truly, I say to you, as you did not do it to one of the least of these, you did not do it to me.' And these will go away into eternal punishment, but the righteous into eternal life."

141 *Rinklerin*: Could be the wife of the ring maker or the wife of the wrestler.

142 A punishment for theft or heresy or to bring shame upon the accused. Ralf Hübner, "Ohr abgeschnitten und an die Tür genagelt," Sächsische.de (Dresden), November 30, 2018.

143 Get out of here!

Shoemaker:	No.
Parson:	Dear one, what do you think of Luther?
Shoemaker:	I think he is a Christian teacher such as has not been known since the time of the apostles.
Parson:	Dear one, what necessity[144] has he added to Christianity?
Shoemaker:	He brought all your human doctrine,[145] teaching, traditions, and imagery to light and warned us against it. Another thing he showed to us is the Holy Scripture, in which we recognize that we are bound in sin and are sinners, Romans 5[146]; and another thing, he has shown us that Christ is our only salvation as in 1 Corinthians 1,[147] and these two things the Scripture pushes[148] through and through. In it we learn to set our own hope, faith, and trust in Christ, which is then the true good work of holiness, as Christ says in John 6.[149]
Parson:	Are no other works allowed? Doesn't Christ say in Matthew 5, "Let your light shine before men, that they may

---

144 Needed teachings.

145 Commandments.

146 Romans 5:19: For as by the one man's disobedience the many were made sinners, so by the one man's obedience the many will be made righteous.

147 1 Corinthians 1:26–31: For consider your calling, brothers: not many of you were wise according to worldly standards, not many were powerful, not many were of noble birth. But God chose what is foolish in the world to shame the wise; God chose what is weak in the world to shame the strong; God chose what is low and despised in the world, even things that are not, to bring to nothing things that are, so that no human being might boast in the presence of God. And because of him you are in Christ Jesus, who became to us wisdom from God, righteousness and sanctification and redemption, so that, as it is written, "Let the one who boasts, boast in the Lord."

148 In the sense of exhortation.

149 John 6:37: All that the Father gives me will come to me, and whoever comes to me I will never cast out.

see your good works and glorify your Father who is in heaven"?[150]

Shoemaker: Paul says in Romans 5, "Man is justified through faith, without works."[151] And also in Romans 1, "The righteous shall live by faith."[152]

Parson: James 2 says, "Faith without works is dead."[153]

Shoemaker: A true Christian faith doesn't celebrate but brings forth good fruit, as Christ said in Matthew 7: "A good tree cannot bring forth bad fruit."[154] But such good works occur not to serve heaven, which Christ earned for us; also not from fear of hell, for Christ has redeemed us; [and] also not for honor, for honor should go only to God, as it is written in Matthew 4;[155] but rather in godly love as a thanksgiving to God and to the help and profit of your neighbor. So, dear sir, what do you think of Luther's fruit?

Parson: Is he so righteous that so few learned and powerful men follow[156] him and so many rough and unlearned do follow him?

Shoemaker: Neither Pilate, Herod, Caiphas, nor Annas followed Christ, also not the Pharisees, but rather turned against him; only the common folk followed him. For that reason,

---

150 Matthew 5:16: In the same way, let your light shine before others, so that they may see your good works and give glory to your Father who is in heaven.

151 Romans 5:1: Therefore, since we have been justified by faith, we have peace with God through our Lord Jesus Christ.

152 Romans 1:17: For in it the righteousness of God is revealed from faith for faith, as it is written, "The righteous shall live by faith."

153 James 2:17: So also faith by itself, if it does not have works, is dead.

154 Matthew 7:17–18: So, every healthy tree bears good fruit, but the diseased tree bears bad fruit. A healthy tree cannot bear bad fruit, nor can a diseased tree bear good fruit.

155 Matthew 4:10: Then Jesus said to him, "Be gone, Satan! For it is written, 'You shall worship the Lord your God and him only shall you serve.'"

156 *anhangen:* Cleave to.

Christ rejoiced in the Spirit and said in Luke 10, "Father, I thank you that you have hidden your truth from the wise of the world and have revealed it to the small ones."[157]

Parson: Oh, dear one, the common folk only concede that a small part of Luther's teachings are correct.

Shoemaker: That's what your dumb preachers do who cry out he is a heretic and do so without Scripture. Christ recognized the common folk in Matthew 5:[158] "Go through the narrow gate, for the gate is wide that leads to destruction and there are many who walk through it."[159] And in Matthew 22: "Many are called, but few are chosen."[160]

Parson: Such words are used in the pubs, in the market, and everywhere, like fools, and don't belong in such a place.

Shoemaker: Christ said in Matthew 10, "Whatever I whisper in your ear, you should preach from the rooftops."[161]

Parson: If I am to tell the truth, I consider Luther to be the greatest heretic since Arius's[162] time, and you are his followers, not worthy of skin and hair, as many of you are, and nothing good is in you; nothing good will come of you. Don't you know it? That title[163] I give to Luther and to you together.

---

157 Luke 10:23–24: Then turning to the disciples he said privately, "Blessed are the eyes that see what you see! For I tell you that many prophets and kings desired to see what you see, and did not see it, and to hear what you hear, and did not hear it."

158 The actual verse is found in Matthew 7.

159 Matthew 7:13: "Enter by the narrow gate. For the gate is wide and the way is easy that leads to destruction, and those who enter by it are many."

160 Matthew 22:14: "For many are called, but few are chosen."

161 Matthew 10:27: What I tell you in the dark, say in the light, and what you hear whispered, proclaim on the housetops.

162 Arius, the heretic, declared that Christ was a created being and therefore subordinate to the Father. "Five Heretics."

163 The title of "heretic."

Shoemaker: On one point you are correct: no one is good except God, Matthew 19,[164] for our nature is corrupt as is written in Genesis 8, "The human heart is set on evil from youth."[165] Each man must mortify himself daily with the cross, else he might hinder the spirit. For nature ceases not to be that thing whereunto it is inclined, although the spirit be made righteous through faith. Proverbs 24 says, "The righteous falls seven times a day."[166] For that reason, we pray all day long, "Forgive us our guilt," found in Matthew 6.[167] And Paul says to the Romans in chapter 7, "The good that I want to do, I don't do, but rather the bad, that I don't want to do, is what I do."[168] And he cries further, "O I am a miserable man, who will save me from the body of death?"[169] This shows that we are sinners until death. Let the one without sin cast the first stone, as recorded in John 8.[170]

Parson: You are all unprofitable people, persnickety; I hope you'll be knocked on the head, for there is no other remedy for you.

---

164   Matthew 19:17: And he said to him, "Why do you ask me about what is good? There is only one who is good. If you would enter life, keep the commandments."

165   Genesis 8:21: And when the Lord smelled the pleasing aroma, the Lord said in his heart, "I will never again curse the ground because of man, for the intention of man's heart is evil from his youth. Neither will I ever again strike down every living creature as I have done."

166   Proverbs 24:16: . . . for the righteous falls seven times and rises again, but the wicked stumble in times of calamity.

167   Matthew 6:12: . . . and forgive us our debts, as we also have forgiven our debtors.

168   Romans 7:19: For I do not do the good I want, but the evil I do not want is what I keep on doing.

169   Romans 7:24: Wretched man that I am! Who will deliver me from this body of death?

170   John 8:7: And as they continued to ask him, he stood up and said to them, "Let him who is without sin among you be the first to throw a stone at her."

Shoemaker:	What? Do you want to fight with the sword? That doesn't suit you spiritual ones.[171]
Parson:	Why not? Didn't Christ say in Luke 22[172] that two swords are useful, the spiritual and the worldly?
Shoemaker:	Yet Christ forbade Peter in Matthew 26 and said, "Whosoever fights with the sword will die by the sword."[173]
Parson:	We don't seem to be able to win with sweetness, so we must use sour when the heretics have gotten out of hand. It's high time to strike!
Shoemaker:	Oh no, rather follow the advice of Gamaliel in Acts 5: "If the doctrine be of man, it will fall without the sword,[174] but if it be of God, it cannot be suppressed, because you can't fight against God."[175]

---

171 *euch Geistlichen*: You who are "holier than thou."

172 Luke 22:35–38: And he said to them, "When I sent you out with no moneybag or knapsack or sandals, did you lack anything?" They said, "Nothing." He said to them, "But now let the one who has a moneybag take it, and likewise a knapsack. And let the one who has no sword sell his cloak and buy one. For I tell you that this Scripture must be fulfilled in me: 'And he was numbered with the transgressors.' For what is written about me has its fulfillment." And they said, "Look, Lord, here are two swords." And he said to them, "It is enough."

173 Matthew 26:52: Then Jesus said to him, "Put your sword back into its place. For all who take the sword will perish by the sword."

174 Of its own accord.

175 Acts 5:34–40: But a Pharisee in the council named Gamaliel, a teacher of the law held in honor by all the people, stood up and gave orders to put the men outside for a little while. And he said to them, "Men of Israel, take care what you are about to do with these men. For before these days Theudas rose up, claiming to be somebody, and a number of men, about four hundred, joined him. He was killed, and all who followed him were dispersed and came to nothing. After him Judas the Galilean rose up in the days of the census and drew away some of the people after him. He too perished, and all who followed him were scattered. So in the present case I tell you, keep away from these men and let them alone, for if this plan or this undertaking is of man, it will fail;

Parson:	Nothing will come of it.[176]
Shoemaker:	Certainly, sir, your will be done. Matthew 6[177] says, "The student is not above the teacher."[178] John 15 says, "They have persecuted me, so too they will persecute you,"[179] and Luke 6, "Blessed are you, when men shall revile you and persecute you for my name's sake."[180]
Parson:	Some will remain silent who are now crying out.
Shoemaker:	Christ says in Matthew 10, "Whoever acknowledges me before men, him will I acknowledge before my Father who is in heaven."[181]
Parson:	Silence must be kept or heads will roll.
Shoemaker:	Christ in Matthew 10 says, "Don't fear those who would kill the body, they cannot kill the soul."[182] Oh Lord God, how wonderful to die for your name's sake.
Parson:	Death would be earned. A heretic can be executed after three warnings.
Shoemaker:	You have to prove with the Scripture that we are heretics.
Parson:	That's what we will easily do.

---

but if it is of God, you will not be able to overthrow them. You might even be found opposing God!" So they took his advice.

176 The new doctrine.

177 The verse is actually found in Matthew 10.

178 Matthew 10:24: A disciple is not above his teacher, nor a servant above his master.

179 John 15:20: "Remember the word that I said to you: 'A servant is not greater than his master.' If they persecuted me, they will also persecute you. If they kept my word, they will also keep yours."

180 Luke 6:22: "Blessed are you when people hate you and when they exclude you and revile you and spurn your name as evil, on account of the Son of Man!"

181 Matthew 10:32: So everyone who acknowledges me before men, I also will acknowledge before my Father who is in heaven.

182 Matthew 10:28: And do not fear those who kill the body but cannot kill the soul. Rather fear him who can destroy both soul and body in hell.

Shoemaker: Then God will place our blood on your hands that you allowed us (the poor sheep of Christ) to be lead astray for so long,[183] and you have allowed so many preachers to teach falsely, and their teachings were not disputed.

Parson: It will happen soon; we are paying attention to you ([through] all our sermons).

Shoemaker: Yes, it is true; you have fulfilled Matthew 22: "And the Pharisees went in and counseled together to trap him and sent their servants along with Herod's servants."[184]

Parson: Why not? One has to deal with heretics surreptitiously when they are crafty so that one can shave them bald.[185]

Shoemaker: O God, these preachers want to lead us all to Christ and leave no one out. At the same time, you would lead us all to the hangman. You want fire from heaven to fall on us, as in Luke 9.[186] Hear Christ speak, "Don't you know which spirit you are the children of? The Son of Man did not come to condemn, but rather to save souls."[187] It is written in 2 Corinthians 13, "The Father gave me power not to condemn, but rather to build up."[188]

Parson: That is what we want to do as well.

---

183 An interesting parallel to *The Wittenberg Nightingale*.

184 Matthew 22:15–16: Then the Pharisees went and plotted how to entangle him in his words. And they sent their disciples to him, along with the Herodians, saying, "Teacher, we know that you are true and teach the way of God truthfully, and you do not care about anyone's opinion, for you are not swayed by appearances."

185 Expose the heresy.

186 Luke 9:54: And when his disciples James and John saw it, they said, "Lord, do you want us to tell fire to come down from heaven and consume them?"

187 John 3:17: For God did not send his Son into the world to condemn the world, but in order that the world might be saved through him.

188 2 Corinthians 13:10: For this reason I write these things while I am away from you, that when I come I may not have to be severe in my use of the authority that the Lord has given me for building up and not for tearing down.

Shoemaker:	Well, fire and sword don't suit it[189] but rather the word of God, as is written in Hebrews 4, "which is sharper than a two-edged sword."[190] For that reason, you are not of God, because your doctrine fights against the word of God, which is the power of God, according to 1 Corinthians 1.[191]
Parson:	That doesn't make a difference.
Shoemaker:	Yes, you are not bringing God's words. You seek to protect not the honor of God but rather your own power, honor, and riches. The word of God is against that, which is why you persecute it[192] and work[193] against one another.
Parson:	Yes, but then you can't straighten out the people.[194] When the heart is full, the mouth runs over, it says in Luke 6.[195]
Shoemaker:	With you it is as Christ says in Luke 7, like children sitting in the marketplace and calling to one another and saying, "We have played the flute for you and you have not danced and we have mourned for you and you have not wept."[196] The same goes for you; one tells you the word of God for

---

189 *Reimbt sich aber nit darzu*: Don't rhyme with that.

190 Hebrews 4:12: For the word of God is living and active, sharper than any two-edged sword, piercing to the division of soul and of spirit, of joints and of marrow, and discerning the thoughts and intentions of the heart.

191 1 Corinthians 1:18: For the word of the cross is folly to those who are perishing, but to us who are being saved it is the power of God.

192 The word of God.

193 Struggle.

194 Set them straight.

195 Luke 6:45: The good person out of the good treasure of his heart produces good, and the evil person out of his evil treasure produces evil, for out of the abundance of the heart his mouth speaks.

196 Luke 7:31–32: "To what then shall I compare the people of this generation, and what are they like? They are like children sitting in the marketplace and calling to one another, 'We played the flute for you, and you did not dance; we sang a dirge, and you did not weep.'"

comfort, but you receive it with derision; it is told to you earnestly, but you spurn it.

Parson: Even if you sing like a little bird, you still aren't one.

Shoemaker: Your heart is hardened like that of Pharaoh in Exodus from the seventh to the fifteenth chapters, who accepted neither miracle nor plague; his opinion was that the children of Israel should continue making bricks so that he could continue celebrating with his people.[197] You also think of us as you want to think of us.

Parson: You bet![198] You've figured it out.

Shoemaker: Yes, it seems to me you are like the false bailiff in Luke 16, saying, "What should I do, my Lord has taken my office from me, I cannot dig and I am ashamed to beg."[199] You holy ones are afraid of the same thing; for that reason neither exhortation nor admonishment can help.

Parson: Don't you know, Christ speaks in John 6, "No one comes to me, but that the Father shows him."[200] Time brings roses: Who knows which will convert the other?

Shoemaker: O Lord, I hear this gladly. It is written in John 15, "Without me you can do nothing,"[201] and further, "You did not choose me, I chose you."[202] Therefore, it's not up to us;

---

197 In Exodus 7–15, Egypt was struck by ten plagues. Pharaoh hardened his heart each time and did not allow the Israelites to leave Egypt.

198 *Wett Fritz:* An idiom for "you guessed it right!"

199 Luke 16:3: "And the manager said to himself, 'What shall I do, since my master is taking the management away from me? I am not strong enough to dig, and I am ashamed to beg.'"

200 John 6:44: No one can come to me unless the Father who sent me draws him. And I will raise him up on the last day.

201 John 15:5: I am the vine; you are the branches. Whoever abides in me and I in him, he it is that bears much fruit, for apart from me you can do nothing.

202 John 15:16: You did not choose me, but I chose you and appointed you that you should go and bear fruit and that your fruit should abide, so that whatever you ask the Father in my name, he may give it to you.

	God must convert us. I wish that for all of you with all my heart.
Parson:	It's time for church. Cook, bring me my robe! Dear master,[203] go in peace. It will all be well.
Shoemaker:	If God wills it. Well then, good-bye, peace be with you, dear sir; don't take anything I've said as evil, and forgive me.
Parson:	God forgive us our sins!
Shoemaker:	Amen.[204]
Parson:	Dear cook,[205] how freely the laity speaks against us holy ones. I think the devil has disgruntled the shoemaker; he harassed me, and if I were not so learned, he would have set me on a donkey.[206] Therefore, I won't hire him anymore but rather Hans Zobel;[207] he's a good, easygoing fellow, doesn't care much about the Holy Scripture and the Lutheran heretical writings, which are not appropriate for the laity, nor does he dispute with me. As Solomon said, "Whoever walks in integrity, walks well."[208] I should have thrown that one at the shoemaker. That would have made him stumble.
Cook:	Lord, I was afraid when you couldn't best him with the Scriptures that you would hit him with the slippers.
Parson:	If I had not feared that an uproar might have been stirred up, I would have thrown the slippers in his face. Neither Christ nor Paul could have gotten rid of him in three days, he puts so much faith in them.

---

203 The shoemaker was a master at his craft; thus, the title "master" is appropriate.

204 The shoemaker exits.

205 The cook enters with the robe. The shoemaker exits.

206 *Er het mich auf den Esel gesetzt*: A euphemism for "to make a fool of someone."

207 No reference to this name has been found.

208 Proverbs 10:9: Whoever walks in integrity walks securely, but he who makes his ways crooked will be found out.

Cook: I'm amazed at how smart the laity is getting to be.

Parson: If you want to know, I'll tell you. No one cares about the holy ones anymore. There was a time when the Holy Father, the pope, and the bishops would compel such heretics as Luther and others who preach in the same manner[209] who raise the office of preacher according to the holy rights and who should be made to recant according to the holy canon as with Jon Huss in Constance.[210] If one could only make the evangelical preachers be quiet, then everything would be good. But when they are told to be silent, they come and want to debate with the pope and the bishops. Until now such a thing has been unheard of. That one who is not worthy would debate with the most holy one! But it will get better. Even if the preachers don't want it, they have to be quiet, as it says in Paul's writing,[211] and if the sword has to be used, then it has to be used, if the Holy Father wants to do that, then the laity must also be quiet, and we could return to our normal way of life.

Cook: It would be very good for everyone to debate with you as the shoemaker just did.

Parson: In the old days, we would have excommunicated one like him, but now we must listen to and learn from the laity, like the Pharisees did with Christ. Dear cook, call our heating man.[212] He reads a lot in the Bible, and maybe

---

209 *die auf sein Geigen predigen*: Who preach on his violin, an idiomatic phrase meaning "in the same manner."

210 Martyred in 1415 for his efforts to reform the (Catholic) church.

211 Hebrews 4:12: For the word of God is living and active, sharper than any two-edged sword, piercing to the division of soul and of spirit, of joints and of marrow, and discerning the thoughts and intentions of the heart.

212 *Calefactor*: The servant who kept the fire going (for cooking and heating) and the candles lit to provide light.

	he can quote the Scripture better than I can. He should find some good quotes for me out of curiosity.
Cook:	Heinrich, Heinrich, come see the Lord.
Calefactor:	Worthy Lord, what is it?
Parson:	Our shoemaker has vexed me and showed me much in the Bible, like is the practice of Lutherans. You must find me some chapters that he quoted that I would like to see in the Scripture.
Calefactor:	You should know it yourself. For a long time, you have helped the weak learn the catechism.
Parson:	One only needs an elementary education to understand what people wrote and did and very little about doctrine, which the holy fathers decided in the council.
Calefactor:	It really wasn't determined by the fathers in the council and the people who came later, for the same laws and doctrine and Scripture were from the word and spirit of God, as the prophets, apostles, and preachers were all men.
Parson:	Yes, so they could have been confused, but the Lutherans don't want to believe that.
Calefactor:	No, when Peter speaks in 2 Peter 1, there is no wisdom from man, but rather the holy ones of God have spoken, driven by the Holy Spirit.[213] And afterward Peter denounced the false prophets who led many misguided sects. This is referring to your holy position, rank, rules, and human findings[214] (outside of the word of God), which you are now using to avoid it [the wisdom of the Holy Spirit].
Parson:	Yes, it has been spoken not to us but rather to the ancients, and that was long ago.

---

213 2 Peter 1:21: For no prophecy was ever produced by the will of man, but men spoke from God as they were carried along by the Holy Spirit.

214 Human-created doctrine.

Calefactor: O you fools and hard of heart to believe all that which the prophets have said according to Luke 24.[215]

Cook: Lord, that means for you the cock is still crowing![216] You didn't suffer that from me.[217]

Parson: O you lousy reveler, do you also want to call me to justice? Are you also a Lutheran miscreant? Get out of this house and don't come back, you unashamed animal!

Calefactor: You're sorry that the shoemaker degraded the red beret.[218] Don't be surprised that God let the shepherds announce his good news.[219] Therefore, also the shoemaker has to teach you Pharisees, yes, the stones will cry out.[220] Old man, I make my decision with knowledge![221]

Cook: You are right. I'm surprised that you speak with the rough ones. They take care of neither you nor the holy candles.

Parson: I want to protect myself from him; a burned child fears fire. I need to get to church. Go to the market and buy a thrush or twelve. I have invited the chaplain with some gentlemen to dinner and will hold a banquet. Carry the Bible out of the parlor, and see to it that the dice and games are all together and that we have a fresh deck or two of cards ready.

---

215 Luke 24:25: And he said to them, "O foolish ones, and slow of heart to believe all that the prophets have spoken!"

216 There is still time, but be ready. Mark 13:35: Therefore stay awake—for you do not know when the master of the house will come, in the evening, or at midnight, or when the rooster crows, or in the morning.

217 It wasn't I who said it.

218 The symbol of his rank.

219 Referring to the angel's announcement to the shepherds of Jesus's birth, recorded in Luke 2.

220 Luke 19:40: He answered, "I tell you, if these were silent, the very stones would cry out."

221 The calefactor exits.

Cook: Yes, sir. Will you be back right after church?
Parson: Yes. Be sure the meal is ready.

1524

Philippians 3

Your stomach, your God.[222]

---

222 Philippians 3:19: Their end is destruction, their god is their belly, and they glory in their shame, with minds set on earthly things.

CHAPTER 6

A Discussion on the Public Works of the Spiritual Person and Their Vows, by Which They Suppose Themselves to Be Holy, to the Sacrilege of the Blood of Christ

Eyn geſprech võ den Scheinwerckẽ
der Gayſtlichen/vnd jren gelüßbten/damit
ſy zäuerleſterung des blůts Chriſti
vermaynen ſelig zůwerden.

Hans Sachß.
Schůſter.

ij. Thimot.iij.
Jr thorhait wirt offenbar werden yederman.

Introduction

In this second play, Hans Sachs continues his critique of Catholicism, specifically focusing on the practices, principles, and purpose of monkhood. In contrast to the first dialogue and *The Wittenberg Nightingale*, Sachs takes a less aggressive and ironic tone here, leading to both a more balanced end result and somewhat less popularity than the witty bluntness of the previous dialogue. Of the four Reformation dialogues, this is the most genial and polite between the two parties.

The play opens with monks who have come to beg for candles. They identify as Franciscans, part of an order of Catholics founded in 1209 by Saint Francis of Assisi. As part of this order, they would have taken three primary vows: poverty, chastity, and obedience, which are referenced throughout the play. On the other side of the discussion, we find two members of the laity: Hans the shoemaker and Peter the baker. As is Sachs's pattern, he represents himself in this play as the shoemaker Hans, the primary speaker. Hans exemplifies Sachs's emphasis on the sufficiency of Scripture by incessantly using Scripture to refute the points of the monks. Peter, on the other hand, contributes the practical viewpoint of the common man.

Throughout the play we see the overarching theme of whether the practices of the Franciscan order, and even its existence, are biblical and valuable, centering on the three primary vows already mentioned. Topics include the monks' use of money and possessions, whether they base their beliefs on the Bible or on the teachings of Saint Francis, their service to the community, the state of their hearts compared to their actions, and ultimately the source of their holiness and salvation.

The accompanying picture, illustrated by Erhard Schön, depicts an older, gesturing monk, who would represent the only speaker on behalf of the monks (Heinrich), and a younger monk who is not participating in the conversation. They are wearing sandals and carrying a full basket of candles with them. Both the abundance of candles and the obviously well-fed figures of the monks imply a disconnect from their stated virtues as discussed in the conversation. This depiction must have been satisfactory for Sachs, as Schön went on to become his primary illustrator in the following years.

Footnotes have been used to identify specific German or Latin words or phrases that have been translated other than literally or to add contextual information for the reader. As a reminder to the reader, verse numbers were not added to Scripture until 1551. Sachs cited by chapter only, while we have provided specific verse references.

A Discussion on the Public Works of the Spiritual Person and Their Vows, by Which They Suppose Themselves to Be Holy, to the Sacrilege of the Blood of Christ

Hans Sachs, Shoemaker

2 Timothy 3. Their folly will be clear to all men.[1]

Monk: Peace be with you, dear brothers! For the Lord's sake, give your holy alms to the barefoot monks[2]—for candles,[3] by which we sing and read.

Peter: I won't give such strong beggars anything when begging is forbidden. In Deuteronomy 15, God says, "No beggar should be among you."[4] I want to give my candles to poor, timid[5] neighbors who work as well.

Monk: I see; you are no doubt Lutheran.

Peter: No, we are evangelical.

---

1 2 Timothy 3:9: But they will not get very far, for their folly will be plain to all, as was that of those two men.

2 *Barfußen*: This refers to "discalced" monks, a type of congregation that goes about barefoot or only in sandals. Some parts of the Franciscan order practiced this. The two monks depicted are wearing sandals, while Peter is wearing close-toed shoes. Stephen Donovan, "Discalced," in *The Catholic Encyclopedia* (New York: Robert Appleton Company, 1909), https://www.newadvent.org/cathen/05028a.htm.

3 *Licht*: This literally translates to "light." The specific meaning of "candle" is clear through the accompanying depiction of two monks carrying a basket of candles.

4 Deuteronomy 15:4: But there will be no poor among you; for the Lord will bless you in the land that the Lord your God is giving you for an inheritance to possess.

5 *Hausarmen*: Literally "house poor." The poor who had homes but were too timid to beg. Any handouts they received would be given to them at home.

Monk: Well,[6] then do as the gospel teaches—namely, in Matthew 5, "Give to everyone who asks of you";[7] Luke 6, "Be generous, as your heavenly Father is generous";[8] and Luke 11, "Give alms from what you have, then everything will be pure for you."[9]

Hans: Brother Heinrich has already overcome you with Scripture.

Peter: I admit it; I can go no further. Come here, dear Brother Heinrich. Here is a penny[10] for the sake of the Lord. Buy yourself a candle according to your inclination.

Monk: Oh, God protect me, I may take no money. My order does not keep any.

Hans: Who created your order?

Monk: Our holy Father Franciscus.[11]

Hans: Is Franciscus your father, then? Does Christ not say in Matthew 23, "No one should call himself father on earth, for you have one Father, who is in heaven"?[12]

Monk: Oh, we know that well, but he has taught us as a godly father would his child.

Hans: Then Franciscus is your master, but Christ says in the same chapter, "You should not let yourselves be called master, for you have one Master, Christ."[13] Christ also says in John 14, "I am

---

6 *Ei*: An interjection used in a variety of contexts, including indignation, surprise, and so on. This is translated throughout this dialogue as "well" or "oh."

7 Matthew 5:42: Give to the one who begs from you, and do not refuse the one who would borrow from you.

8 Luke 6:36: Be merciful, even as your Father is merciful.

9 Luke 11:41: But give as alms those things that are within, and behold, everything is clean for you.

10 *Pfennig*: A German coin.

11 Saint Francis of Assisi, who founded the Franciscan order in the early 1200s.

12 Matthew 23:9: And call no man your father on earth, for you have one Father, who is in heaven.

13 Matthew 23:10: Neither be called instructors, for you have one instructor, the Christ.

the way, the truth, and the life,"[14] and in John 10, "I am the door to the sheep; whoever gets in elsewhere, he is a thief and a murderer."[15]

Monk: Well, you do not understand it correctly. He has not taught us from his own mind but has taken all his precepts from the holy gospel.

Hans: Where does it say then in the gospel that you shouldn't take or touch money? I would show you the opposite.

Monk: Where?

Hans: In Matthew 17, Christ said to Peter, "Go to the sea and cast your line. In the mouth of the first fish that comes out you will find a golden coin. Take it and give it for yourself and me."[16]

Monk: Matthew 6 says, however, "You should not collect for yourself treasure on earth,"[17] and further, "You cannot serve God and mammon."[18] In Luke 12, "Protect yourself from greed, for no one lives because of having abundance in his goods";[19] and Luke 18, "How difficult will it be for the rich to come into the

---

14 John 14:6: Jesus said to him, "I am the way, and the truth, and the life. No one comes to the Father except through me."

15 John 10:1, 7: "Truly, truly, I say to you, he who does not enter the sheepfold by the door but climbs in by another way, that man is a thief and a robber." . . . So Jesus again said to them, "Truly, truly, I say to you, I am the door of the sheep."

16 Matthew 17:27: "However, not to give offense to them, go to the sea and cast a hook and take the first fish that comes up, and when you open its mouth you will find a shekel. Take that and give it to them for me and for yourself."

17 Matthew 6:19: Do not lay up for yourselves treasures on earth, where moth and rust destroy and where thieves break in and steal.

18 Matthew 6:24: No one can serve two masters, for either he will hate the one and love the other, or he will be devoted to the one and despise the other. You cannot serve God and money.

19 Luke 12:15: And he said to them, "Take care, and be on your guard against all covetousness, for one's life does not consist in the abundance of his possessions."

kingdom of God";[20] and Matthew 19, Mark 10, and Luke 18, "If you want to be complete, go, sell what you have, and give it to the poor. In this way you will accumulate a treasure in heaven. And come and follow me."[21] You have there a reason and a source from the gospel for our willing poverty.

Hans: Well said. Do you barefoot monks hold to this?

Monk: Yes. We take no money, so we have none, neither little nor much.

Hans: Yes, though you have your collectors and distributors outside of the monastery, such as the princes,[22] and collect (under the guise of willing poverty) great treasure, buying cardinals' hats for many thousand ducats[23] and building exquisite monasteries like the palaces, as is going on today. If that isn't called collecting treasure and taking or touching money, then I don't know what I should call it.

Peter: It is called greed, under sleight of hand.[24]

---

20 Luke 18:24: Jesus, seeing that he had become sad, said, "How difficult it is for those who have wealth to enter the kingdom of God!"

21 Matthew 19:21: Jesus said to him, "If you would be perfect, go, sell what you possess and give to the poor, and you will have treasure in heaven; and come, follow me."

Mark 10:21: And Jesus, looking at him, loved him, and said to him, "You lack one thing: go, sell all that you have and give to the poor, and you will have treasure in heaven; and come, follow me."

Luke 18:22: When Jesus heard this, he said to him, "One thing you still lack. Sell all that you have and distribute to the poor, and you will have treasure in heaven; and come, follow me."

22 *Fürsten*: Territorial princes.

23 *Ducaten*: Gold or silver coins used across Europe.

24 *Under dem Hütlein gespilt*: Literally "played under the little hat." A common sixteenth-century idiom for sleight of hand or doing something secretly with the intent to deceive.

Monk: Oh dear one, it is not so serious. It is true, we do have caretakers, whom we allow to handle this. We, however, do not concern ourselves at all with the money and attend to our service to God.

Hans: Christ says, however, in Matthew 6, "Where your treasure is, there your heart is also."[25] Therefore, your heart is not in the monastery but perhaps in a citizen's house with your treasure. Therefore, you cannot serve God, because you serve mammon with your heart. From this follows that you have no contentment in your possessions, as it says in Luke 12, but constantly beg and scrape together worldly goods. How then will you enter the kingdom of God through your poverty, in which you pride yourselves?[26]

Monk: Well, dear master,[27] we left our possessions willingly. Should we thereafter never again accept holy alms from pious people?

Peter: Yes, some of you left barely one guilder[28] worth and came into an easy living,[29] well worth two hundred guilder. He is provided his whole life long with all needs and knows nothing of poverty but cuts off poor Christians from their bread just as they are about to eat.[30] Peter has testified of you in 2 Peter 2, "They lead

---

25   Matthew 6:21: For where your treasure is, there your heart will be also.

26   Luke 12:27–31: Consider the lilies, how they grow: they neither toil nor spin, yet I tell you, even Solomon in all his glory was not arrayed like one of these. But if God so clothes the grass, which is alive in the field today, and tomorrow is thrown into the oven, how much more will he clothe you, O you of little faith! And do not seek what you are to eat and what you are to drink, nor be worried. For all the nations of the world seek after these things, and your Father knows that you need them. Instead, seek his kingdom, and these things will be added to you.

27   Used to address a master at his craft, not someone in a position of authority.

28   *Gulden*: A gold coin.

29   *Pfründ*: Sinecure. A position that does not require much effort but provides status and financial benefit.

30   Literally cutting off the bread from in front of their mouths.

a tender life off your love, and live on what is yours."[31] I don't call that selling one's possessions and giving to the poor.

Monk: Do not hold me in disdain. You and those like you do not give us much; rather, great lords, rich citizens, and merchants feed us out of their abundance.

Peter: Well and good. Where do those take it from? Solely from us: we, the eleven thousand martyrs,[32] must pay, for they deceive, pressure, force, and coerce us, often to the point of losing blood. Afterward they eat with your awful fathers (holy fathers, I should say),[33] who are strong and lazy. These themselves could well work and might feed other poor Christians along with themselves.

Hans: Yes, if Christian love were in them, as Paul writes in 2 Thessalonians 3: "We have not taken bread from anyone in vain, but rather we have labored day and night with toil and work, so that we would burden none among you."[34] And further, "He who does not work, should not eat."[35]

---

31 An exact match to Sachs's verse was not found; 2 Peter 2:3 is the closest to his meaning: "And in their greed they will exploit you with false words."

32 Possibly a reference to the legend of Saint Ursula and the eleven thousand martyred virgins. Ben Johnson, "The Legend of St. Ursula and the 11,000 British Virgins," Historic UK, November 15, 2016, https://www.historic-uk.com/HistoryUK/HistoryofEngland/Saint-Ursula-the-11000-British-Virgins/.

33 A play on words. *Heillos*, meaning awful, terrible, or hopeless, is contrasted with *heilig*, meaning holy.

34 2 Thessalonians 3:8: . . . nor did we eat anyone's bread without paying for it, but with toil and labor we worked night and day, that we might not be a burden to any of you.

35 2 Thessalonians 3:10: For even when we were with you, we would give you this command: If anyone is not willing to work, let him not eat.

Monk: Does it not say in 1 Corinthians 9, "Do you not know, those who work in the temple feed themselves through the temple, and those who care for the altar live off of the altar"?[36]

Hans: It says, however, in the text directly following, in 1 Corinthians 9, "So the Lord has commanded: those who preach the gospel should feed themselves from the gospel."[37] But like you say, this became practice in the Old Testament because of the servants of the temple and altar, as in Leviticus 7.[38] This is in the past, however, for in the New Testament we have no physical temple made from wood and stone. Rather, we ourselves are the temple of God, as in 1 Corinthians 3: "Do you not know that you are the temple of God, and that the spirit of God lives in you?"[39] Therefore, we do not allow temple servants anymore. Since we also have no altar for sacrifices, we do not allow altar servants anymore. For Christ alone is high priest, as it says in Hebrews 7, "who offered himself once for us all."[40] Therefore, we only allow servants for proclaiming the holy gospel in the New Testament, just as Christ sent out his disciples to this end. In the final chapter of Mark it says, "Go out into the whole world and preach the gospel to all creatures."[41] According to Paul, those who

---

36 1 Corinthians 9:13: Do you not know that those who are employed in the temple service get their food from the temple, and those who serve at the altar share in the sacrificial offerings?

37 1 Corinthians 9:14: In the same way, the Lord commanded that those who proclaim the gospel should get their living by the gospel.

38 Leviticus 7: This refers to the whole chapter, which describes the proper practice for sacrifices.

39 1 Corinthians 3:16: Do you not know that you are God's temple and that God's spirit dwells in you?

40 Hebrews 7:27: He has no need, like those high priests, to offer sacrifices daily, first for his own sins and then for those of the people, since he did this once for all when he offered up himself.

41 Mark 16:15: And he said to them, "Go into all the world and proclaim the gospel to the whole creation."

do this should be supported by it. You, however, eat your bread in idleness, against the will of God. Genesis 3 says, "By the sweat of your brow should you enjoy your bread."[42]

Monk: Well, but we also proclaim the gospel to you. Therefore, like Matthew 10[43] says, a worker is deserving of his wages.

Hans: Yes, there are some among you, though sadly not many, who purely preach Christ. Other than this, your whole monasteries lie sated together[44] and are useful to neither God nor the world.

Monk: I think you are absurd. What else do we do day and night, except for serving God?

Hans: Yes, you are stuffed full of service to God and good works yet miss the most necessary works, which Christ will demand at the last judgment (Matthew 25)—namely, the work of mercy. "I was hungry, and you have not fed me," and so on.[45]

Monk: Dear one, do we not give alms? Come tomorrow around noon to our monastery. There you will see a crowd of poor people, whom we feed daily.

Peter: Yes, you give out the food to them that you do not like and pour them out soup and peas, kraut and fish soup mixed together. Aren't you ashamed that you have given the Lord Christ such scraps?[46] For he says in Matthew 25, "What you have done to the least of mine, you have done to me."[47]

---

42 Genesis 3:19: By the sweat of your face you shall eat bread, till you return to the ground, for out of it you were taken; for you are dust, and to dust you shall return.

43 Matthew 10:10: . . . no bag for your journey, or two tunics or sandals or a staff, for the laborer deserves his food.

44 In the sense of one on top of the other.

45 Matthew 25:42: For I was hungry and you gave me no food, I was thirsty and you gave me no drink . . .

46 *Geschlepper*: Thin, bad soup.

47 Matthew 25:40: And the King will answer them, "Truly, I say to you, as you did it to one of the least of these my brothers, you did it to me."

Monk: Yes, I admit, our material alms are small, but we give out spiritual comfort to those who ask us.

Peter: Yes, you go to the sick gladly, since you are well rewarded for going. However, when you go to someone in vain and comfort him, his case certainly does not stand well. They cannot eat well from your good words.

Hans: It says, however, in 1 John 3, "Who of this world has goods, sees his brother in need, and closes his heart to him, how does the love of God remain in him?"[48] And further, "My children, let us not love with words, nor with the tongue, but rather by deed and in truth."[49] Now, you may have some poor men among you, but you pass by in front of the poor, as the priest and the Levite passed by in front of the wounded man in Luke 10.[50] If we of the world, despised by you as Samaritans, did not come to their aid, they would languish on your account (as the beggar Lazarus before the rich man's house in Luke 16).[51]

Monk: We really have no authority. We are spiritual people; therefore, we give out only spiritual goods, and that willingly.

Peter: Yes, you give out your vigils,[52] requiems,[53] and church services generously enough, like I my rolls and Master Hans his shoes, yet with the difference: Who pays for what he has? And if someone owed a coffer keeper[54] five guilder for an offering

---

48 1 John 3:17: But if anyone has the world's goods and sees his brother in need, yet closes his heart against him, how does God's love abide in him?

49 1 John 3:18: Little children, let us not love in word or talk but in deed and in truth.

50 Luke 10:25–37, the parable of the Good Samaritan.

51 Luke 16:19–31, the Rich Man and Lazarus.

52 *Vigilg*: Nightly watches and prayers.

53 *Selmesse*: Literally "soul's Mass." This is a Mass that would be sung to free a soul from purgatory.

54 *Seckeldario*: An intentional, facetious misstatement of *Säckelmeister*, literally "master of the coffer." It is blended here with *secretarius* (Latin) and declined accordingly.

and lacked one ort,[55] the coffer keeper wouldn't take the money but would bring the man for justice: so you give out your good works generously.

Monk: May God protect you; we are spending this time unprofitably with you. We must go on so that someone may give us something.

Hans: Dear Brother Heinrich, tell me one more thing.

Monk: What is it?

Hans: Do you hold to eternal chastity, like you have praised?

Monk: Yes, why not? If we did not know that we should hold to it, we would not praise it.

Hans: Does Christ not say in Matthew 19, "Not everyone takes this word, but those to whom it is given"?[56] Therefore, Christ holds that living chaste is not in one's own power but must be given by God.

Peter: The peasant women become well aware of your chastity when the monks collect cheese.[57]

Monk: Where have you discerned this in our order?

Peter: I do not mean you alone but all begging monks who collect cheese.

Monk: Yes, when a weed is already among such a great assembly, how the whole lot is judged accordingly.

Hans: I worry, if you similarly abstain from natural works, if you nevertheless defile yourselves in other unseemly ways.

Monk: Yes. This is why one must castigate the flesh and be sure to align with the entire rule and statute so that the flesh is suppressed.

Hans: Paul spoke of your rules and statutes in Colossians 2: "Let yourselves not be taken captive by statutes that have an appearance of wisdom through self-imposed spirituality and humility, and

---

55 *Ort*: One-quarter of a guilder.

56 Matthew 19:11: But he said to them, "Not everyone can receive this saying, but only those to whom it is given."

57 The monks who collect cheese (called *Käsebrüder* or *Käsesammler*) were notorious among the peasant women because of their lack of chastity.

because they do not spare the body or use any food to satisfy the needs of the flesh."[58]

Peter: The monks are so gaunt due to their afflictions, while the peasants, who do not fast as much as the monks, are quite fat.

Monk: It is not because of fasting but our various castigations.

Peter: Dear Brother Heinrich, tell us more.

Monk: Gladly. We do not wear any linen underneath, we gird ourselves with monks' belts,[59] and we go barefoot in only sandals.[60] We have no hair on our heads and do not bathe our whole life long, until after death. We do not lie down on feathers and never completely take off our clothes. We eat meat barely half of the time and never eat out of tin. We must often hold *silentium*,[61] meaning to keep complete silence. We must also stand or kneel every day for one or five hours at the altar[62] and each night go to midnight Mass.

Peter: I also have to work all day with my servants, eat poorly, and often not lie down until barely midnight; my children often

---

58 Colossians 2:20–23: If with Christ you died to the elemental spirits of the world, why, as if you were still alive in the world, do you submit to regulations—"Do not handle, Do not taste, Do not touch" (referring to things that all perish as they are used)—according to human precepts and teachings? These have indeed an appearance of wisdom in promoting self-made religion and asceticism and severity to the body, but they are of no value in stopping the indulgence of the flesh.

59 *Stricken*: Monks' belts, or cinctures. Franciscan monks wore rope belts tied in three knots, symbolizing their three vows (poverty, chastity, and obedience). "The Meaning of Our Corded Belts," Franciscan Missionaries of the Eternal Word, 2017, https://franciscanmissionaries.com/meaning-corded-belts/.

60 *Zuschnitten Schuhen*: Shoes made of cut materials. These meet the requirements of discalced monks, who either go barefoot or only wear sandals.

61 The original text uses this Latin word, meaning "silence." This was an imposed silence at certain times or places.

62 *Chor*: This refers to the place in the church around the altar itself, where the choir would stand.

sing midnight Mass for me before then. I am part of a much more difficult order than you.

Monk: Yes, well, if you were there when we held our assembly, the smile would leave your face when you heard the whipping rod singing.

Peter: You do not hold to the whipping rod. You make only a mock attack, which does nothing.

Monk: Then you send the man to prison and let him waste there.

Hans: Oh, you blind men—how you lead one another in your severe, fruitless works of men.

Monk: Does God not say, "Man, help yourself, then I will also help you"?[63]

Hans: Where is that written? So you come with your severe sayings when it is clearly written in Hosea 13, "O Israel, in you lies your degeneration, and in me alone lies your help."[64] Therefore, your hypocritical reverence does nothing to suppress the flesh, for it says in Genesis 13,[65] "The man's heart is inclined to evil from his youth."[66] Therefore, it says in Proverbs 20, "Who

---

63 Though the modern English phrase "God helps those who help themselves" is attributed to Algernon Sydney, a seventeenth-century politician, versions of the same concept date back to ancient Greece. Even today this is commonly mistaken as being a scriptural concept, though it is not found anywhere in the Christian Bible. Clarence Haynes, "Why 'God Helps Those Who Help Themselves' Is Presumed to Be Biblical," Christianity.com, July 7, 2020, https://www.christianity.com/wiki/christian-life/why-god-helps-those-who-help-themselves-is-presumed-to-be-biblical.html.

64 Hosea 13:9: He destroys you, O Israel, for you are against me, against your helper.

65 The actual reference is found in chapter 8, not chapter 13.

66 Genesis 8:21: And when the Lord smelled the pleasing aroma, the Lord said in his heart, "I will never again curse the ground because of man, for the intention of man's heart is evil from his youth. Neither will I ever again strike down every living creature as I have done."

may say, my heart is pure?"[67] Now you eat, drink, and sleep in abundance and yet celebrate this. This kindles one's ingrained nature, for Genesis 1 and 9 state clearly, "Increase and multiply yourselves."[68] Therefore, your heart is stained with evil, burning lust (without the particular high grace of God).

Monk: Well, if we didn't consent to this willingly, then we would deserve such objections.

Hans: You play with these thoughts in your hearts, however, like a cat with a mouse. Now, God is an investigator of all hearts, as it says in Acts 1: "Therefore God judges according to one's heart."[69] Therefore, Paul says in 1 Corinthians 7, "It is better to marry than to burn."[70] And in the same chapter, "If a virgin marries, they do not sin."[71]

Monk: Yes. However, we have pledged eternal chastity in our vows, alongside willing poverty and holy obedience.

Hans: You should hear clearly that you do not keep yourselves perfect. Why have you taken another vow on yourselves and not contented yourselves with the baptism by which you renounced the devil and all his spirits?

---

67 Proverbs 20:9: Who can say, "I have made my heart pure; I am clean from my sin"?

68 Genesis 1:28: And God blessed them. And God said to them, "Be fruitful and multiply and fill the earth and subdue it, and have dominion over the fish of the sea and over the birds of the heavens and over every living thing that moves on the earth."

   Genesis 9:7: And you, be fruitful and multiply, increase greatly on the earth and multiply in it.

69 Acts 1:24: And they prayed and said, "You, Lord, who know the hearts of all, show which one of these two you have chosen."

70 1 Corinthians 7:9: But if they cannot exercise self-control, they should marry. For it is better to marry than to burn with passion.

71 1 Corinthians 7:28: But if you do marry, you have not sinned, and if a betrothed woman marries, she has not sinned. Yet those who marry will have worldly troubles, and I would spare you that.

Monk: Oh, that is the other baptism, in which we are given new names so that we may be born again as new.

Hans: Yet Paul says in Ephesians 4, "There is one Lord, one faith, one baptism, one God and Father of all."[72] Therefore, your baptism is no baptism at all but rather something established by men, who are all liars (Psalm 115[73]).[74] Therefore, you go about with false, worldly wisdom, holding to chastity even as to poverty. I believe this applies to your obedience as well.

Monk: How so? Do we not adhere to complete obedience? No one joins the monastery without permission from our worthy father, the abbot.[75]

Hans: Yes, you maintain obedience in the things that you do gladly, though sometimes with an unwilling heart toward your highest authority. This, however, is not the true obedience that the Scriptures demand from us in 1 Peter 2: "Be subject to all worldly establishments, to the king as chief," and so on,[76] and in Romans 13, "Be subject to all worldly authority" and "give to everyone what they are due, levy to whom levies are owed, tolls to whom tolls are owed."[77] Also in Matthew 22, "Give to

---

72 Ephesians 4:5–6: . . . one Lord, one faith, one baptism, one God and Father of all, who is over all and through all and in all.

73 The actual reference is found in Psalm 116, not 115.

74 Psalm 116:11: I said in my alarm, "All mankind are liars."

75 *Gardian:* Literally guardian or protector. This would refer to the highest among the monks in this particular monastery.

76 1 Peter 2:13: Be subject for the Lord's sake to every human institution, whether it be to the emperor as supreme . . .

77 Romans 13:1: Let every person be subject to the governing authorities. For there is no authority except from God, and those that exist have been instituted by God.

Romans 13:7: Pay to all what is owed to them: taxes to whom taxes are owed, revenue to whom revenue is owed, respect to whom respect is owed, honor to whom honor is owed.

Caesar what is Caesar's, and to God what is God's."[78] You, however, have smoothly evaded this obedience that God desires of you and have taken on an obedience you established yourselves, in which you are free from indulgences, tithes, wartime contributions,[79] watchman's wages, taxes, interest, rent, tolls, superfluous taxes,[80] and all other burdens that we bear together as brothers.

Monk: Well, we are spiritual people and not of this world; therefore, we have been freed from worldly tributes.

Hans: By whom?

Monk: By the blessed Pope Honorius III and by Kaiser Friedrich II, over three hundred years ago.[81] And now you Lutherans want to reform us?

Hans: One blind man has led the others, as it says in Luke 6: "If one blind man leads the other, do they not both fall into the pit?"[82] Tell me, though, what is your obedience based on?

Monk: On our rules and statutes, as they have been recorded word for word.

Hans: Now, if your rules and statutes only ever consist of cowls, bald heads, monks' belts, shoes, avoiding meat, silence, singing, reading, going to midnight Mass, singing in a chorus, bowing, kneeling, and other such outwardly established works, then the judgment of Matthew 15 speaks directly to you: "In vain they serve me while they teach such doctrine, which is nothing more

---

78　Matthew 22:21: They said, "Caesar's." Then he said to them, "Therefore render to Caesar the things that are Caesar's, and to God the things that are God's."

79　*Reisgelt*: From *Reisiger*, which were armed fighters of the time, often mercenaries.

80　Implying a tax that is unnecessary and therefore unjust.

81　This is referring to the confirmation of the Franciscan order by Pope Honorius III in 1223.

82　Luke 6:39: He also told them a parable: "Can a blind man lead a blind man? Will they not both fall into a pit?"

than the commands of men,"[83] and further, "All plants which God, my heavenly Father, has not planted will be uprooted."[84]

Monk: Are these spiritual practices of ours not good, then?

Hans: No.

Monk: How so?

Hans: God neither commanded nor asked for them.

Monk: Well, but we do them with the good intent of honoring God.

Hans: Nothing pleases God but that for which he has asked, as in Leviticus 10.[85] There Aaron's sons Nadab and Abihu took fire in their bowls and meant to burn them before the Lord. So the fire of the Lord consumed them, because they had offered strange fire, which God had not commanded, though they did it to honor God. Now all your orders are full of nothing but strange, invented service to God. Outwardly the appearance is holy and glittering, but inwardly the foundation is nothing but worm-eaten and full of deceitful spirits, as in Matthew 23: "Woe to you hypocrites and Pharisees, who are like the whitewashed tombs. Outwardly they seem beautiful, but inwardly they are full of corpses and filth."[86] So you also seem outwardly holy, but internally you are full of hypocrisy and vice.

Monk: Oh, dear one, how so?

---

83 Matthew 15:9: "In vain do they worship me, teaching as doctrines the commandments of men."

84 Matthew 15:13: He answered, "Every plant that my heavenly Father has not planted will be rooted up."

85 Leviticus 10:1–2: Now Nadab and Abihu, the sons of Aaron, each took his censer and put fire in it and laid incense on it and offered unauthorized fire before the Lord, which he had not commanded them. And fire came out from before the Lord and consumed them, and they died before the Lord.

86 Matthew 23:27–28: Woe to you, scribes and Pharisees, hypocrites! For you are like whitewashed tombs, which outwardly appear beautiful, but within are full of dead people's bones and all uncleanness. So you also outwardly appear righteous to others, but within you are full of hypocrisy and lawlessness.

Hans: You have already heard it in part. You hold to poverty, but without lack. You hold to chastity that has been defiled and to obedience that is invented.

Monk: Say what you will, we each have full status according to the gospel, as in Matthew 19: "If you want to be complete, sell what you have," and so on.[87]

Hans: Well, that must be understood spiritually so that we set our hope and trust not in earthly things but rather only in God, as Paul describes in 1 Corinthians 7: "Beloved brothers, those who have wives should act as if they had none, and that buy as if they did not possess it, and they that use the world, as if they do not need it," and so on.[88] It is also good to notice, along with this, that not all of us could leave what is ours and become monks. Who would farm the grain? Now, we must all be complete if we are to enter the kingdom of God, as it says in Revelation 21: "Nothing unclean shall enter into the heavenly Jerusalem."[89]

Peter: Oh, the Franciscans[90] have found a way around this. If one of us laity is going to die, they put a gray cowl on him, now making a monk out of him, cut his hair and bathe him so that he

---

87 Matthew 19:21: Jesus said to him, "If you would be perfect, go, sell what you possess and give to the poor, and you will have treasure in heaven; and come, follow me."

88 1 Corinthians 7:29–31: From now on, let those who have wives live as though they had none, and those who mourn as though they were not mourning, and those who rejoice as though they were not rejoicing, and those who buy as though they had no goods, and those who deal with the world as though they had no dealings with it.

89 Revelation 21:27: But nothing unclean will ever enter it, nor anyone who does what is detestable or false, but only those who are written in the Lamb's book of life.

90 *Observanzer*: Observants. This is a part of the Franciscan order primarily known as the Order of Friars Minor. Michael Bihl, "Order of Friars Minor," in *The Catholic Encyclopedia* (New York: Robert Appleton Company, 1909), https://www.newadvent.org/cathen/06281a.htm.

goes heavenward as a fuller (as perfect, I should say),[91] like a cow into a mouse hole.

Hans: Dear Brother Heinrich, what brought you into the order?

Monk: So that I will become holy, as has been promised to us in our vows.

Hans: Do you hope to become holy through your work as a monk?

Monk: Yes, what else would I be doing in the monastery?

Hans: Yet Paul says in Ephesians 2, "You have been made holy by grace, through faith, and that is not from you, it is a gift from God, not by works, so that no one may boast."[92]

Monk: Yet Christ promises to many that work will be rewarded at the end, like in Matthew 25,[93] Luke 6,[94] John 5,[95] and Paul in 1 Corinthians 3.[96]

Hans: There you are taking works as belief, out of which they have flowed. But so that you understand it more clearly that God does not reward works, listen to Christ himself in Luke 17: "If you have done everything that is commanded of you, then say: we are unprofitable servants. We have done only what we were

---

91 A play on words. *Voller*, referring to a tradesman who works as a fuller (a worker who fulls cloth, purifying dirt and stains from the wool), is contrasted with *Volkomner*, meaning one who is perfect or complete.

92 Ephesians 2:8–9: For by grace you have been saved through faith. And this is not your own doing; it is the gift of God, not a result of works, so that no one may boast.

93 Matthew 25: This refers to whole chapter.

94 Luke 6:35: But love your enemies, and do good, and lend, expecting nothing in return, and your reward will be great, and you will be sons of the Most High, for he is kind to the ungrateful and the evil.

95 John 5:28–29: Do not marvel at this, for an hour is coming when all who are in the tombs will hear his voice and come out, those who have done good to the resurrection of life, and those who have done evil to the resurrection of judgment.

96 1 Corinthians 3:14: If the work that anyone has built on the foundation survives, he will receive a reward.

obligated to do."[97] Here you hear that no one earns anything through proper Christian work, as it says in Isaiah 64: "Our unrighteousness is as an unclean cloth of a sick woman."[98] How would you then become holy through your self-imposed, self-serving works?

Peter: How do you survive with all of your merchant's treasure? You have sold us holiness, and you have a large amount remaining.

Monk: If I knew that I was not becoming holy through my monastic life, I would hang my cowl on the fence and throw stones at it.

Peter: Well, leave your bondage[99] then. It says in Matthew 21, "Whores and open sinners will go before you into the kingdom of heaven."[100]

Monk: Oh, now I am old and can't do anything. What could I begin to do?

Hans: I would give you an ax so that you could support yourself with work.

Monk: I cannot let you.

Hans: How so? That way you would feel actual, true poverty for the first time, your unchastity would leave you, and you would finally become truly obedient to everyone.

Monk: No, no! I know the monastery better.

Hans: I am hearing clearly that you are of the people that Paul speaks of in Philippians 3, "the enemy of the cross of Christ, whose end is damnation and whose belly is their god."[101] So you fear

---

97 Luke 17:10: "So you also, when you have done all that you were commanded, say, 'We are unworthy servants; we have only done what was our duty.'"

98 Isaiah 64:6: We have all become like one who is unclean, and all our righteous deeds are like a polluted garment.

99 *Notstal*: A stall for wild horses, leading to their captivity.

100 Matthew 21:31: Jesus said to them, "Truly, I say to you, the tax collectors and the prostitutes go into the kingdom of God before you."

101 Philippians 3:18–19: "For many, of whom I have often told you and now tell you even with tears, walk as enemies of the cross of Christ. Their end is

poverty although you have praised it and remain in error despite awareness of the truth.

Monk: Indeed, I hear not much good spoken of monks who have left but rather how they chase after pretty women, barely one out of ten works gladly, and otherwise they live wantonly, one doing this, another that, so that they may support themselves without working. Some of them chase after evil things. How can a good spirit have driven them from the monastery?

Peter: This is how one can see what good there is beneath the cowls. Those who used to act like the living saint in the monasteries, who now live like rakes outside, these still did the same things in their hearts even in the monastery, which they now do with works on the outside.

Hans: I worry, sadly, that many leave the monasteries out of curiosity and wantonness (to suffer their evil lust in the world), though against their own conscience. This cannot come from faith, and whatever does not come from faith is sin, as in Romans 9.[102] The same lead an evil life afterward, though their conscience will convict them. Though it does not have an effect now, it will not stay behind in the misery of death—God have mercy on them! However, those who recognize through knowledge of the word of God that you are incapable of holding to the foolish vows, and with free and secure conscience leave this status established by men, and enter the status established by God—namely, into marriage, Genesis 2, "The man will leave his father and mother and cleave to his wife"[103]—and who sustain themselves through

---

destruction, their god is their belly, and they glory in their shame, with minds set on earthly things."

102 Referenced incorrectly—this verse is found in Romans 14:23: But whoever has doubts is condemned if he eats, because the eating is not from faith. For whatever does not proceed from faith is sin.

103 Genesis 2:24: Therefore a man shall leave his father and his mother and hold fast to his wife, and they shall become one flesh.

work, to which they are born (as a bird to flight) as in Job 5.[104] These I cannot judge wrongly.

Monk: I do not want to leave, though, and if Saint Peter spoke, it would not be wrong.

Hans: You are one of the righteous, of which Isaiah says in chapter 6, "He has blinded their eyes and hardened their hearts, that they might not see with their eyes or understand with their hearts and turn themselves, and be made holy."[105]

Monk: Oh dear one, if you think we are in such a dangerous state, what do you take us for?

Hans: I take you for the people who Peter warned us of in 2 Peter 2: "There will be false teachers among you, who bring in destructive sects on the side, and renounce the Lord who bought them."[106] The whole chapter speaks further of your seduction.

Monk: Dear one, that is not spoken of us. Where do we renounce Christ the Lord?

Hans: You renounce his salvation and sanctification and want to make yourselves holy through your public works. You direct others also to attain holiness through their own works instead of Christ, selling good works in a simonish[107] way.

---

104 Job 5:7 . . .but man is born to trouble as the sparks fly upward.

  In the Luther translation: . . .sondern der Mensch wird zu Unglück geboren, wie die Vögel schweben, emporzuflieben (as the birds hover [in order to] fly upward).

105 Isaiah 6:10: Make the heart of this people dull, and their ears heavy, and blind their eyes; lest they see with their eyes, and hear with their ears, and understand with their hearts, and turn and be healed.

106 2 Peter 2:1: But false prophets also arose among the people, just as there will be false teachers among you, who will secretly bring in destructive heresies, even denying the Master who bought them, bringing upon themselves swift destruction.

107 *Simoneiisch:* Simony, the act of selling sacred things. This references Acts 8, in which Simon offered the apostles money to give him their power.

Monk: Oh, dear one, you are then opposed to us; this is why you taunt us.

Hans: No, by my soul's salvation, it is only from brotherly love.

Monk: Dear one, if you are evangelical, you should not deal with us so derisively, for you must give account of every useless word in the final judgment, Matthew 12.[108]

Hans: You would not accept the Scriptures that speak of you; therefore, we must convince you by your own deeds (which by your own admittance is derisive and laughable) that you are what they speak of.

Monk: But who is helped by this?

Hans: You, if you (through so many indications) just once recognized yourself at your core what wretched, blind, and hard-hearted people you are. Not acting so high class like the hypocrites in the temple, Matthew 18,[109] praising your works and boasting that you are holy by them, but rather, saying humbly with the open sinner: "God be gracious to me, a poor sinner,"[110] and being poor in spirit, hungry and thirsty after the righteousness of God, as in Matthew 5.[111] Then you will be filled with goods, as in Luke 1[112]—that is, with the unsearchable treasure of Jesus

---

108 Matthew 12:36–37: I tell you, on the day of judgment people will give account for every careless word they speak, for by your words you will be justified, and by your words you will be condemned.

109 Referenced incorrectly—this discussion of hypocrites is found in Matthew 23. Matthew 23:1–36 lists seven woes to the scribes and Pharisees who would make themselves great because of their temple service.

110 Luke 18:13: "But the tax collector, standing far off, would not even lift up his eyes to heaven, but beat his breast, saying, 'God, be merciful to me, a sinner!'"

111 Matthew 5:6: "Blessed are those who hunger and thirst for righteousness, for they shall be satisfied."

112 Luke 1:53: He has filled the hungry with good things, and the rich he has sent away empty.

Christ, Ephesians 3.[113] These are the comforting promises of Christ, which would surely become delicious and pleasant to you. Therefore, dear Brother Heinrich, what I and my brother Peter have said to you has happened for the best (without all jealousy and hate). Would God that all monks from all orders had heard it. We bid you for God's sake to not take it ill of us if we have spoken to you somewhat too harshly.

Peter: See here, Brother Heinrich, two candles. Do not read Scotus[114] or Bonaventure[115] with them but rather read the Bible. Eventually God will also illuminate you with his divine word. Take nothing amiss from us.

Monk: Nothing, dear brothers. I would like to search into these things further and go to do so now. God be with you!

Peter: Amen.

1524.

Isaiah 59. They shall not be covered by their works, for their works are worthless works.[116]

Year 1524.

---

113 Ephesians 3:8: To me, though I am the very least of all the saints, this grace was given, to preach to the Gentiles the unsearchable riches of Christ . . .

114 Duns Scotus, a Scottish Catholic priest, Franciscan friar, and philosopher-theologian living in the 1200s. A. Bernard Wolter, "Blessed John Duns Scotus," in *Encyclopedia Britannica*, online ed., 2021, https://www.britannica.com/biography/Blessed-John-Duns-Scotus.

115 Bonaventure, an Italian Franciscan friar from the 1200s who wrote on the subjects of theology and philosophy. J. Francis Quinn, "Saint Bonaventure," in *Encyclopedia Britannica*, online ed., 2021, https://www.britannica.com/biography/Saint-Bonaventure.

116 Isaiah 59:6: Their webs will not serve as clothing; men will not cover themselves with what they make. Their works are works of iniquity, and deeds of violence are in their hands.

CHAPTER 7

A Dialogue on the Content of an Argument between a Roman Catholic and a Christian Friend concerning Greed and Other Common Vices

Ein Dialogus/des inhalt/ein ar gument der Römischen/wider das Christlich heüflein/den Geytz/auch ander offenlich laster zc. Betreffend.

Ephesios.v.
Hürerey vnd vnrainigkait/oder geytz/laßt nit von euch gesagt werden/wie den heyligen zū steet.

Introduction

In this third play, written in 1524, Hans Sachs pits a Roman Catholic and a Protestant against each other in a series of back-and-forth conversations mostly concerning the topic of greed. He uses this discussion between the Catholic and the Protestant to further describe the ways in which he sees greed apparent in the practices of the Catholic Church and its *Heiligen*, or "holy ones." Sachs also addresses many counterarguments from the point of view of the Catholic priest that give cultural insights into the social issues at the time. According to Richard Zoozmann, the dialogue opens with a letter written by Sachs to a citizen of Breslau (modern-day Wrocław, Poland[1]) that further teaches us about the social context of the time period, specifically pertaining to the Catholic-Protestant relationship.[2]

The principal theme explored by this dialogue is greed. Greed as a theme is explored in the contexts of the Catholic Church, the society as a whole, and the Protestant's personal life. As a theme, it is developed with examples of greed in society and evaluated throughout the text with biblical references to either contest what is defined as greed or support an action being declared as greedy. Topics in this dialogue about greed include the collection of money by the Catholic Church, the practice of loaning money at interest, deceitful financial practices, the hoarding of goods, and the treatment of the poor.

While the principle discussion is about greed, it is also clear that it is inherently a debate about the authority of tradition versus *Sola Scriptura*, or the Scriptures alone, and an exploration of the practices of the Catholic Church at the time. This is made evident by Sachs as the character Reichenburger, using Scripture references, continually points to Catholic practices of the day as examples of the presence of greed in the Catholic Church as well as the defense of forms of financial transactions. Sachs points to the traditions in the Catholic Church that he finds greedy and indefensible by Scripture by naming the practices of indulgences, excommunication, sacrifices, the sacraments, and other forms of offerings to the church. These form the basis of the Protestant's, and ultimately Sachs's, argument against the authority of tradition, which is supported by plentiful scriptural references. The Protestant also uses Scripture to support his financial dealings, which are contested by the

---

1 "Breslau," Local Life: Wroclaw, continually updated at https://www.local-life .com/wroclaw/articles/breslau#.

2 Richard Zoozmann, *Hans Sachs und die Reformation: In Gedichten und Prosastücke* (Hamburg, Germany: SEVERUS Verlag, 2017), 23.

Catholic, using church tradition and the Scripture (including the Apocrypha) to support his claims and form the base of the argument against tradition and for the interpretation of Scripture in daily life alone.

There are two main characters in this dialogue: the Roman Catholic priest, who is called (Father) Romanus, and the wealthy Protestant, who is called Reichenburger, whose name means "wealthy citizen." Reichenburger makes known his perception of the practices of the Catholic Church as inherently greedy throughout the discussion between the two characters, and Romanus, similarly, makes known his thoughts of the greedy practices of the laity. Throughout the dialogue, these two characters joust with scriptural references in pointed accusations of sinful, greedy conduct. It is interesting to note that many of these verses that Reichenburger and Romanus use against each other pertain to how to treat the poor and needy. While both use scriptural references, when Reichenburger refers to examples of greed in the Catholic Church, he uses the practices and traditions of the church as the basis of his arguments. However, Romanus does not strictly refer to practices of Protestants but rather refers to the community at large for the basis of his arguments.

The accompanying image to this dialogue shows Romanus standing, wearing monk's robes, and pointing at the table before him. Reichenburger sits at the table facing Romanus, wearing clothing with fur and a hat, which are symbols of his status as a wealthy man. Romanus points at the pouch of coins lying in front of Reichenburger on the table as Reichenburger seemingly nudges them toward him.

Sachs relies solely on Scripture to support the claims of both the evangelical and the Catholic in this dialogue. He cited by chapter only, as verse numbers were not added to Scripture until 1551. As an aid to the reader, we have provided specific verse references. Footnotes have been used to identify specific German or Latin words or phrases that have been translated other than literally or to add contextual information for the reader.

A Dialogue on the Content of an Argument between a
Roman Catholic and a Christian Friend concerning
Greed and Other Common Vices

Ephesians 5:3

But sexual immorality and all impurity or covetousness must not
even be named among you, as is proper among saints.

To the esteemed Hans Odrer[3] at Preisla,[4]
Hans Sachs wishes grace and joy in Jesus Christ our beloved Lord. Amen.

Beloved brother in the Lord, it is by the manifold requests of our beloved
brother in Christ Ulrich Lauthi that I should bless you with my talent,
which I have received according to the teaching of 1 Peter 4.[5] So that I
may not be found to be like the wicked servant in Matthew 25,[6] I am
submitting to his will with a dialogue, which I am hereby sending to
you. Its content consists of an argument where our Roman Catholics cry
out with a raised voice from the pulpit, or wherever they have room, to
blaspheme the evangelical teachings, specifically with cursed greediness
and continuing with other public offenses. These offenses (Lord have
mercy) are in full swing in those among us who have not truly come to
know Christ by the Spirit, as if the teaching of Christ were false. With
disputes and writing, they have received little honor, and still much less
with their countless hidden acts of malice, falling now into sinful living

---

3 A citizen of Breslau whose relation to Sachs is unknown.

4 Preisla is Sachs's dialect for the name Breslau (today Wrocław, Poland). Breslau
   was a thriving city in Silesia inhabited in Sachs's day by Germans. It was also
   known as Prezzla.

5 1 Peter 4:10: As each has received a gift, use it to serve one another.

6 Matthew 25:26: But his master answered him, "You wicked and slothful servant!
   You knew that I reap where I have not sown and gather where I scattered no
   seed?"

that I hope will collapse soon from the resonating echoes of the evangelical horn, just like the wall of Jericho (Joshua 6).[7] I hope for this, because
then they would have nothing against us and would potentially wash their
hands in the blood of Christ so that the full number of fellow believers
who were slain according to the will of God's word would be fulfilled
(Revelation 6),[8] which has already begun. God strengthen us all that we
may abide in his Word to the end and be blessed. Amen. Matthew 24.[9]

Given at Nürnberg on the day of Michael in the year 1524.

Matthew 26.

The spirit is willing, but the flesh is weak.[10]

Romanus:[11] Peace be upon you,[12] my dear squire Reichenburger!
Reichenburger:[13] And God welcome you a thousand times, dignified
Father Romanus![14] Your return to my house is truly

---

7 Joshua 6:20: As soon as the people heard the sound of the trumpet, the people
   shouted a great shout, and the wall fell down flat, so that the people went up
   into the city, every man straight before him, and they captured the city.

8 Revelation 6:11: Then they were each given a white robe and told to rest a little
   longer, until the number of their fellow servants and their brothers should be
   complete, who were to be killed as they themselves had been.

9 Matthew 24:46: Blessed is that servant whom his master will find so doing
   when he comes.

10 Matthew 26:41: The spirit indeed is willing, but the flesh is weak.

11 The Roman Catholic is given the name Romanus, which would translate to
   "the Roman."

12 The greeting is given in Latin (*Pax vobis*), which would be recognized as church-
   related speech.

13 The Christian friend's name, Reichenburger, translates literally to "rich
   citizen."

14 Reichenburger addresses Romanus with the respectful title "dignified father"
   or *wirdiger Vater* (worthy father).

	rare as a snowfall,[15] since you have avoided my house for nearly three years. What are you looking for?
Romanus:	Really, not much. I just want to speak with you about a matter that happened three years ago, which you are a witness of.
Reichenburger:	When you unexpectedly snuck to my place all alone, I wrongly wanted to believe that you truly wanted to disrobe yourself of your garments of greed (or should I have said of holiness[16]) and that you wanted to become a Christian.
Romanus:	I want to continue to wear my monk's hood because of meekness; in the same way[17] you new evangelicals practice and carry on among one another and are loving to me, I would otherwise respond to you differently.
Reichenburger:	Tell me, dignified father, what you know, and only the truth; and do not spare me anything.
Romanus:	Look in the mirror of your hearts and how pure they are because of greed. And not just you alone, but look at all this world from the greatest to the least, and you will find that it is all overflowing with greed. As Isaiah says in Jeremiah chapter 6, "From the least to the greatest of them, all follow greed."[18] You new evangelicals set your sights on us monks and priests alone, as if we were the only greedy ones, and you

---

15 *bedeutet wahrlich eine Schnee*, which literally translates to "truly means a snow." This is a metaphor referring to the rarity of a snowfall and relating it to the rarity of Romanus's visits.

16 An instance of wordplay to disguise an insult: *Geizigkeit* (greed) versus *Geistlichkeit* (holiness).

17 Romanus is returning the insult with a sarcastic jab at the evangelicals for lack of meekness and love.

18 Jeremiah 6:13: For from the least to the greatest of them, everyone is greedy for unjust gain.

forget your own greed. You, however, will not be par-
doned with us. Christ says in Luke 13, "Do you think
that those eighteen on whom the tower in Siloam fell
and crushed are to blame for all those who live in
Jerusalem? I say no; but rather if you do not better
yourselves, you will all die."[19] Therefore, dear evangelicals, first remove the beam out of your eye, and then
the splinter out of your brother's eye (Matthew 7).[20]

Reichenburger: Well,[21] when do we so greedily deceive the people as you
clergymen for so long have deceived us? You deceived
us with indulgences, excommunication, sacrifices,
vigils, the sacred Mass, good works, with all the sacraments, all of which you sold to us for money, and
what was left over, you won over with little prayers
and other tricks.

Romanus: Well, but in the same way you deceived one another
in financial transactions and judicial proceedings, in
extortion and in sum, through and through. Who
wants to recount all of the transactions in which greed
reigns? What frequently comes up in confessions is not
lost to me and my memory! If only I could tell of it!

Reichenburger: Dignified father, tell it to me in confession here and
in confidence![22] I would love to hear the truth, if you
please.

---

19 Luke 13:4–5: Or those eighteen on whom the tower in Siloam fell and killed
them: do you think that they were worse offenders than all the others who lived
in Jerusalem? No, I tell you; but unless you repent, you will all likewise perish.

20 Matthew 7:5: You hypocrite, first take the log out of your own eye, and then
you will see clearly to take the speck out of your brother's eye.

21 *Ei*: This interjection in the original text denotes an emotional response of
indignation, contradiction, or offense. Due to the context, there is not a
suitable English equivalent, thus it is represented in multiple fashions.

22 *Unter der Rosen*: Under the roses (Latin *sub rosa*), which means "in confidence."
The rose is a symbol of secrecy in Latin.

Romanus: Where does the hoarding of wine, grain, salt, and everything that one could even imagine or desire come from? Does it not come from greed?

Reichenburger: Hey! Don't say such things! If there were no one like that in the entire city, it would often lead to price inflation, burdens of war, and other hardships. Doesn't Proverbs 6 say, "O lazy one, look at the ant and notice her ways and learn her wisdom, she prepares her meal in summer and gathers in harvest what she eats."[23]

Romanus: I am not talking about storing up where one seeks to benefit the whole community and takes just a single penny for a prize and, even less, where a governing body stores up and seeks common good. Rather, I am only talking about the hoarders who hoard for their own profit and prize. The hoarder suffers when wine, grain, and other goods are in abundance, rejoicing in the scarce year and concealing his hoarding in the midst of urgent need in hopes of gaining more money from the hoarded goods. Proverbs 11 speaks of this: "He who hides his grain is cursed among the people."[24] And Leviticus 25: "You shall not give your food to the poor with extortion."[25] And Deuteronomy 23: "You shall not extort your brother, neither with money, nor with food, nor with anything that can be extorted."[26] And

---

23 Proverbs 6:6–8: Go to the ant, O sluggard; consider her ways, and be wise. Without having any chief, officer, or ruler, she prepares her bread in summer and gathers her food in harvest.

24 Proverbs 11:26: The people curse him who holds back grain, but a blessing is on the head of him who sells it.

25 Leviticus 25:37: You shall not lend him [your poor brother] your money at interest, nor give him your food for profit.

26 Deuteronomy 23:19: "You shall not charge interest on loans to your brother, interest on money, interest on food, interest on anything that is lent for interest."

Amos 8: "Hear this, you who trample on the poor
and take from the needy of the earth, say, as the new
moon wanes, we sell the wage, and the Sabbath, that
we [sell] wheat, we may make the measure small and
increase the shekel and sell the chaff of the grain
that we possess to the thirsty for silver.' And the Lord
swore: 'I will not forget any of their works even until
the end.'"[27]

Reichenburger: But hoarding in such quantities is not strictly a Christian behavior. Anyone can do so if they want.

Romanus: Greed also reigns in communities where they completely buy out some goods out of their neighbor's
hands and bring those goods back to them, like spices
or whatever their trade is, applying an additional
charge to it whenever they feel, and they burden the
people and land. Is that right for the evangelical?

Reichenburger: That is also unfair, because everything that you want
people to do to you, do also to them (Matthew 7).[28]

Romanus: Greed also reigns with bad merchandise, forcibly
burdening some, often causing the poor to perish.
This is forbidden according to Leviticus 19: "You shall
not steal, lie, nor deal falsely with one another."[29] And

---

27 Amos 8:4: Hear this, you who trample on the needy and bring the poor of
the land to an end, saying, "When will the new moon be over, that we may sell
grain? And the Sabbath, that we may offer wheat for sale, that we may make
the ephah small and the shekel great and deal deceitfully with false balances,
that we may buy the poor for silver and the needy for a pair of sandals and
sell the chaff of the wheat?" The Lord has sworn by the pride of Jacob: "Surely
I will never forget any of their deeds."

28 Matthew 7:12: "So whatever you wish that others would do to you, do also to
them, for this is the Law and the Prophets."

29 Leviticus 19:11: "You shall not steal; you shall not deal falsely."

Sirach 34:[30] "Whoever deceives the poor is a man of blood."[31] [And] 1 Thessalonians 4: "Let no one reach too far, nor judge his brother in trade, because the Lord accounts for all these things."[32] Where do those who use their power to counterfeit good merchandise persist? Is that right for the evangelical?

Reichenburger: Well that is not Christian behavior. Malachi 1 says, "Cursed be the one who cheats."[33]

Romanus: Greed also reigns with a false scale, measure, number, being too quick to calculate the sum, and in the process of taking on credit, which are forbidden according to Leviticus 19: "You shall not deal unfairly at the court with measures of length, weight, quantity," and so on.[34] And Proverbs 11: "A dishonest scale is an insult to God."[35] And Luke 6: "With the measure you use you will be measured."[36] Are these right for evangelicals?

Reichenburger: Well, who can call good what is against God and the love of your neighbor?

Romanus: In addition, greed violently reigns among the merchants and distributors who employ these methods to oppress their employees and workers. Whenever workers take up the fruits of their labor or carry home their penny's worth, their work is rebuked to the extreme,

---

30 Sirach, also known as Ecclesiasticus, is a book of the Apocrypha. The Catholic priest references the Apocrypha; however, the evangelical Christian does not.

31 Sirach 34:24: Like one who kills a son before his father's eyes is the person who offers a sacrifice from the property of the poor (NRSVUE).

32 1 Thessalonians 4:6: . . . that no one transgress and wrong his brother in this matter, because the Lord is an avenger in all these things.

33 Malachi 1:14: Cursed be the cheat.

34 Leviticus 19:35: "You shall do no wrong in judgment, in measures of length or weight or quantity."

35 Proverbs 11:1: A false balance is an abomination to the Lord.

36 Luke 6:38: For with the measure you use it will be measured back to you.

and then the poor worker stands trembling at the door with folded hands, frozen in silence, so that he does not lose the favor of his boss, the merchant, having borrowed some money from his work. Consequently, the merchant deals with him as he wants. When the poor man suffers the loss of his own money to his work, the rich man is overjoyed in the poor man's worthless purchases and says that he has done good to the poor man. Hear now what Leviticus 25 says: "If you sell to or buy from your neighbor, you shall not mistreat them."[37] And Deuteronomy 24: "Don't hold back the wages of the needy and poor, so that he won't call to the Lord and you be guilty."[38] And Sirach 34: "He who sheds the blood and cheats the workers, his brothers, and he who takes the bread of his sweat, is guilty of killing his neighbor."[39]

Reichenburger: You failed to mention how proud the worker is. If he needs something from you, you cannot pay him enough for it, and no one can get anything from him.

Romanus: Your objection will not last long. It will undoubtedly pierce you, as it often goes, and in the winter when it is so damp, they will give you next to nothing. In the summer you stripped him of his skin. In the winter you draw the marrow from his bones. Is it right for evangelicals that the poor work and work, and though

---

37 Leviticus 25:14: And if you make a sale to your neighbor or buy from your neighbor, you shall not wrong one another.

38 Deuteronomy 24:15: "You shall give him his wages on the same day, before the sun sets (for he is poor and counts on it), lest he cry against you to the Lord, and you be guilty of sin."

39 Sirach 34:25–27: The bread of the needy is the life of the poor; whoever deprives them of it is a murderer. To take away a neighbor's living is to commit murder; to deprive an employee of wages is to shed blood (NRSVUE).

they hunger, they cannot nourish their wives and children? I don't think so! God hears their groaning, as Exodus 6 says: "I have heard the groaning of the children of Israel whom the Egyptians burden with drudgery."[40]

Reichenburger: In my whole life, I have never been pleased by such injustices. These, above all else, are not Christlike.

Romanus: Still, greed reigns in the exchange, whose many guises are without count. Further, greed reigns: if someone sells a ware in cash for the amount of one hundred gulden[41] and the other needs a loan for a half of a year, the borrower must pay back five or six more gulden in interest. This is not evangelical behavior.

Reichenburger: Well, dear friend, the vendor would earn just as much with the cash in the meantime as the buyer is giving him.

Romanus: How about if he were to lose so much as the entire sum itself? Thus, if one is to lend to another, he should do so without obligation, as it says in Matthew 5: "Whoever wants to borrow from you, don't turn him away."[42]

Reichenburger: I hear you. If someone wanted to borrow one hundred gulden from me and I had it available to lend, would I be obligated to lend it to him? No; rather, I am only obligated to lend to those who lack and not those in abundance, and likewise with loaning. Luke 6: "And lend, hoping for nothing in return."[43] This refers only to your neighbor's lack and not to abundance. Should someone loan to someone according to their coveting (one would find some such vagabonds), one

---

40 Exodus 6:5: Moreover, I have heard the groaning of the people of Israel whom the Egyptians hold as slaves.

41 Gulden is a medieval German currency in the form of gold coins.

42 Matthew 5:42: "And do not refuse the one who would borrow from you."

43 Luke 6:35: And lend, expecting nothing in return.

would stipulate more than three outcomes, including gambling, squandering it,[44] and more; thus it would facilitate him and would go against God.

Romanus: It very well could be. Greed also reigns in untold ways through loaning when the moneylender seeks after his own interest by applying many conditions to the detriment of the poor. Here he loans a bad coin for a good one, or a bad product for a good one, and there he loans a sum of money one year of a gulden or more over, which is essentially extortion. Scripture then would be wrong, as Exodus 22: "If you make it easy for any of my people with you who are poor, don't be like a extortioner to him, nor drive him to an extortioner."[45] And Leviticus 25: "If your brother becomes poor and takes from you, you shall support him and not extort him, but rather you should fear your God, so that your brother may live beside you, then you should not loan him money with interest."[46]

Reichenburger: Should no one make a living for the trouble and the work of loaning out great sums of money? Is the trouble not worth it?

Romanus: One should be concerned with neither a gift, tip, nor whatever someone wants to call it, as Christ says in Luke 6: "You should lend, where you expect nothing

---

44 *Brassen:* In Latin *heluor,* translating to immoderate spending, squandering, or gluttony.

45 Exodus 22:25: "If you lend money to any of my people with you who is poor, you shall not be like a moneylender to him, and you shall not exact interest from him."

46 Leviticus 25:35–37: If your brother becomes poor and cannot maintain himself with you, you shall support him as though he were a stranger and a sojourner, and he shall live with you. Take no interest from him or profit, but fear your God, that your brother may live beside you. You shall not lend him your money at interest.

in return, so your reward will be great, and you will be children of the Most High."[47] Are we going to turn up our noses to the saying "One should not hope; rather, give the sum total and gift something in addition and they will take it gladly," but the saying in Ezekiel 18 directs, "A man who does the cursed work of loaning at interest to extort and takes more than the capital, should he then live since he is doing the cursed thing? He will not live. He will die and his sin will stay on him, says the Lord."[48] Here you hear clearly, whatever is taken above the principal, be it little or much, whether the principal be large or small, whatever name you give it, the Scripture states here that it is called extortion. More to the lending or selling at interest of the yield from vineyards, gardens, fields, meadows, forests, fish-abundant bodies of water, houses, barns, or other such real estate to be named, I leave to the titles and names that are found in chapter 5 of the prophetic book of Nehemiah.[49] The Rhine[50] will not cleanse him.

Reichenburger: It is no less a great violation in lending and unfortunately has spread widely.

---

47 Luke 6:35: Lend, expecting nothing in return, and your reward will be great, and you will be sons of the Most High.

48 Ezekiel 18:13: [A man] lends at interest, and takes profit; shall he then live? He shall not live. He has done all these abominations; he shall surely die; his blood shall be upon himself.

49 In chapter 5, Nehemiah admonishes nobles, priests, and officials (no names given) who had returned to Jerusalem after the Babylonian captivity to keep their promises to help the poor. Nehemiah 5:10: Moreover, I and my brothers and my servants are lending them money and grain. Let us abandon this exacting of interest.

50 The Rhine River was used heavily in the Middle Ages for the salt trade, and salt was also seen as a wound-cleansing substance due to the burning sensation it gave wounds.

Romanus: Yes, it has been so widely spread that what is said in Psalm 55 has been fulfilled in our time: "Extortion and deception do not cease in their streets."[51] This concerns, above all, the poor, as Proverbs 28 says, "Whoever collects his wealth by interest and profit does so to the detriment of the poor."[52] God threatens the extortionist in Ezekiel 22: "You have taken the interest and excess, you have greedily coerced your neighbor, and you have forgotten me, says the Lord. I struck my hands together at the greediness that you had."[53] And Amos 4: "You fat cows, hear the Word of the Lord. You, who are on the mountain of Samaria, you oppress the thirsty, and crush the poor."[54] We see daily that the extortionist grows fat from the blood of the poor.

Reichenburger: Oh, oh, oh! What am I supposed to say? The truth is too apparent these days.

Romanus: Greed deals so violently with the poor debtors who have nothing to pay up! It takes for itself all that they have and throws them in the tower. Is this evangelical?

Reichenburger: If we push for the organization of rights, is that wrong?

Romanus: You want to be evangelicals? Even Saint Paul doesn't praise the courts among the Christians, 1 Corinthians 6,[55] and not unreasonably, when it is not Christlike,

---

51 Psalm 55:11: Oppression and fraud do not depart from its marketplace.

52 Proverbs 28:8: Whoever multiplies his wealth by interest and profit gathers it for him who is generous to the poor.

53 Ezekiel 22:12–13: You take interest and profit and make gain of your neighbors by extortion; but me you have forgotten, declares the Lord God. "Behold, I strike my hand at the dishonest gain that you have made."

54 Amos 4:1: "Hear this word, you cows of Bashan, who are on the mountain of Samaria, who oppress the poor, who crush the needy, who say to your husbands, 'Bring, that we may drink!'"

55 1 Corinthians 6:5–6: I say this to your shame. Can it be that there is no one among you wise enough to settle a dispute between the brothers, but brother

how it often occurs with false witness, swearing oaths, directing the truth, bending it, making appeals, stretching the truth. So it goes, while there is money, there is a defense; with no money, there is no defense. Greed reigns in full power here as members of the jury become rich from bribes and money smuggling. God paints an image of these false jurists in Jeremiah 5: "For godless men are found among my people concealing themselves like fowlers. They lay out the rope and the shackle to capture men. Like a cage is full of birds, so their houses are full of deceit; therefore, they have become powerful and rich[56] and they evilly trod on my Word. They don't judge the affairs of the widow and don't judge the affairs of the orphan, and don't judge the conviction of the poor. Shall I not strike down these things?"[57] And God curses these false jurists in Deuteronomy 27, saying, "Cursed be anyone who perverts the rights of the foreigner, the orphan, and the widow. And all the people shall say, Amen."[58] Therefore, you should not bring the poor to court but should handle everything with them according to the word of God in Proverbs 22: "Do not act in violence against the poor man because he is poor, nor crush

---

goes to law against brother, and that before unbelievers?

56 *grossmechtigt und greicht*: Carries the meaning word for word from the Latin Vulgata: *magnificati sunt et ditati*.

57 Jeremiah 5:26–29: "For wicked men are found among my people; they lurk like fowlers lying in wait. They set a trap; they catch men. Like a cage full of birds, their houses are full of deceit; therefore they have become great and rich; they have grown fat and sleek. They know no bounds in deeds of evil; they judge not with justice the cause of the fatherless, to make it prosper, and they do not defend the rights of the needy. Shall I not punish them for these things?"

58 Deuteronomy 27:19: "'Cursed be anyone who perverts the justice due to the sojourner, the fatherless, and the widow.' And all the people shall say, 'Amen.'"

the thirsty before the court, for the Lord judges his case and punishes those that have punished the poor man's spirit."[59]

Reichenburger: How then must we live with debtors in a Christian way when, as you say, we would be blamed?[60]

Romanus: Deuteronomy 24 states, "When you make your neighbor a loan of any sort, you shall not go into his house to collect his deposit. You shall stand outside, and the man to whom you make the loan shall bring the pledge out to you. And if he is a poor man, you shall not sleep in possession of his deposit. You shall restore to him the deposit before the sun sets, that he may sleep in his cloak and bless you. And it shall be righteousness for you before the Lord your God."[61] And Isaiah 58: "Is not this the fast that I chose: loosen the straps of the yoke, tear up the promissory note, and let the weak be."[62] And Ezekiel 18: "Give back the deposit to the debtor, don't take anything by force."[63] The new law is overall love, love, love.

---

59 Proverbs 22:22–23: "Do not rob the poor, because he is poor, or crush the afflicted at the gate, for the Lord will plead their cause and rob of life those who rob them."

60 *es sei fuer Schuld (it would be for blame)*: Similar to the construction *fuer Schuld geben* (to place blame) in modern German.

61 Deuteronomy 24:10–13: "When you make your neighbor a loan of any sort, you shall not go into his house to collect his pledge. You shall stand outside, and the man to whom you make the loan shall bring the pledge out to you. And if he is a poor man, you shall not sleep in his pledge. You shall restore to him the pledge as the sun sets, that he may sleep in his cloak and bless you. And it shall be righteousness for you before the Lord your God."

62 Isaiah 58:6: "Is not this the fast that I choose: to loose the bonds of wickedness, to undo the straps of the yoke, to let the oppressed go free, and to break every yoke?"

63 Ezekiel 18:7: . . . does not oppress anyone, but restores to the debtor his pledge, commits no robbery, gives his bread to the hungry and covers the naked with

Reichenburger: But one finds many bad debtors who would have had it well, such as many drunkards, gamblers, and whores who in this way lost what was theirs unnecessarily and are liable. Even with love and goodness, no one can get anything from them, they lie around and procrastinate on and on, holding no faith. Should we really not require anything of them?

Romanus: Of course, the worldly authorities should hold them to this, for they hold the sword that avenges evil, as Romans 8[64] says. I'm only talking about the poor who did not lose what was theirs unnecessarily but who became poor due to sickness and emergencies. And then you find some misers who are not in need of it and nevertheless drive the poor from the privilege of their homes. Micah 2 speaks of this: "They have coveted the fields and violently taken them, and they have robbed the houses. Therefore, thus says the Lord: I think evil things of these people, and you will not remove your necks from this."[65] And Proverbs 14: "Whoever oppresses a man in need insults his Maker."[66] Later, Proverbs 22: "Whoever oppresses the poor to increase his wealth, he will give it to the rich

---

a garment.

64   From God's righteous punishment. This is actually Romans 13:4: . . . for he is God's servant for your good. But if you do wrong, be afraid, for he does not bear the sword in vain. For he is the servant of God, an avenger who carries out God's wrath on the wrongdoer.

65   Micah 2:2–3: They covet fields and seize them, and houses, and take them away; they oppress a man and his house, a man and his inheritance. Therefore thus says the Lord: behold, against this family I am devising disaster, from which you cannot remove your necks.

66   Proverbs 14:31: Whoever oppresses a poor man insults his Maker.

and become thirsty."[67] This runs through the chest
of some unmerciful men or at least their children,
as after the death of the elderly, the goods disappear
like frost on a fence. Although the stingy man stays
sitting in his wealth for the span of his life, he is constantly scratching and clawing for it with previously
mentioned division and malice (for the stomach of
the greedy is insatiable, Proverbs 8[68]), and he does
not truly need his riches. As it says in Sapientia[69] 5,
"The greedy one will not be fulfilled with money and
he who loves riches will not take the fruits of them."[70]
And Amos 5: "Therefore because you have afflicted
the poor and taken from him the chosen spoils, you
will build houses of hewn stone, but you will not live
in them; you will plant the most lovely vineyards, but
you will not drink the wine from them."[71] Also, as
it happened to the rich man in Luke 12, who says, "Eat
and drink, dear Soul, you have a large abundance to
last many years, be merry!" But God says, "You fool!
This night one will demand of you your soul, and
who will those things that you have prepared belong
to?" Likewise (says Christ), it happens to him who

---

67 Proverbs 22:16: Whoever oppresses the poor to increase his own wealth, or
gives to the rich, will only come to poverty.

68 This is actually from Proverbs 13:25: The righteous has enough to satisfy his
appetite, but the belly of the wicked suffers want.

69 Sapientia, also known as Wisdom, is found in the Apocrypha.

70 Wisdom (Sapientia) 5:1: Then the righteous will stand with great confidence
in the presence of those who have oppressed them and those who make light
of their labors.

71 Amos 5:11: Therefore because you trample on the poor and you exact taxes of
grain from him, you have built houses of hewn stone, but you shall not dwell in
them; you have planted pleasant vineyards, but you shall not drink their wine.

collects treasure for himself and is not rich in God.[72] Christ speaks about this in Matthew 16: "For what help would it be to a man if he gains the whole world and yet suffers damage to his soul?"[73] It also says in Sirach 5, "Do not depend on dishonest wealth, for it will not benefit you on the day of your burial or on the day of revenge."[74] And Ezekiel 7 and Zephaniah 1: "Their silver and gold are not able to help them in the day of the wrath of the Lord."[75] Therefore, dear squire, it would be much better if it were as in Proverbs 15: "Little with the fear of the Lord is better than much treasure and is irreplaceable,"[76] and as it says in Habakkuk 2, "Woe to him who collects evil greediness."[77] And Ecclesiasticus[78] 10, "Nothing is more criminal than the greedy, nothing is more evil

---

72 Luke 12:19–21: "Soul, you have ample goods laid up for many years; relax, eat, drink, be merry." But God said to him, "Fool! This night your soul is required of you, and the things you have prepared, whose will they be?" So is the one who lays up treasure for himself and is not rich toward God.

73 Matthew 16:26: For what will it profit a man if he gains the whole world and forfeits his soul?

74 Sirach 5:8: Do not depend on dishonest wealth, for it will not benefit you on the day of calamity (NRSVUE).

75 Ezekiel 7:19: Their silver and gold are not able to deliver them in the day of the wrath of the Lord.

    Zephaniah 1:18: Neither their silver nor their gold shall be able to deliver them on the day of the wrath of the Lord. In the fire of his jealousy, all the earth shall be consumed; for a full and sudden end he will make of all the inhabitants of the earth.

76 Proverbs 15:16: Better is a little with the fear of the Lord than great treasure and trouble with it.

77 Habakkuk 2:9: "Woe to him who gets evil gain for his house."

78 Ecclesiasticus, also known as Sirach, is found in the Apocrypha.

than the love of money, for he has sold his soul."[79] And Christ says in Luke 12, "Guard yourself against greed, for no one lives from being fully satisfied with his possessions."[80]

Reichenburger: A good Christian knows that he is only a steward over the temporary goods and that nothing will be buried with him, as it says in Ecclesiastes 5: "As he came out from his mother's womb, so will he return, and takes nothing with him from his toil."[81] And 1 Timothy 6: "We brought nothing into the world, and so it is clear that we won't take anything out."[82] Thus, a true Christian is not consumed with worry for temporary things that he would collect much treasure, as in Matthew 6.[83] Rather, like in 1 Timothy 6, "if we have food and clothing, then let us be content. But those who desire to be rich fall into temptation, and traps, and many harmful desires that plunge people into ruin and damnation."[84] Why then would a Chris-

---

79 Sirach 10:31: And one dishonored in wealth, how much more in poverty! (NRSVUE).

80 Luke 12:15: "Take care, and be on your guard against all covetousness, for one's life does not consist in the abundance of his possessions."

81 Ecclesiastes 5:15: As he came from his mother's womb he shall go again, naked as he came, and shall take nothing for his toil that he may carry away in his hand.

82 1 Timothy 6:7: . . . for we brought nothing into the world, and we cannot take anything out of the world.

83 Matthew 6:19–20: "Do not lay up for yourselves treasures on earth, where moth and rust destroy and where thieves break in and steal, but lay up for yourselves treasures in heaven, where neither moth nor rust destroys and where thieves do not break in and steal."

84 1 Timothy 6:8–9: If we have food and clothing, with these we will be content. But those who desire to be rich fall into temptation, into a snare, into many senseless and harmful desires that plunge people into ruin and destruction.

tian who is strong in his faith[85] defile himself with such apparent division and malice? Where then is it not possible that a rightly acquired good through the passing of inheritance, marriage, or rightful purchasing, in itself, is dependent upon God?

Romanus: Christ says in Matthew 6, "Where your treasure is, there your heart is also,"[86] and "No one can serve two masters, for either way he will hate one and love the other. You cannot serve God and riches,"[87] for "the seed of the word of God, that fell among the thorns of wealth, will suffocate through worry, and it will not come to pass that it brings forth fruit" (Matthew 13).[88] Therefore, the message is not well received, as Christ says in Matthew 19,[89] Mark 10,[90] and Luke 18: "How difficult will the rich come into the kingdom of God! It is easier for a camel to go through the eye of a needle."[91]

Reichenburger: It is stated in Mark 10 with the words "How difficult it is that those who put their trust in wealth enter the

---

85 *Rechtgläubiger*: True believer.

86 Matthew 6:21: For where your treasure is, there your heart will be also.

87 Matthew 6:24: "No one can serve two masters, for either he will hate the one and love the other, or he will be devoted to the one and despise the other. You cannot serve God and money."

88 Matthew 13:22: As for what was sown among thorns, this is the one who hears the word, but the cares of the world and the deceitfulness of riches choke the word, and it proves unfruitful.

89 Matthew 19:24: "Again I tell you, it is easier for a camel to go through the eye of a needle than for a rich person to enter the kingdom of God."

90 Mark 10:25: "It is easier for a camel to go through the eye of a needle than for a rich person to enter the kingdom of God."

91 Luke 18:24–25: "How difficult it is for those who have wealth to enter the kingdom of God! For it is easier for a camel to go through the eye of a needle than for a rich person to enter the kingdom of God."

kingdom of God!"[92] Abraham, Isaac, Jacob, David, Job, and many of the patriarchs were also rich, but they did not put their hope in it. Isn't it possible, then, that one can be rich without setting his heart on his riches? As Paul teaches in 1 Corinthians 7, "Those who buy should do so as if they had no goods, and those who make use of this world as if they didn't need it."[93] If the heart is also made free and uncoupled from temporary goods and puts its sights on God and not on those things, then it is made content and does not greedily strive after them. Rather, the heart is prepared to leave these things, as God wills, and his Christians need to give to the poor, as Luke 16: "Make friends for yourselves by means of unrighteous wealth,[94] so that when you starve they may receive you into eternal dwellings."[95]

Romanus: Yes, that would lead to a certain amount of wealth. Where the rich man forgets the poor, [and] instead draws riches to himself, as was said previously, or consumes riches with much splendor and lust of the body like the rich man in Luke 16, gloriously clothed, who ate and drank seemingly all day and left poor Lazarus lacking even crumbs and sitting wretchedly before his gate. It will also be said to such rich men in

---

92 Mark 10:23: How difficult it will be for those who have wealth to enter the kingdom of God!

93 1 Corinthians 7:30–31: . . . and those who mourn as though they were not mourning, and those who rejoice as though they were not rejoicing, and those who buy as though they had no goods, and those who deal with the world as though they had no dealings with it. For the present form of this world is passing away.

94 Mammon.

95 Luke 16:9: And I tell you, make friends for yourselves by means of unrighteous wealth, so that when it fails they may receive you into the eternal dwellings.

this world as to the rich man,[96] "Son, think of how you received good in this lifetime, but the poor received bad, but now the poor will be comforted and you will be tormented."[97]

Reichenburger: Well, since the word of God is so clearly preached, one finds many rich men, God be praised, who charitably give assistance to, lend to, and give to those who are poor, timid neighbors[98] and others.

Romanus: Oh, but the poor are received sourly by some rich men as in Proverbs 18: "The poor speaks with supplication, but the rich answers roughly."[99] But in 1 John 3, it says, "Whoever has the world's goods and sees his brother in need, yet closes his heart against him, where does God's love abide in him?"[100] And later in 4: "He who does not love his brother, whom he sees, how can he love God, whom he does not see?"[101] By this, you know that you have received the evangelical Word but lack the works. When one feels so little love, they themselves become a noisy gong, as Paul names them in 1 Corinthians 13.[102]

---

96 In the parable of the rich man in Luke 16.

97 Luke 16:25: "Child, remember that you in your lifetime received your good things, and Lazarus in like manner bad things; but now he is comforted here, and you are in anguish."

98 *Hausarmen*: House poor; the poor who had homes but were too timid to beg. Any handouts they received would be given to them at home.

99 Proverbs 18:23: The poor use entreaties, but the rich answer roughly.

100 1 John 3:17: But if anyone has the world's goods and sees his brother in need, yet closes his heart against him, how does God's love abide in him?

101 1 John 4:20: If anyone says, "I love God," and hates his brother, he is a liar; for he who does not love his brother whom he has seen cannot love God whom he has not seen.

102 1 Corinthians 13:1: If I speak in the tongues of men and of angels, but have not love, I am a noisy gong or a clanging cymbal.

Reichenburger: Should one give to anyone according to what he requests, some would rely on it and lie around begging and not work. Not all who beg are needy and therefore one is not obligated to give in all cases, for whoever will not work should not eat, 2 Thessalonians 3.[103]

Romanus: Whoever is clearly able to work but doesn't do so, relying instead on lazy begging, should be punished so that other poor people must not undergo their punishment. In any case, some of you are a little too hard on the poor. If a poor person occasionally drinks wine (which they may also be in need of), you rich say, "What should we give the poor? They devour everything like animals and waste everything on drink!" Such excuses and the like seek to conceal greed in the heart. If you will not be faithful with the least, who will entrust to you more (Luke 16)?[104] By this, they will know that you are children of the world and not children of the light. Paul calls greed an idolization in Ephesians 5,[105] and it is even true when it causes the rich to worship not only goods but any kind of status. See how the builders and manual laborers are so selfish, and each of them hauls around their bags, and envy, hate, disputes, and fighting have no end among them. Though they all want to be good evangelicals, everyone is full of greed (as previously stated), from the least to the most, without needing much testing. Their daily dealings make it very clear

---

103 2 Thessalonians 3:10: If anyone is not willing to work, let him not eat.

104 Luke 16:11: If then you have not been faithful in the unrighteous wealth, who will entrust to you the true riches?

105 Ephesians 5:5: For you may be sure of this, that everyone who is sexually immoral or impure, or who is covetous (that is, an idolater), has no inheritance in the kingdom of Christ and God.

to see with new findings, lounging, hauling, offering, betrayal, stealing, robbery, murder, bad handling, hanging themselves, [and] drunkenness, [of] which Paul says in 1 Timothy 6, "Greed is a root of all kinds of evils."[106] Did you really think, dear squire, that you laity would carry water on a pole equally with us clergymen in terms of greed?[107] Who among you is without sin that they may cast the first stone at us (John 8)?[108]

Reichenburger: I recognize, unfortunately, that there are many stingy, selfish rich men among us, as you have displayed, but there are also good Christians who give floods of handouts, not in the Pharisees' manner of blowing their own horn, but as Matthew 6 describes, where the left hand does not know what the right hand does.[109] That is why you clergy folk think that we never give, gift, or donate much. There is no one who gives more to charity, and the poor are strong. The real poor people don't make much noise; only the foul vagabonds do. Therefore, you are not allowed to defile the evangelical teaching with the greed of these misers who live more like heathens than Christians. Luke 6 says that out of the abundance of the heart, the mouth speaks, and this applies also to you.[110]

---

106 1 Timothy 6:10: For the love of money is a root of all kinds of evils.

107 Romanus is expressing that the clergymen (Catholics) do not carry the same guilt of greed as the laity (evangelicals).

108 John 8:7: And as they continued to ask him, he stood up and said to them, "Let him who is without sin among you be the first to throw a stone at her."

109 Matthew 6:3–4: But when you give to the needy, do not let your left hand know what your right hand is doing, so that your giving may be in secret. And your Father who sees in secret will reward you.

110 Luke 6:45: The good person out of the good treasure of his heart produces good, and the evil person out of his evil treasure produces evil, for out of the abundance of the heart his mouth speaks.

Romanus: I will say what I know: that the majority of those who boast of being evangelicals are up to their ears in greed.

Reichenburger: I hold the hope that the word of God will force greed, along with evil dealings and public crimes, to the ground over time, according to what God says through Isaiah 55: "For as the rain and the snow come down from heaven and do not return there but water the earth, making it green and giving seed to the sower and bread to the eater, so is my word that comes out of my mouth. It will not return to my mouth, but it will gladly go in all that which I send it forth to do."[111]

Romanus: You have preached the word of God (or so you call it) for a long time, but I have yet to see any changes, and then you chase us clergymen away.

Reichenburger: We do so out of necessity when your dishonest teachings and commandments have rooted themselves too deeply. Then we need to uproot them and plant the true word of God in their stead, and God will cause it to thrive, as it says in 1 Corinthians 3:10[112] and also in Mark 4: "As the sown seed bears fruit by itself, without the help of the farmer, bringing first grass, then the ear, then the completed grains of the wheat."[113] Therefore, we do not need to worry when the grain will

---

111 Isaiah 55:10–11: "For as the rain and the snow come down from heaven and do not return there but water the earth, making it bring forth and sprout, giving seed to the sower and bread to the eater, so shall my word be that goes out from my mouth; it shall not return to me empty, but it shall accomplish that which I purpose, and shall succeed in the thing for which I sent it."

112 1 Corinthians 3:10: According to the grace of God given to me, like a skilled master builder I laid a foundation, and someone else is building upon it. Let each one take care how he builds upon it.

113 Mark 4:28: The earth produces by itself, first the blade, then the ear, then the full grain in the ear.

follow because where the gospel is preached correctly, the grains will come by themselves.

Romanus: I hear you clearly! All I have to do is preach "Believe! Believe! Love! Love!" and the hellish deposits of greed, divorce, and other open crimes that go against God's law in full power daily will be silenced. Then the bad reasoning will unravel itself, and your things will be rightfully displayed. However, God says in Jeremiah 51, "You wouldn't want to silence your misdoing, for the time of your vengeance is from the Lord."[114] And in Ezekiel 22: "Son of man, will you judge the city of sin and show them all of their cursed works?"[115] Such things happen, and I believe that you would be unlikely to take a step back like Zacchaeus in Luke 19, where he says, "Behold, Lord, the half of my goods I give to the poor, and if I have deceived anyone, I give fourfold more."[116] Rather, many more of you would step back and say to yourselves, "That is a difficult message; who can listen to it?!" Like the disciples in John 6,[117] you would have probably in the end gotten into a fistfight wherever (among whomever) you went, or your shame and insult would clearly come to light.[118] You really like to hear this, because it talks about monks and priests, as Herod heard John

---

114 Jeremiah 51:6: "Be not cut off in her punishment, for this is the time of the Lord's vengeance."

115 Ezekiel 22:2: "And you, son of man, will you judge, will you judge the bloody city? Then declare to her all her abominations."

116 Luke 19:8: "Behold, Lord, the half of my goods I give to the poor. And if I have defrauded anyone of anything, I restore it fourfold."

117 John 6:60: When many of his disciples heard it, they said, "This is a hard saying; who can listen to it?"

118 In order to prevent your shame from coming to light (being brought before everyone for them to see).

preaching about Christ and obeyed him in many things. But when he showed Herod his own wrongdoings, John had to be put in a dungeon and lose his head. When your evangelical preachers experience[119] this,[120] they keep themselves behind closed doors.[121]

Reichenburger:　Well, let's move on.[122] The day will come with time when God's law must be explained and displayed alongside the gospel, and man will be shown his depraved heart to frighten and humble him, since his heart has been inclined to evil from his youth (Genesis 8).[123] So then, he will be zealous for grace, as the gospel will be reported and provided to him through Christ. Also, the law does not justify the heart before God, but it prepares the heart for justification that occurs through the gospel. It changes the heart with a living trust in Christ wherein God works, Colossians 2.[124] When this is done, godly fruit follows.

Romanus:　I don't see any good fruits among you except when it does the body good. No confessions, fasting, prayers, churchgoing, sacrifices, pilgrimage, [instead] eating meat, and leaving the monastic orders, and the like are common practices among you. And you remain unashamed of these things in previous heathenish

---

119 *Schmecken*: To get a taste of.

120 Being shown their own wrongdoing.

121 *Hinter dem Berg halten*: Hiding or concealing something.

122 *Verziehen*: To procrastinate or postpone.

123 Genesis 8:21: And when the Lord smelled the pleasing aroma, the Lord said in his heart, "I will never again curse the ground because of man, for the intention of man's heart is evil from his youth. Neither will I ever again strike down every living creature as I have done."

124 Colossians 2:2: . . . that their hearts may be encouraged, being knit together in love, to reach all the riches of full assurance of understanding and the knowledge of God's mystery, which is Christ.

vices, such as greed, divorce, fornication, hostility, mutiny, wrath, quarreling, envy, hate, slander, murder, infidelity, gambling, cursing God, drunkenness, wastefulness, dancing, pride, stabbing, hunting, disobedience. You are judged by these fruits as heathens and not Christians, as Christ says in Matthew 7: "By their fruits you will recognize them."[125]

Reichenburger: Those that boast of the gospel are unfortunately the smallest portion of Christians, if what is said in Matthew 22 is true: "Many are called, but few are chosen."[126] These only have an artificial hope created from flesh and blood, and they turn evangelical freedom into lust and opportunity of the flesh, which Paul warns against (Galatians 5).[127] They tread over precious pearls[128] in dung like swine (Matthew 7)[129] and stay in their previous heathenish vices, stubbornly refusing to change their ways and drowning in them as nuisances and a dishonor to the gospel. But with time, such people and others will be dealt with as Paul teaches in 1 Corinthians 5.[130] God have mercy on you and all of us, for we are all sinners and there is no one who is without sin, 1 Kings 8.[131]

Romanus: If I hear you clearly, true Christians also do not live without sin.

---

125 Matthew 7:20: Thus you will recognize them by their fruits.

126 Matthew 22:14: "For many are called, but few are chosen."

127 Galatians 5:13: For you were called to freedom, brothers. Only do not use your freedom as an opportunity for the flesh, but through love serve one another.

128 *Margariten*: Romans called pearls *margarita*, using the Greek term.

129 Matthew 7:6: "Do not give dogs what is holy, and do not throw your pearls before pigs, lest they trample them underfoot and turn to attack you."

130 1 Corinthians 5:13: God judges those outside. "Purge the evil person from among you."

131 Sachs uses the ordering of the Clementine Vulgate, so the original reference is "iii. Regum viii."

Reichenburger: Yes, it says in 1 John 1, "If we say we have no sin, we deceive ourselves, and the truth is not in us."[132] So long as the flesh and blood are alive, they seek at all times to be against the Holy Spirit; as Galatians 5 says, "For the desires of the flesh are against the Spirit, and the desires of the Spirit are against the flesh."[133] Here, the cross and suffering serve us, according to 1 Peter 4: "Whoever suffers in the flesh ceases from sin."[134] Also, God occasionally allows his elect to give in to outer temptations, as David did in adultery (2 Samuel 11)[135] and Peter in denying Christ (Matthew 26).[136] Everything came to be good for them, and they were thirsty for God's mercy after their sins, crying, "Abba, dear Father, forgive us our sins!" (Romans 8; Matthew 6),[137] and then they are received by God with

---

1 Kings 8:46: "If they sin against you—for there is no one who does not sin—and you are angry with them and give them to an enemy, so that they are carried away captive to the land of the enemy, far off or near."

132 1 John 1:8: If we say we have no sin, we deceive ourselves, and the truth is not in us.

133 Galatians 5:17: For the desires of the flesh are against the Spirit, and the desires of the Spirit are against the flesh.

134 1 Peter 4:1: For whoever has suffered in the flesh has ceased from sin.

135 2 Samuel 11:4: So David sent messengers and took her, and she came to him, and he lay with her. (Now she had been purifying herself from her uncleanness.) Then she returned to her house.

136 Matthew 26:74–75: Then he began to invoke a curse on himself and to swear, "I do not know the man." And immediately the rooster crowed. And Peter remembered the saying of Jesus, "Before the rooster crows, you will deny me three times." And he went out and wept bitterly.

137 Romans 8:15: For you did not receive the spirit of slavery to fall back into fear, but you have received the Spirit of adoption as sons, by whom we cry, "Abba! Father!"

Matthew 6:9–13: Pray then like this: "Our Father in heaven, hallowed be your name. Your kingdom come, your will be done, on earth as it is in heaven.

grace as the prodigal son (Luke 15)[138] and firmer in their faith. Falling and rising continues on and on; as Proverbs 22 says, "The righteous falls seven times in the day"[139] until eventually, in death, the old Adam, in flesh and blood, succumbs to death. Only then will come the perfect, holy life, which we are not able to experience here in our sinful bodies.

Romanus: I am worried, dear squire, that few people receive this teaching to the extent that you say. They feel neither the call to worship God nor the work of love and so on.

Reichenburger: You always say, "Feel, feel." Don't you know that the kingdom of God does not come with observations so that you can say, "See here or there," but it is within the heart (Matthew 17)?[140] He who worships God does not do so with outer gestures. True worshippers praise God in the Spirit and in truth (John 4).[141] Thus, the work of love toward your neighbor is just simple in manner and without all the splendor. For this reason, the Catholics[142] think that no one worships God, as in the

---

Give us this day our daily bread, and forgive us our debts, as we also have forgiven our debtors. And lead us not into temptation, but deliver us from evil."

138 Luke 15:32: It was fitting to celebrate and be glad, for this your brother was dead, and is alive; he was lost, and is found.

139 The actual reference is Proverbs 24:16: For the righteous falls seven times and rises again.

140 Possibly Matthew 16:1: And the Pharisees and Sadducees came, and to test him they asked him to show them a sign from heaven.

141 John 4:23: But the hour is coming, and is now here, when the true worshipers will worship the Father in spirit and truth, for the Father is seeking such people to worship him.

142 *Werkheiligen*: A term that Luther coined for the Catholics. A translation of the term would be "those made holy by works," and it is to be contrasted with Luther's belief in salvation, *Sola Christus* (faith in Christ alone).

time of Elijah (1 Kings 19).[143] He thought he alone in all of Israel served the true God when there were seven thousand who did not bend the knee before the idol of Baal and worshipped God. You Catholics, who lack the Holy Spirit, also think that the healing evangelical teaching does not better anyone, since outward sins are still in full power, coming out from those who pride themselves in being evangelicals along with all the other children of the world. And it has to be like the Philistines, Canaanites, Sidonians, and Hivites who lived among Israel (Judges 3),[144] and the good and evil have to live among one another. "But God knows how to free the godly from temptation, and yet punish the unrighteous until the day of judgment," 2 Peter 2.[145] God also preserves those who are his in the depraved world, just as the three youths in the fiery oven (Daniel 3),[146] and they grow up among the children of the world being despised, persecuted, and oppressed, unobservant like the lily among the thorns (Song of Solomon 2),[147] not knowing the world until the time of harvest. For the children of the world will be gathered with the weeds and thrown into the fire,

---

143 1 Kings 19:10: He said, "I have been very jealous for the Lord, the God of hosts. For the people of Israel have forsaken your covenant, thrown down your altars, and killed your prophets with the sword, and I, even I only, am left, and they seek my life, to take it away."

144 Judges 3:5: So the people of Israel lived among the Canaanites, the Hittites, the Amorites, the Perizzites, the Hivites, and the Jebusites.

145 2 Peter 2:9: Then the Lord knows how to rescue the godly from trials, and to keep the unrighteous under punishment until the day of judgment.

146 Daniel 3:20: And he ordered some of the mighty men of his army to bind Shadrach, Meshach, and Abednego, and to cast them into the burning fiery furnace.

147 Song of Solomon 2:1: I am a rose of Sharon, a lily of the valleys.

	but the children of God will be gathered with the wheat and will be stored forever in the barn.
Romanus:	Listen! Listen! They rang for the vespers! How did we come to bicker? I didn't accomplish what I came to do.
Reichenburger:	You have held us up quite enough. I believe, since you were not able to disgrace our teaching, you would like to blaspheme it with our sinful lives.
Romanus:	Well, then put off your heathenish lives (1 Peter 4),[148] live Christlike according to the will of God! Then one could say, "This new teaching is from God," when the people are holier from it, for a good tree cannot bring forth bad fruit. A good man brings forth good out of the good treasure of his heart (Luke 6).[149]
Reichenburger:	You are arrogant, seeing only from your high place down on the large worldly crowds, who then (as before) conduct themselves with shameful sins. You are then blinded by the stars and fall back down to your gaudy hypocrisy that you hold to as holy. If you really want to be right, you must search the Scriptures for what God has commanded, forbidden, or allowed freely. When you by grace grasp this, then you won't hold the monks' caps and statutes in such high regard.
Romanus:	I don't have any desire for your crowds, who are a mangy, snotty mess. If there were a shepherd and a sheep's

---

148 1 Peter 4:1–2: Since therefore Christ suffered in the flesh, arm yourselves with the same way of thinking, for whoever has suffered in the flesh has ceased from sin, so as to live for the rest of the time in the flesh no longer for human passions but for the will of God.

149 Luke 6:45: The good person out of the good treasure of his heart produces good, and the evil person out of his evil treasure produces evil, for out of the abundance of the heart his mouth speaks.

pen,[150] then I would hang up my monk's cap and step
into the crowd. There are other ways if this one fails.
It's high time to go.

Reichenburger: You are of the people who God talks about in Isaiah 65:
"The whole day I have stretched out my hands to the
people who do not call on my name and who speak
out against me."[151] Therefore, see that your flight
does not happen too late in the winter or Sabbath
(Matthew 24).[152]

Romanus: Once again, I am parting with knowledge, dear squire
Reichenburger. God be with you!

Reichenburger: Amen.

Psalm 1:1–3
Blessed is the man who practices the law of the Lord day and night.
He will be as a tree, planted at the streams of water,
so that it bears its fruit in its time.[153]

---

150 "Shepherd and a sheep's pen" refers to organized leadership as opposed to the
mangy, snotty mess.

151 Isaiah 65:2–3: I spread out my hands all the day to a rebellious people . . . a
people who provoke me to my face continually.

152 Matthew 24:20: Pray that your flight may not be in winter or on a Sabbath.

153 Psalm 1:1–3: Blessed is the man who walks not in the counsel of the wicked,
nor stands in the way of sinners, nor sits in the seat of scoffers; but his delight
is in the law of the Lord, and on his law he meditates day and night. He is like
a tree planted by streams of water that yields its fruit in its season, and its leaf
does not wither. In all that he does, he prospers.

CHAPTER 8

A Conversation between an Evangelical Christian and a Lutheran Where the Angry Idiot Who Calls Himself a Lutheran Is Admonished Brotherly

---

Ain Gespꝛꝛch aines Euangeli⸗
schen Chꝛisten/ mit ainem Lutherischen
darinn der Ergerlich wandel etli⸗
cher/ die sich Lutherisch nennē
angezaigt/vnd bꝛüderlich
gestrafft wirdt.
M.D.xxiiij.

Hans Sachs Schuchmacher.

Secunda Corinth. vj.

Last vns nyemant yrgent ain ergernuß
geben/ auff das vnnser ampt nicht gele⸗
stert werd/ sonnder in allen dingen laßt
vns beweysen / wie die diener Gottes.

Introduction

In this fourth and final play, Hans Sachs introduces a dispute between a self-professed Protestant and a Lutheran, by name and not practice, based on the Lutheran's witness and insensitivity to his Catholic father-in-law. Through this dispute, Sachs provides a criticism of the culture and practices of those who claimed to be non-Catholic, Reformed Christians at the time. According to Richard Zoozmann, this dialogue expands on the apostolic saying "Let no one bring another to offense so that our office may not be blasphemed" (2 Corinthians 6:3). Zoozmann continues by saying that this play also focuses on the overzealous and eccentric in the Protestant Christian community, who see the value and goal of the Reformation as being found in their external freedoms.[1] In doing so, these Christians offend others, who then seek to harm the new teachings out of anger with rumors, threats, and blasphemy.

In the beginning of the play, Hans mentions to Peter a "little book about the freedom afforded to Christians," which is in reference to the book *On the Freedom of a Christian* by Martin Luther, written in 1520. The reference to Luther's book by the character Hans foreshadows the discussion that follows. It is evident that Sachs knows the contents of this book very well while also having an intimate knowledge of Luther's translation of the Scriptures, of which the New Testament had been published only two years prior, in 1522. Sachs portrays the character Hans as a silhouette of himself, knowing the Scriptures well and using them accurately to defend his position (and subsequently that of Luther). He also demonstrates awareness of theological and cultural issues of the time, which he portrays through the character Peter, who quotes Scripture out of context or chooses to ignore parts that he does not wish to abide by and who misunderstands the freedom afforded to a Christian as freedom to do as he pleases. Master Ulrich, Peter's father-in-law, serves to represent the Catholic laity to whom a Christian is meant to be a witness; thus, his character is initially strong in his resolve but softens as he finds common ground with Hans. Unlike for the other three plays, there is no accompanying image.

It is possible that throughout these four plays, there is a continuation of characters—specifically Hans and Peter. In three of the plays, it is clear that the character Hans is in fact Sachs himself. There is no clear evidence to support that Peter the baker from the second dialogue is the same Peter, the Lutheran, in the fourth dialogue. However, there are similarities in the characterization of Peter among the dialogues, specifically pertaining to his role in representing the common man.

The principal themes presented by Sachs in this dialogue concern freedom in Christ, avoiding offending your neighbor, and the

---

1 Richard Zoozmann, *Hans Sachs und die Reformation: In Gedichten und Prosastücke* (Hamburg, Germany: SEVERUS Verlag, 2017), 23.

responsibility of the Christian as a witness of the gospel. Throughout the discussion between the Protestant and the Lutheran, Sachs explores what the Scriptures say about the freedom of the believer in Christ and the appropriateness of their practice, specifically discussing such freedoms as eating meat on Friday, which was forbidden by the Catholic Church. Throughout the dialogue, Sachs also highlights the theme of avoiding offending others. This theme is expressed as Sachs delves into Scripture to look at how practicing freedoms that the Christian possesses because of faith in Christ can coincide with not causing offense to others. Sachs unites the exploration of these themes with the responsibility of Christians as witnesses to those around them, looking to the Scripture for what makes a good witness.

The Protestant, Lutheran, and Catholic characters support their contentions with Scripture. As an aid to the reader, each Scripture reference has been supplied with chapter and verse number. (Verse numbers were not added to Scripture until 1551.) Footnotes have been used to identify specific German or Latin words or phrases that have been translated other than literally or to add contextual information for the reader.

A Conversation between an Evangelical Christian and a Lutheran Where the Angry Idiot Who Calls Himself a Lutheran Is Admonished Brotherly

2 Corinthians 6

Let us not be a nuisance to anyone, so as not to blaspheme our position, but rather in all things let us prove we are the servants of God.[2]

Hans: Greetings in the name of God, my beloved brother in Christ!

Peter: Thanks be to God, beloved brother Hans! How is it going? You are a rather infrequent guest in my house.

Hans: The preaching is going well! We announced what was most important,[3] and my little book[4] about the freedom afforded to Christians was with me through it all. Have you received any letters at all from your father-in-law, the old Romanist?[5]

Peter: Oh, no!

Hans: How so? Didn't he convert yet?

Peter: Well,[6] eight days ago on Friday, I threw him right out of the cradle.[7]

Hans: With what?

---

2 2 Corinthians 6:3–4: We put no obstacle in anyone's way, so that no fault may be found with our ministry, but as servants of God we commend ourselves in every way.

3 *das Erst*: The first things, the most important things.

4 Reference to *On the Freedom of a Christian* by Martin Luther (1520).

5 The original term is "Romanist," which was a slang term for Roman Catholics.

6 *Ei*: An interjection used in a variety of contexts, including indignation, shock, contradiction, and so on.

7 Referring to the figurative cradle of a new believer or someone who is considering conversion.

Peter: Well,[8] he came to my house unexpectedly, and then we ate a roasted calf. Oh how the man threw out curses and scolded us as if we'd committed a murder, like all those Romanists do.[9] Since then, he hasn't spoken a word to me and hasn't come to my house at all.

Hans: Well, well, you've done the man an injustice. You know well that your father-in-law isn't ready for evangelical freedom yet.

Peter: But how is eating meat a sin? I think you're trying to trick me. In Matthew 15, Christ calls the people to him and says, "Listen and understand this: what goes in the mouth does not defile a man."[10] Also, in Luke 10 he says, "Whenever you enter a town, eat what is brought before you."[11] And in John 8 he says, "So if the Son sets you free, you will be truly free."[12] And Paul says in 2 Corinthians 3, "Where the Spirit of the Lord is, there is freedom."[13] And in Romans 14 he says, "I know and am assured in the Lord Jesus that no food is unclean in itself, but it is unclean for anyone who finds it unclean."[14] And according to Titus 1, "To the pure, all things are pure, but to the defiled and unbelieving, nothing is pure; for both their minds

---

8 *Ei.*

9 Eating meat on Friday was forbidden by the Catholic Church at that time.

10 Matthew 15:10–11: "Hear and understand: it is not what goes into the mouth that defiles a person."

11 Luke 10:8: Whenever you enter a town and they receive you, eat what is set before you.

12 John 8:36: So if the Son sets you free, you will be free indeed.

13 2 Corinthians 3:17: Now the Lord is the Spirit, and where the Spirit of the Lord is, there is freedom.

14 Romans 14:14: I know and am persuaded in the Lord Jesus that nothing is unclean in itself, but it is unclean for anyone who thinks it unclean.

and their consciences are unclean."[15] And according to Romans 14, "Blessed is the one whose conscience is not bothered by that which he intakes."[16] Brother, what do you have to say about these sayings?

Hans: You are right in that eating meat is not in and of itself a sin, as God no longer forbids us from eating it. However, Paul says in 1 Corinthians 10, "I have done everything, but not everything is helpful. I have done everything, but it does not improve everything. No one seeks what is his, but that which belongs to another."[17] And 1 Corinthians 8 says, "But see to it that your freedom does not become a stumbling block to the weak."[18] And in Romans 14, "The one who is weak in faith, take him in and do not confuse his conscience. One person believes he may eat anything, but the weak person eats only vegetables."[19] It continues later on in the chapter, "It is much better that you eat no meat and drink no wine or do that which causes your brother to stumble, to be offended or to be weak. If you have faith, then keep it between yourself and God."[20]

---

15 Titus 1:15: To the pure, all things are pure, but to the defiled and unbelieving, nothing is pure; but both their minds and their consciences are defiled.

16 Romans 14:22: Blessed is the one who has no reason to pass judgment on himself for what he approves.

17 1 Corinthians 10:23–24: "All things are lawful," but not all things are helpful. "All things are lawful," but not all things build up. Let no one seek his own good, but the good of his neighbor.

18 1 Corinthians 8:9: But take care that this right of yours does not somehow become a stumbling block to the weak.

19 Romans 14:1–2: As for the one who is weak in faith, welcome him, but not to quarrel over opinions. One person believes he may eat anything, while the weak person eats only vegetables.

20 Romans 14:21–22: It is good not to eat meat or drink wine or do anything that causes your brother to stumble. The faith that you have, keep between yourself and God.

Peter: It also says otherwise in 1 Corinthians 10, "Why should I let my freedom be judged by someone else's conscience? If I partake with thankfulness, should I be blasphemed because of that for which I give thanks?"[21]

Hans: In the text that follows, Paul says, "Be inoffensive to both the Jews or the Greeks or to the congregation of God, just as I join with everyone in all things, not seeking things for myself, but what is beneficial to many, that they may be saved."[22]

Peter: I don't care about that. In Galatians 5 it says, "Therefore stand firm in freedom with which Christ has freed us, and do not let yourselves be bound to a yoke of slavery."[23] And in Colossians 2, "Let no one judge you about food or drink, or about any (holy) day."[24] And later it says, "Then as you have died with Christ to the laws of man, why do you let yourselves be ensnared with these laws, as if you were still alive, saying: 'You should not touch that, you should not eat or drink that, you should not handle that!'"[25] And it says it even clearer in 1 Corinthians 10: "Whatever is for sale in

---

21 1 Corinthians 10:29–30: For why should my liberty be determined by someone else's conscience? If I partake with thankfulness, why am I denounced because of that for which I give thanks?

22 1 Corinthians 10:32–33: Give no offense to Jews or to Greeks or to the church of God, just as I try to please everyone in everything I do, not seeking my own advantage, but that of many, that they may be saved.

23 Galatians 5:1: For freedom Christ has set us free; stand firm therefore, and do not submit again to a yoke of slavery.

24 Colossians 2:16: Therefore let no one pass judgment on you in questions of food and drink, or with regard to a festival or a new moon or a Sabbath.

25 Colossians 2:20–22: If with Christ you died to the elemental spirits of the world, why, as if you were still alive in the world, do you submit to regulations—"Do not handle, Do not taste, Do not touch."

the meat market, eat it and do not seek to spare your conscience."[26]

Hans: Brother, it follows this up later in 1 Corinthians 10 with "But if someone were to say to you, 'This is an offering to our gods'" (as our avoidance of meat may also be a sacrifice to gods whenever we avoid meat according to man's commandments and not God's), Paul says, "Then do not eat it and spare the conscience of the one who declared it."[27] And in Romans 14, "For if your brother is grieved by what you eat, you are no longer walking in love. Beloved one, do not pollute them with your food, for whose sake Christ died."[28] And in 1 Corinthians 8, "And so by your knowledge this weak person is destroyed, the brother for whom Christ died. When you then sin against your brothers and strike down their weak conscience, you sin against Christ. Therefore, if food offends my brother, I would never eat meat."[29] How do you feel about these sayings by Saint Paul?

Peter: What use is our freedom to us if we're not allowed to use it?

Hans: It's extremely helpful for us to know that no food is detrimental to us. But we should avoid it for the sake

---

26 1 Corinthians 10:25: Eat whatever is sold in the meat market without raising any question on the ground of conscience.

27 1 Corinthians 10:28: But if someone says to you, "This has been offered in sacrifice," then do not eat it, for the sake of the one who informed you.

28 Romans 14:15: For if your brother is grieved by what you eat, you are no longer walking in love. By what you eat, do not destroy the one for whom Christ died.

29 1 Corinthians 8:11–13: And so by your knowledge this weak person is destroyed, the brother for whom Christ died. Thus, sinning against your brothers and wounding their conscience when it is weak, you sin against Christ. Therefore, if food makes my brother stumble, I will never eat meat, lest I make my brother stumble.

of the weak. As it says in Romans 15, "We who are strong should bear the frailty of the weak, and not please ourselves."[30] Also, as 1 Corinthians 10 states, "Let anyone who thinks that he is standing take heed that he does not fall."[31] I worry, though, that there are many among you who eat meat on Friday not from a basis in faith but out of insolence, profanity, and lust, and the least of these falters in their conscience. This is what Paul says in Romans 14: "But whoever would falter is condemned, because the eating is not from faith. For whatever does not come from faith is sin."[32]

Peter: Ach, dear brother Hans. How long then are we supposed to lie in the Babylonian prison wearing Roman chains and deprive ourselves of freely using our Christian freedom to eat meat and all else?

Hans: My dear brother Peter, be patient! In 2 Thessalonians 2, Paul says, "The Lord Jesus will extinguish him with the Spirit of his mouth and will bring an end to him."[33] Therefore, dear brother, allow yourself to be satisfied along with me and our brethren that our consciences are free and unrestrained by such man-made commands concerning the salvation of the soul. Let us then bear such and the same burdens with our fellow brethren outwardly and willingly, as we do with

---

30 Romans 15:1: We who are strong have an obligation to bear with the failings of the weak, and not to please ourselves.

31 1 Corinthians 10:12: Therefore let anyone who thinks that he stands take heed lest he fall.

32 Romans 14:23: But whoever has doubts is condemned if he eats, because the eating is not from faith. For whatever does not proceed from faith is sin.

33 2 Thessalonians 2:8: And then the lawless one will be revealed, whom the Lord Jesus will kill with the breath of his mouth and bring to nothing by the appearance of his coming.

other statutes and customs of the state, like in Galatians 6: "Bear one another's burdens, so the law of
Christ will be fulfilled."[34]

Peter: I hear what you're saying.[35] I need to show love to men
and women who differ in what food is acceptable to
eat, though they'll be cast away by Christ regardless.
Matthew 15 says, "A single plant that God, my heavenly
Father, has not planted will be uprooted."[36]

Hans: Listen to what Paul says in Romans 14: "The kingdom
of God is not eating nor drinking, but righteousness,
peace, and joy in the Holy Spirit."[37] And in 1 Corinthians 8, "We eat and are not better, we don't eat and
we are not worse."[38] It is just better that we avoid meat
to ease our unknowing brother's conscience, as this
avoidance is an act of faith and love and is pleasing to
God, when it was previously an abomination to him.

Peter: Oh, I hear what you're saying. I have to become a
hypocritical Romanist again and follow the ordinances
and ceremonies with them.

Hans: Well, anything that you can do without irritating your
neighbor, you are allowed to do. You only act this
way for the sake of irritating your neighbors. That's
why you should do as Paul says in 1 Corinthians 9:
"For though I am free from everyone, I have made
myself a servant, that I might win more of them. To

---

34 Galatians 6:2: "Bear one another's burdens, and so fulfill the law of Christ."

35 In saying "I hear what you're saying," he is not saying "I agree with you."

36 Matthew 15:13: "Every plant that my heavenly Father has not planted will be
rooted up."

37 Romans 14:17: For the kingdom of God is not a matter of eating and drinking
but of righteousness and peace and joy in the Holy Spirit.

38 1 Corinthians 8:8: We are no worse off if we do not eat, and no better off if
we do.

the Jews I became as a Jew, in order to win Jews. To the
heathens as a heathen, to the weak as a weak man
and have become all things to all people."[39] And in
2 Corinthians 11, "Who is weak, and I am not weak
and who is offended and I do not burn?"[40] Let's also
follow Christ's commandment in John 13: "A new
commandment I give to you, that you love one another
as I have loved you. By this all people will know that
you are my disciples."[41] Did you hear that? Love is the
true test of a Christian, not eating meat, because even
dogs and cats can do that well.

Peter: Brother, that's not helpful to them[42] at all; even if we
continue for a while to spare them [the offense],[43] it
will only make them all the angrier and more stubborn. For that reason, it doesn't matter whether you
eat meat or leave it.

---

39 1 Corinthians 9:19–22: For though I am free from all, I have made myself a
servant to all, that I might win more of them. To the Jews I became as a Jew,
in order to win Jews. To those under the law I became as one under the law
(though not being myself under the law) that I might win those under the law.
To those outside the law I became as one outside the law (not being outside
the law of God but under the law of Christ) that I might win those outside the
law. To the weak I became weak, that I might win the weak. I have become all
things to all people.

40 2 Corinthians 11:29: Who is weak, and I am not weak? Who is made to fall,
and I am not indignant?

41 John 13:34–35: "A new commandment I give to you, that you love one another:
just as I have loved you, you also are to love one another. By this all people will
know that you are my disciples."

42 "Them" refers to the Romanists—that is, the Catholics who have not accepted
the teachings of the Reformation.

43 *verschonen:* To spare someone; here to spare them the offense.

Hans: Dear brother, if you offend[44] them instead, they will immediately berate and insult the gospel and the word of God due to your heresy and meat eating, because of all of the stumbling blocks and annoyances of the evangelical teachings, eating meat is the absolute worst to the common man. Let God remove your blindness with his good word! They have fulfilled what Paul says in 2 Thessalonians 2: "Because they have not accepted the love of the truth so they might be saved. Therefore, God sends them a strong delusion, so that they believe the lies by which everyone who has not accepted the truth will be judged."[45]

Peter: Sadly, it's true. I actually have neighbors who are so moved by their conscience if they eat even a bite of meat on a Friday that they feel as if they lied or betrayed someone else's honor and goodness.

Hans: Well then, dear brother, just avoid eating meat or only eat it secretly, so you don't offend anyone.

Peter: Well then, I'll do it. So far, I hadn't considered that so much bad would come of it.

Hans: Come on, then, let's go! They're ringing the three o'clock call[46] for the sermon.

Peter: Another thing first. Brother, my father-in-law is coming. Go talk to him about the gospel!

Master Ulrich:[47] Greetings and God bless you, you Lutherans!

---

44 *nicht verschonen:* Not spare.

45 2 Thessalonians 2:10–12: . . . because they refused to love the truth and so be saved. Therefore God sends them a strong delusion, so that they may believe what is false, in order that all may be condemned who did not believe the truth but had pleasure in unrighteousness.

46 Ringing the church bells for the Protestant service.

47 The father-in-law Master Ulrich, a Catholic, enters the conversation.

Hans: Many thanks! You've come just in time. Come with us to our sermon, Master Ulrich!

Master Ulrich: I'd rather that your preacher be hung. He is a heretic.

Hans: Really, dear Master Ulrich, why is that?

Master Ulrich: Whenever my son-in-law comes over, he says, "Our pastor says that you are not allowed to pray, worship the saints, fast, tithe, make pilgrimage, take part in Catholic Mass and Holy Eucharist,[48] celebrate Vigil, celebrate All Souls' Day,[49] or pay indulgences and that no good works will help you achieve holiness." He says all this and still more foul antics that my son-in-law and his companions hold to. He knows exactly what I mean.

Hans: O Peter, Peter! You and your companions are going about it all wrong, saying "Our preacher says this and that" but not telling them the reason why and how the pastor explained it to you. Simple people are rushing away from the teachings because of this. They curse the Christian pastor and flee from teachings like yours because they want to hear the reasoning. They unknowingly blaspheme the holy word of God, saying, "Is this what they're teaching now? I'll keep my old faith, then." Whose fault is that? Only you crude rascals. It doesn't matter to me whether you and your like are my friends or my foes; I say this out of necessity. If you were truly Christians, you would handle

---

48 In the original text, this is referred to as the Holy Mass. The Holy Eucharist, or liturgy of the Eucharist, is seen as the holiest and most sacred part of the Catholic Mass.

49 *Jartag* or *Jahrestag* (more commonly *Gedenktag*) is the anniversary of a major event such as a birth, the founding of a church, or a death. As the list refers to Roman Catholic traditions, All Souls' Day (*Allerseelen*) seems to be what is referred to here.

yourselves like Christians and tell those who don't know the comforting word of Christ what you heard from the pastor—namely, that Christ's death is the only act of our salvation and how the heavenly Father has given Christ governance over heaven and earth. Because of this, we should only listen to Christ. What he says, we should do. What he forbids, we should leave be. What he freely permits, let no one forbid, neither in heaven nor on earth, by the salvation of souls.[50] If you told people such things, it could wake the hearts of the unknowing so that they might come to such sermons and hear the reasons themselves, by which they would come to a true knowledge of the truth of God. Then other laws of man and such clowning[51] around would fall flat on the ground at their own hand.

Master Ulrich: I'd also have a higher opinion of all that if people told me good things, but I don't hear much of that from Lutherans. A table full of Lutherans came over to my son-in-law's place, and even then, you truly don't hear a single good Christian word from them. They launch into criticizing monks and bishops, but a dog couldn't get even a slice of bread from them, and whoever the worst may be is the master among them. For that reason, your Lutheran ways don't tempt me one bit.

Hans: Peter, Peter, this is contrary to loving your neighbor. Matthew 7 says, "Whatever you want others to do to

---

50 *Selen Heil*: Used here as an intensifier to emphasize the gravity of what was just said.

51 *Gaukelwerk*: Normally translated "juggling," but in this case it refers to a meta-phorical juggling of ideals by people considered to be foolish.

you, do also to them."[52] You really don't want your
reputation to be based on when your neighbors were
so blind, poor, and stubborn that others easily sympa-
thized with them and prayed on their behalf to God,
crying out that he would bring shame, crime, [and]
injustice to you and telling your story at the table as a
lesson.

Peter: Well, they're allowed to do it, then. You have to let
them say so because it's the truth.

Hans: If that's true, then listen to what Paul says in Romans 2:
"O man, you cannot excuse yourselves, every one of you
who judges. For in passing judgment on another
you condemn yourself because you do the very same
things."[53] Judge your own heart first before you judge
another.

Peter: Dear brother, you all led us by the fool's cord[54] for
so long, we'd like to repay you exactly like it says in
Revelation 18: "Pay her back as she has paid you back
and repay her double for her deeds."[55]

Hans: But it says in Matthew 5, "Love your enemies and
bless those who curse you. Do well to those who hate
you, pray for those who torment and persecute you."[56]
And in 1 Peter 3, "Finally, all of you, have unity of
mind, sympathy, brotherly love, a tender heart, and

---

52 Matthew 7:12: "So whatever you wish that others would do to you, do also to
them."

53 Romans 2:1: Therefore you have no excuse, O man, every one of you who
judges. For in passing judgment on another you condemn yourself, because
you, the judge, practice the very same things.

54 *Narrenseil*: Refers to the practice of leading fools with a rope through public
spaces.

55 Revelation 18:6: Pay her back as she herself has paid back others, and repay
her double for her deeds.

56 Matthew 5:44: Love your enemies and pray for those who persecute you.

be friendly. Do not repay evil for evil, not reviling for reviling, but on the contrary, bless," and so on.[57]

Peter: Are we supposed to laugh it off, then? Did you think we would be alright with that? I can already see it: they will shout for us to be treated like the Christians who, because of the gospel, were stormed, sacked, burned, and exiled and their land divided as loot in the Babylonian kingdom.

Hans: Dear brother, through Christ, how all of this will go was already announced to us. Read Matthew 10,[58] Mark 12,[59] Luke 21,[60] and John 15.[61] You'll find persecu-

---

57 1 Peter 3:8–9: Finally, all of you, have unity of mind, sympathy, brotherly love, a tender heart, and a humble mind. Do not repay evil for evil or reviling for reviling, but on the contrary, bless, for to this you were called, that you may obtain a blessing.

58 Matthew 10:16–18: "Behold, I am sending you out as sheep in the midst of wolves, so be wise as serpents and innocent as doves. Beware of men, for they will deliver you over to courts and flog you in their synagogues, and you will be dragged before governors and kings for my sake, to bear witness before them and the Gentiles."

59 Mark 12:2–8: When the season came, he sent a servant to the tenants to get from them some of the fruit of the vineyard. And they took him and beat him and sent him away empty-handed. Again he sent to them another servant, and they struck him on the head and treated him shamefully. And he sent another, and him they killed. And so with many others: some they beat, and some they killed. He had still one other, a beloved son. Finally he sent him to them, saying, "They will respect my son." But those tenants said to one another, "This is the heir. Come, let us kill him, and the inheritance will be ours." And they took him and killed him and threw him out of the vineyard.

60 Luke 21:16–17: You will be delivered up even by parents and brothers and relatives and friends, and some of you they will put to death. You will be hated by all for my name's sake.

61 John 15:18–21: "If the world hates you, know that it has hated me before it hated you. If you were of the world, the world would love you as its own; but because you are not of the world, but I chose you out of the world, therefore

tion in all of them, as well as every attack against Christians.

Peter: It would surely be better, though, if we were to strike back with our fists according to Revelation 18: "With the cup that she has given to you, give her double (speaking of the Babylonian harlot). As she glorified herself and lived in luxury, give her that much torment and mourning."[62]

Hans: No, in Deuteronomy 32 it says, "Vengeance is mine, says the Lord."[63] And in Revelation 13, "Whoever puts people in prison, to prison he will go, and he who kills with the sword must be killed with the sword."[64] And in Matthew 26, "He who strikes with the sword will perish by the sword."[65] The Lord will find you to be as it says in 2 Peter 2, "They will be destroyed in their destruction."[66] Therefore, be at peace and continue with Christlike patience. Luke 6 says, "He who strikes

---

the world hates you. Remember the word that I said to you: 'A servant is not greater than his master.' If they persecuted me, they will also persecute you. If they kept my word, they will also keep yours. But all these things they will do to you on account of my name, because they do not know him who sent me."

62 Revelation 18:6–7: Pay her back as she herself has paid back others, and repay her double for her deeds; mix a double portion for her in the cup she mixed. As she glorified herself and lived in luxury, so give her a like measure of torment and mourning.

63 Deuteronomy 32:35: Vengeance is mine, and recompense, for the time when their foot shall slip; for the day of their calamity is at hand, and their doom comes swiftly.

64 Revelation 13:10: If anyone is to be taken captive, to captivity he goes; if anyone is to be slain with the sword, with the sword must he be slain.

65 Matthew 26:52: For all who take the sword will perish by the sword.

66 2 Peter 2:13: . . . suffering wrong as the wage for their wrongdoing. They count it pleasure to revel in the daytime. They are blots and blemishes, reveling in their deceptions, while they feast with you.

you on the cheek, offer the other also, and the one
who takes away your cloak, it is nothing to him to take
your tunic either."[67]

Peter: What then?! Are we supposed to say their seductive lies
are true?

Hans: No! When you are being watched by them and they blaspheme the evangelical truth, don't be silent. Instead,
lay their fabricated laws against the word of God, and
don't handle things with rumors or shouting again,
because that is wrong and annoying to everyone.

Peter: Ah, but even Christ himself dealt with these deceptive wolves in sheep's clothing whether they were
present or absent. Namely, in Matthew 7[68] and 24,[69]
Mark 13,[70] and Luke 21.[71] Saint Paul wrote about them
in 1 Corinthians 15,[72] 2 Corinthians 11,[73] Galatians 5,[74]

---

67 Luke 6:29: To one who strikes you on the cheek, offer the other also, and from
one who takes away your cloak do not withhold your tunic either.

68 Matthew 7:15: "Beware of false prophets, who come to you in sheep's clothing
but inwardly are ravenous wolves."

69 Matthew 24:11: And many false prophets will arise and lead many astray.

70 Mark 13:6: "Many will come in my name, saying, 'I am he!' and they will lead
many astray."

71 Luke 21:8: And he said, "See that you are not led astray. For many will come in
my name, saying, 'I am he!' and, 'The time is at hand!' Do not go after them."

72 1 Corinthians 15:34: Wake up from your drunken stupor, as is right, and do not
go on sinning. For some have no knowledge of God. I say this to your shame.

73 2 Corinthians 11:12–15: And what I am doing I will continue to do, in order
to undermine the claim of those who would like to claim that in their boasted
mission they work on the same terms as we do. For such men are false apostles,
deceitful workmen, disguising themselves as apostles of Christ. And no wonder,
for even Satan disguises himself as an angel of light. So it is no surprise if his
servants, also, disguise themselves as servants of righteousness. Their end will
correspond to their deeds.

74 Galatians 5:7: You were running well. Who hindered you from obeying the truth?

> Ephesians 4,[75] Philippians 3,[76] Colossians 2,[77] 2 Thes-
> salonians 2,[78] 1 Timothy 4,[79] and 2 Timothy 2.[80] And
> Saint Peter also wrote about them in 1 Peter 5,[81]
> 2 Peter 2,[82] 1 John 4,[83] and 2 John 1.[84]

Hans: Pay attention. That is why it says in Romans 15:4,
"Whatever was written for us, was written for our
instruction, on which we have hope through patience

---

75 Ephesians 4:25: Therefore, having put away falsehood, let each one of you speak the truth with his neighbor, for we are members one of another.

76 Philippians 3:2: Look out for the dogs, look out for the evildoers, look out for those who mutilate the flesh.

77 Colossians 2:4: I say this in order that no one may delude you with plausible arguments.

78 2 Thessalonians 2:9–11: The coming of the lawless one is by the activity of Satan with all power and false signs and wonders, and with all wicked deception for those who are perishing, because they refused to love the truth and so be saved. Therefore God sends them a strong delusion, so that they may believe what is false.

79 1 Timothy 4:2: . . . through the insincerity of liars whose consciences are seared.

80 2 Timothy 2:20: Now in a great house there are not only vessels of gold and silver but also of wood and clay, some for honorable use, some for dishonorable.

81 1 Peter 5:8: Be sober-minded; be watchful. Your adversary the devil prowls around like a roaring lion, seeking someone to devour.

82 2 Peter 2:1: But false prophets also arose among the people, just as there will be false teachers among you, who will secretly bring in destructive heresies, even denying the Master who bought them, bringing upon themselves swift destruction.

83 1 John 4:1: Beloved, do not believe every spirit, but test the spirits to see whether they are from God, for many false prophets have gone out into the world.

84 2 John 1:7: For many deceivers have gone out into the world, those who do not confess the coming of Jesus Christ in the flesh. Such a one is the deceiver and the antichrist.

and comfort."[85] We've also been warned by the Holy Scriptures about them and their seduction so that we don't lay our consciences at their feet but hold onto the unchanging word of God alone.

Peter: Why then do our pastors cry out false and deceptive teachings, commandments, and worship to God and display false and deceptive lives from the podium? Doctor Martin even does so, along with many of his followers, who write such predictable and unnecessary pieces about the Christian community. Whatever is right in his eyes is right for us too.

Hans: Yes, such sermons and calls to action are compelled by a Christlike love for the good of the unknowing and deceived people. This causes those people to hand over their consciences to the deceivers. It would be good for the deceived if God struck down the deceivers through his powerful Word, as he did with Saul[86] before Damascus in Acts 9,[87] and if he made lambs of Christ out of those devil's wolves. But whoever gives such sermons and writings out of evil intent and not out of Christlike love, it is unrighteous and sinful, and it is as useful in and of itself as it says in 1 Corinthians 13:3: "If I gave away all I had to the poor, and if I let my body be burned, and I did not

---

85 Romans 15:4: For whatever was written in former days was written for our instruction, that through endurance and through the encouragement of the Scriptures we might have hope.

86 *Paulum*: Paul is referred to as Saul before he goes to Damascus in Acts 9 and is first referred to as Paul in Acts 13, when he is in Cyprus.

87 Acts 9:3–6: Now as he went on his way, he approached Damascus, and suddenly a light from heaven shone around him. And falling to the ground, he heard a voice saying to him, "Saul, Saul, why are you persecuting me?" And he said, "Who are you, Lord?" And he said, "I am Jesus, whom you are persecuting. But rise and enter the city, and you will be told what you are to do."

have love, it would not be useful to me for anything."[88]
It's pretty clear here that when you all sit there under
the influence of wine and defile monks and priests
with your words, it isn't out of Christlike love but
rather out of pride, envy, hate, or bad habits. This
kind of slander is forbidden in Scripture—namely,
in Ephesians 4:29: "Let no foul blabber come out of
your mouths, but only what is useful for betterment,
as it is needed." And it continues: "Let all bitterness
and rage and wrath and clamor and blaspheming be
put away from you."[89] And in Titus 3, "Remind them
not to blaspheme anyone, not to quarrel, to be gentle,
demonstrating meekness toward all people."[90] And in
1 Peter 2, "So put away all evil and all deceit and
hypocrisy and hate and all slander."[91]

Peter: They don't care about that at all. It doesn't matter if
you sing sweetly or badly to them, they are stubborn
as the Pharisees.

Hans: Well, then let them go like the heathens in Matthew 18.[92]
When you continually slander and curse them, it is of

---

88 1 Corinthians 13:3: If I give away all I have, and if I deliver up my body to be
burned, but have not love, I gain nothing.

89 Ephesians 4:29–31: Let no corrupting talk come out of your mouths, but only
such as is good for building up, as fits the occasion. . . . Let all bitterness and
wrath and anger and clamor and slander be put away from you.

90 Titus 3:1–2: Remind them to be submissive to rulers and authorities, to be
obedient, to be ready for every good work, to speak evil of no one, to avoid
quarreling, to be gentle, and to show perfect courtesy toward all people.

91 1 Peter 2:1: So put away all malice and all deceit and hypocrisy and envy and
all slander.

92 Matthew 18:15–17: "If your brother sins against you, go and tell him his fault,
between you and him alone. If he listens to you, you have gained your brother.
But if he does not listen, take one or two others along with you, that every
charge may be established by the evidence of two or three witnesses. If he refuses

no use to anyone, and other people sitting around you
will hear and get angry about it, saying, "The Lutherans can't do anything except blaspheme the saints and
want to strike and stab them. How can there possibly
be something good behind them and their teachings? Their teachings are the devil's." Then they flee
onward from the evangelical teachings and hold
onto their old falsehoods. That is the fruit of your
slander. Therefore, if you want to be a true Christian, avoid doing this, and spare others from it. You
all want to look for a disguise for your indecency in
the godly man Luther, but you don't properly hold
to his teachings. Although Luther announced the
end of imprisonment of the poor captive conscience
through the freedom of Christ, he also warned us—as
he does through and through and many, many times
throughout his writings and sermons—to guard ourselves from deceptive, irritating, and non-Christian
interactions and not to swarm[93] the gospel and the
word of God with confusion or talk nonsense[94] with
those who lack reason. This is so that you don't drape[95]
a cloak of shame over the Christian man, the Christlike and well-meaning Doctor Luther, because of your
blundering interactions. Then what merciful Christian minds, what founded faith and trust that those
who act outwardly like the saints who chase after honor

---

to listen to them, tell it to the church. And if he refuses to listen even to the
church, let him be to you as a Gentile and a tax collector."

93 *schwürmen*: A verb meaning "to swarm" or collectively rush in a state of confusion or disorder.

94 *rasen*: To rush or to rage. The original text does not provide this reclarification.
It rather states, "Not to swarm [. . .] with this deed/action."

95 *Schanddeckel*: Coat of shame, referring to a shameful covering.

and goodness with their bodies are offensive to their neighbor by eating meat and more, and they appear to be Christians! But then their fruit shows that the tree is actually evil and rotten, Matthew 7.[96]

Master Ulrich: Yes, Master Hans, if you were only there when the Lutherans were gathered together and brought someone with them who was not a Lutheran, you would hear how they spare people, surely holding themselves back.[97] They celebrate Shrove Tuesday with him and they lay into him, saying that he must be some Romanist, pope-loving hypocrite and holier-than-thou saint,[98] sneering and taunting him so much that he sits there among them like a piper who has ruined the dance and doesn't know where to look.[99]

Hans: Oh you filthy boor![100] Your heart should be glad (if you really were a Christian), when you come across lost[101] people, to brotherly share with them the word of God (which is the task that was given to you in Matthew 25[102]). But you drive them away and mock them.

---

96 Matthew 7:17–20: So, every healthy tree bears good fruit, but the diseased tree bears bad fruit. A healthy tree cannot bear bad fruit, nor can a diseased tree bear good fruit. Every tree that does not bear good fruit is cut down and thrown into the fire. Thus you will recognize them by their fruits.

97 This is said in a sarcastic manner.

98 *Werkheilige*: One who believes works lead to salvation of the soul.

99 ... *weiß nit in welche Ecken er sehen sol*: Literally, "Doesn't know which corner to look at," or refused to make eye contact because he felt ashamed.

100 Directed toward Peter.

101 *unwissende*: "you unknowing ones," referring to people who don't know / believe in the gospel.

102 Matthew 25:45: "Then he will answer them, saying, 'Truly, I say to you, as you did not do it to one of the least of these, you did not do it to me."

Peter: Dear friend, you don't understand anything at all from the Scriptures, and you stumble through them like a dog getting in a carriage; he needs help to get in.

Hans: Oh no, by the will of Christ! Spare the lost and weak-minded because they're not accustomed to the word of God. You, who care more to stuff your face than to feed hungry souls,[103] have taught them not of the word of God but of your fictitious works of man. Uselessness and mocking words are also forbidden in the Scriptures. Ephesians 5:4 says, "Avoid indecent words and foolishness and jests and whatever is not suitable."[104] And 2 Timothy 2:16 says, "Avoid the ungodly and lawless, for it will lead many to ungodly ways."[105] Instead, as Paul says in Colossians 3:16, "let the word of Christ dwell richly in you in all wisdom and teach one another."[106]

Peter: Dear friend, there are many old, gray-haired men who pride themselves in knowing the gospel, but they tell it how they see it in their own heads, and when you ask them for their reasoning, you'll glean as much from them as you would from a cow at a board game.[107] Shouldn't they be mocked and punished for this?

Hans: Listen to Paul in 1 Timothy 5:1: "Do not rebuke an older man but encourage him as a father, younger

---

103 *Kuchenprediger*, or *Küchenprediger*: Referring to saints who care more about food than about the state of people's souls.

104 *Was sich nit zur Sach reimt*: Whatever does not rhyme to the matter.

  Ephesians 5:4: Let there be no filthiness nor foolish talk nor crude joking, which are out of place.

105 2 Timothy 2:16: But avoid irreverent babble, for it will lead people into more and more ungodliness.

106 Colossians 3:16: Let the word of Christ dwell in you richly, teaching and admonishing one another in all wisdom.

107 ... *als ein Kuwe im Bretspil*: They understand as much as a cow does a board game.

men as brothers, older women as mothers, younger women as sisters."[108] Pay attention; this must be instructed personally and in a friendly manner.

Peter: But there are always puffed-up saints among them who run around to all the churches and want to purchase heaven from God with their works, and whenever someone tells them what truly worshipping God is, they spring about here and there, and no one can get any nearer to them.

Hans: Right, you have to show them their faults in a friendly manner, as Galatians 6:1 says: "Beloved brothers, if anyone is seized by any transgression, discipline them with a spirit of gentleness so they become godly."[109]

Peter: Yes, they don't accept this, though, saying that we should take care of our own problems.[110]

Hans: One of those who I'm talking about comes around saying they are offended by your crude lifestyle.[111]

Peter: Should we live a hypocritical lifestyle like a monk, then?

Hans: No, rather, a lifestyle like a Christian, as Paul says in Romans 13: "Let us walk properly as in the daytime, not in orgies and drunkenness, not in sexual immorality and sensuality, not in quarreling and zeal."[112] And in Ephesians 4, "I encourage you, dear brethren,

---

108 1 Timothy 5:1–2: Do not rebuke an older man but encourage him as you would a father, younger men as brothers, older women as mothers, younger women as sisters.

109 Galatians 6:1: Brothers, if anyone is caught in any transgression, you who are spiritual should restore him in a spirit of gentleness.

110 . . . *wir söln uns selber bei der Nasen nemen*: We should take ourselves by the nose.

111 *Leben*: Referring not to the person's life but rather to the way the life is lived.

112 Romans 13:13: Let us walk properly as in the daytime, not in orgies and drunkenness, not in sexual immorality and sensuality, not in quarreling and jealousy.

to walk as you are charged by your profession to which you have been called, with all humility and gentleness, with patience, and to bear one with another in love."[113] And Paul describes the reason for this in Philippians 2: "Do all things without grumbling or disputing, that you may be blameless and innocent, children of God without blemish in the midst of a crooked and twisted people."[114]

Peter: They despise the Scriptures and want to keep their old habits. Tell a man something's black, he says it's white, and if you say that the biblical texts are all true, and if you persuade them with the absolute most diligent Christian doctrine, they say all the same, "Have you not seen my opposite opinion?" How do you keep them silent?

Hans: Paul writes in 2 Timothy 2, "The Lord's servant must not be quarrelsome but fatherly to everyone, able to teach, able to endure evil, who disciplines his opponents with gentleness, that God may perhaps grant them repentance to know the truth."[115] And in 1 Peter 2, saying, "For this is the will of God, that by doing good you should obstruct people's ignorance, as people

---

113 Ephesians 4:1–2: I therefore, a prisoner for the Lord, urge you to walk in a manner worthy of the calling to which you have been called, with all humility and gentleness, with patience, bearing with one another in love.

114 Philippians 2:14–15: Do all things without grumbling or disputing, that you may be blameless and innocent, children of God without blemish in the midst of a crooked and twisted generation.

115 2 Timothy 2:24–25: And the Lord's servant must not be quarrelsome but kind to everyone, able to teach, patiently enduring evil, correcting his opponents with gentleness. God may perhaps grant them repentance leading to a knowledge of the truth.

who are free, and not using your freedom as a cover-
up for evil."[116]

Peter: Dear friend, you're being too rude. You're handing
out bad words and throwing insults[117] among us, and
we can't bite back. You cry out, "What joy! We've won!
We've won! Thus it's necessary that they display their
kinship on their shield."[118]

Hans: Oh, so you want to know and teach Christ but don't
want to suffer evil words? How then would you suffer
strikes or death? Pay attention to Paul in Romans 12:
"Bless those who persecute you; bless and do not
curse them, repay no one evil for evil, never avenge
yourselves."[119] Here you hear that you must handle
things with Christlike love and meekness and without crying out and not dealing with people so rudely
and that this should bring forth fruit. It clearly plays
a role in turning people away from the evangelical
doctrine when a few people would come and accept
the doctrine but along the way find the word of God
to be hostile and, in addition, call you heretics and the
word of God heresy. You alone would be to blame for
this with your meat eating, rumors, threats, defiling
and blaspheming the saints, fighting and quarreling, and the one-sided hate that you spew about them

116 1 Peter 2:15–16: For this is the will of God, that by doing good you should put
to silence the ignorance of foolish people. Live as people who are free, not
using your freedom as a cover-up for evil.

117 *Ketzerkoepfen*: An insult meaning a person with a head full of heresy.

118 Coat of arms.

119 Romans 12:14–17: Bless those who persecute you; bless and do not curse them.
Rejoice with those who rejoice, weep with those who weep. Live in harmony
with one another. Do not be haughty, but associate with the lowly. Never be
wise in your own sight. Repay no one evil for evil, but give thought to do what
is honorable in the sight of all.

whenever they see you. They blame just the same the
other godly Christians, who aren't like you but follow
after the gospel of Christ and lead a Christlike lifestyle
transformation.

Peter: Dear friend, if someone is our enemy, we know it well
in advance, and we know well who they are. We aren't
friendly to them either, and if it came to a battle, we
would surely ride on horseback against each other.

Hans: Ugh, I've noticed that it is already that time that it's only
yelling and little will [to change] with you. You don't
have love for your neighbor, and even out of necessity,
no one would know you as a disciple of Christ.

Peter: Why do you say that?

Hans: It says in 1 John 3, "Whoever does not have love for his
brother abides in death. Whoever hates his brother is a
murderer."[120] And in 1 John 4 it says, "If anyone says,
'I love God,' and hates his brother, he is a liar; for if
he who has seen his brother does not love him, how
can he love God, whom he has not seen?"[121] That's why
I fear that you, dear brother Peter, and your hostile
crew don't have true faith in Christ through the work
of God, as in Colossians 2;[122] rather, you have such a
man-made[123] faith of flesh and blood. That's why all of

---

120 1 John 3:14–15: We know that we have passed out of death into life, because
we love the brothers. Whoever does not love abides in death. Everyone who
hates his brother is a murderer, and you know that no murderer has eternal
life abiding in him.

121 1 John 4:20: If anyone says, "I love God," and hates his brother, he is a liar;
for he who does not love his brother whom he has seen cannot love God whom
he has not seen.

122 Colossians 2:12: . . . having been buried with him in baptism, in which you
were also raised with him through faith in the powerful working of God, who
raised him from the dead.

123 *menschlichen gedichten Glauben*: A "humanly invented faith."

your thoughts, words, and works are also about flesh and blood and are harmful and useless to yourselves and offensive to others. That's because being aligned with the flesh is being hostile toward God, as Paul says in Romans 8. But those who chase after the Holy Spirit are the true children of God, Romans 8.[124]

Peter: How can you recognize them,[125] though?

Hans: By love alone, as Christ says in John 13: "By this all people will know that you are my disciples, that you have love for one another."[126] And in 1 John 4 it says, "Beloved, let us love one another, for love is from God, and whoever loves has been born of God and knows God, and anyone who does not love does not know God, because God is love. Whoever abides in love, abides in God, and God in him."[127] To this end, I would like to tell you, as Christ tells the Jews in John 8, "If you were Abraham's children, you would do the works Abraham

---

124 Romans 8:12–17: So then, brothers, we are debtors, not to the flesh, to live according to the flesh. For if you live according to the flesh you will die, but if by the Spirit you put to death the deeds of the body, you will live. For all who are led by the Spirit of God are sons of God. For you did not receive the spirit of slavery to fall back into fear, but you have received the Spirit of adoption as sons, by whom we cry, "Abba! Father!" The Spirit himself bears witness with our spirit that we are children of God, and if children, then heirs—heirs of God and fellow heirs with Christ, provided we suffer with him in order that we may also be glorified with him.

125 The true children of God.

126 John 13:35: "By this all people will know that you are my disciples, if you have love for one another."

127 1 John 4:7–8: Beloved, let us love one another, for love is from God, and whoever loves has been born of God and knows God. Anyone who does not love does not know God, because God is love.

1 John 4:12: No one has ever seen God; if we love one another, God abides in us and his love is perfected in us.

did."[128] Similarly, for you too, if you were evangelical (as you claim to be), you would do the work of the gospel because the gospel is a wonderfully joyful and lovely command from Christ. Thus, when you've been born of the gospel, you proclaim the gospel to your brethren in Christ gently and with all decency, leading a transformation blessed by God as the apostles, who dealt so friendly with people, like how you read in their stories throughout every chapter.[129] With that, my dear brother Peter, see how I talk about the will of God and tell your brethren about me, even if they will call me a hypocrite and take me to be a dissident. It wouldn't remotely touch a hair on my head because I've told them the truth, which must always be persecuted by the godless. And God would want that all who heard the truth, who call themselves Lutherans, might lay down their reputation and learn a little to become true evangelical Christians.

Master Ulrich: Peter, what do you think? Whenever Master Hans comes around, he can really unravel your ideas.[130] One thing is true: whenever you Lutherans conduct yourselves in such self-restrained and inoffensive ways, your doctrine has a much better appeal to everyone. Those who currently call you heretics would call you Christians. Those who curse at you now would praise you. Those who talk badly of you now would speak well of you. Those who flee from you would visit you at home. Those who currently despise you would learn

---

128 John 8:39: "If you were Abraham's children, you would be doing the works Abraham did."

129 In reference to the chapters of Acts and the acts of the apostles throughout the biblical books written by Paul.

130 *aufnesteln*: To undo or untie the laces on articles of clothing.

| | from you. But with your meat eating, rumors, defiling of priests, quarreling, mocking, hatred, and all conduct lacking self-control, you Lutherans have made the Protestant doctrine itself greatly despised. |

Hans: Unfortunately, the day's about over. Let God impart on all of us his Holy Spirit so that we can live according to his godly will. They've rung the three o'clock chime. Let's go to the sermon!

Master Ulrich: Come on, then! You've made me interested. I want to come with you to your sermon so I might become a better Christian.

Hans: A gift of God!

Master Ulrich: Amen.

Philippians 2

Dear brothers, there is among you such an encouragement in Christ, such a comfort of love, such a congregation of the spirit, such a heart-filled love and charity, that so fills my joy, that you have such boldness and sensibility, as well as love, do nothing out of strife or vain honor, but rather out of humility. Take care of each other among yourselves, superior each to the other and similarly don't look after what is yours, but after what belongs to others.[131]

---

131 Philippians 2:1–4: So if there is any encouragement in Christ, any comfort from love, any participation in the Spirit, any affection and sympathy, complete my joy by being of the same mind, having the same love, being in full accord and of one mind. Do nothing from selfish ambition or conceit, but in humility count others more significant than yourselves. Let each of you look not only to his own interests, but also to the interests of others.

CHAPTER 9

The Impact of Hans Sachs's Reformation Writings

Hans Sachs was a tradesman who as a *Meister*—a master at his trade—owned his own business, employed others, and even provided training for apprentices who wanted to pursue the trade of shoemaking. As was the practice, he had apprenticed and traveled extensively as a journeyman before establishing his own business. He was also a *Meister* in the art of verse writing, having been recognized by the prestigious Nürnberg *Meistersinger* school. He was a member of the trade organizations in the bustling trade center of Nürnberg. He was a member not of the nobility but rather of the middle class, a regular man, a *gemeiner Mann*,[1] which was not unusual in sixteenth-century Nürnberg.

Being a member of the middle class placed Sachs in the right place at the right time as far as the Reformation was concerned. As a citizen of Nürnberg, he lived and worked in one of the most important business, political, and cultural centers of the Holy Roman Empire.[2] Nürnberg was at that time a free city, bound to no king or duke. The city fathers quickly adopted Reform ideas, changing the way worship was conducted in the city's main churches—St. Lorenz, the largest parish church in Nürnberg, became Lutheran in 1525—as well as making doctrinal changes in the schools, which were strongly influenced by the church, as early

---

1 Berndt Hamm, "'Ist das gut Evangelisch?' Hans Sachs als Wortführer und Kritiker der Reformation," *Luther* 66, no. 3 (1995): 126.

2 Barbara Könneker, *Hans Sachs* (Stuttgart: J. B. Metzlersche Verlagsbuchhandlung, 1971), 3.

as 1535.[3] The average man,[4] as Sachs referred to himself and his peers, was important to the progress of the city; it was this average man who latched onto new ideas of church reform.

Sachs was part of a pre-Reformation, Pietistic movement in the city that asked how sins could be forgiven. He and others were curious and interested when Luther's Reformation movement began to spread. Although he was not clergy, he studied Luther's writings, carefully comparing them to Scripture. As Sachs began to write in support of the Reformation, we see that his writings were antipope and pro-Luther but strongly focused on a peaceful desire to spread God's word and to call others to accept the work of the Holy Spirit. He wrote as a layman for the laity.[5] His focus was to bring the movement to individuals. As Sachs studied Luther's writings and his translation of the Bible, he found solace in learning that forgiveness of sins is possible through faith in Christ alone. This is the message he wanted to bring to the citizenry.

Sachs was a prolific writer and composer of *Fastnachtspiele*,[6] with his earliest known publication appearing in 1514. He wrote and published until his death in 1576. Before publishing his Reformation writings in 1523 and 1524, Sachs had a well-established reputation as a popular writer, a *Dichter des Volkes*[7]—a poet of the people—whose influence among the populace cannot be denied. He was a journalist who presented the news in verse, such as his poems about the visit of the emperor to Nürnberg,

---

3 Gerald Strauss, *Luther's House of Learning* (Baltimore: Johns Hopkins University Press, 1978), 297.

4 It should be noted that Sachs was not "average" in comparison to the feudal population of the Holy Roman Empire, but he was "average" in the city of Nürnberg, where there was a thriving middle class made up of educated tradesmen.

5 Hamm, "'Ist das gut Evangelisch?'," 126.

6 "Plays" written for the *Fasching* season for the purpose of pointing out the foibles of the rich and famous, the notorious and the sacred.

7 Karl Pannier, *Hans Sachs' Ausgewählte Poetische Werke* (Leipzig: Verlag von Philipp Reclam, 1879), Projekt Gutenberg, https://www.projekt-gutenberg.org/sachs/poetwerk/poetwerk.html.

the Turkish invasions, and in later years, the death of Luther.[8] When he published his Reformation poem and dialogues in quick succession, the public took notice and joined him in this new movement.[9] Political and popular support at all levels of society provided the impetus for the city of Nürnberg to become one of the strongest areas of support for the Reformation[10] and helps explain how the Reformation movement led to the *Bauernkriege* (the peasants' wars that took place in 1524–25). Even after the publication of his Reformation poem and dialogues, Sachs retained his influence with the public.

Sachs did not simply join the movement to gain popularity or to push for political change. He studied Luther's writings and read deeply in the newly translated Scriptures.[11] The list of his publications contains no works written between 1520 and 1523. It was during this time that he immersed himself in study of the Scriptures and Luther's teachings. By 1521, he already owned more than forty texts by Luther and other Reformers.[12] Sachs quickly recognized the validity of Luther's claims against the papacy and that the new teaching came not from human thought but straight from the Bible.[13] This time of study explains how Sachs was able to clearly present the problems of the church through Scripture in his Reformation writings.

That Sachs supported efforts to reform the church is clear in his Reformation dialogues and in *The Wittenberg Nightingale*. What becomes apparent with a deeper reading of these works is that Sachs developed his own purpose and goal in writing—that is, to make it clear to the

---

8 Könneker, *Hans Sachs*, 5.

9 Pannier, foreword to *Ausgewählte Poetische Werke*.

10 Guenther Vogler, "Imperial City Nuremberg, 1524–1525: The Reform Movement in Transition," in *The German People and the Reformation*, ed. and trans. R. Po-chia Hsia (Ithaca: Cornell University Press, 1988).

11 Hamm, "'Ist das gut Evangelisch?,'" 128.

12 Barbara Könneker, *Die deutsche Literatur der Reformationszeit* (Munich: Winkler Verlag, 1975); Pannier, foreword to *Ausgewählte Poetische Werke*.

13 Pannier.

average man that the message of the Scripture is to the individual as well as to the institution of the church. He sought to clarify that the purpose of Luther's call for change was more than a demand to change worship practices and lessen the hold of papal authority on the church. It was a call to individual believers to recognize their responsibility to live as Christians in their everyday lives outside of the church. As one reads through the dialogues, it becomes clear that Sachs's central message was one of *Nächstenliebe*, or brotherly love. Additionally, he was a proponent of order and discipline for the Christian community, for individuals as well as government entities.

Sachs's wish for the movement was more focused on the individual than the church itself, and he agreed with Luther about the relationship of the individual to the governmental authority. The new freedom of the Christian was a spiritual freedom, not a political freedom. He, like Luther, did not support the overthrow of the current political system.[14] He viewed the Schmalkaldic Wars as being just as dangerous and disruptive to the world order as the on-again, off-again battles between the Holy Roman Empire and the French or the Turks.[15] He condemned the *Bauernkriege*, noting that the farmers must bear their cross (their place in society) until the end.[16]

Reading Sachs's Reformation writings clarifies the legacy of the poet. As time passes, minor authors in any era are often set aside as playing insignificant roles within the movement. Unfortunately, as time has passed, that is what has happened with the works of Hans Sachs. Anthologies and collections of literature often include only passing examples of his poetry and prose and rarely, if ever, mention his Reformation writings. Nevertheless, the call for change that Sachs conveys through his five Reformation writings clearly establishes him as an important force within

---

14 Harold John Grimm, *Lazarus Spengler: A Lay Leader of the Reformation* (Columbus: Ohio State University Press, 1978), 93; Steven Ozment, *Protestants: The Birth of a Revolution* (New York: Doubleday, 1991), 86.

15 Pannier, foreword to *Ausgewählte Poetische Werke*.

16 Könneker, *Hans Sachs*, 10.

the movement. Sachs has certainly earned a place in German historical and literary traditions. He has left a legacy of change and influence that cannot be dismissed.

Sachs's Reformation Writings and the German Literary Canon

After Sachs's death in 1576, the popularity of his writings waned. In the realm of the *Meistersinger*, his style and talent were considered passé, and Sachs was often ridiculed as new approaches were developed within the *Meistersinger* schools. As the Reformation spread and developed, as wars and conflicts swirled around religious issues, Sachs's explanations of the doctrinal relevance of the Reformation for the common man were forgotten. Despite the proliferation of his approximately six thousand *Fastnachtspiele* and other poetic works, these too were quickly relegated to the level of trivial literature.

As the Enlightenment dawned, his work once again became relevant. Gotthold Ephraim Lessing (1729–81) asserted that Sachs's dialogues were a distinctive monument to the history of the Reformation.[17] Nevertheless, his vast body of work and his reputation as a *Meistersinger* might still have been forgotten had it not been for Johann Gottfried Herder (1744–1803) and Johann Wolfgang von Goethe (1749–1832). Herder is most well known as one of the earliest linguistic theorists. He called for a renewal of Sachs's work, noting that along with the study of language must come the study of the literature of a people group. An examination of Sachs's poetic works provided evidence of language use during the sixteenth century. Goethe, a student of Herder, also championed Sachs as a true German author whose works were to be revived and brought into the canon of Germanic literature. Goethe's poem "Hans Sachsens poetische Sendung" imitated Sachs's unique language use and verse. This serves as a monument to the legacy of the *Meistersinger* of Nürnberg.[18] Heinrich Heine (1797–1856), perhaps Germany's best-known poet

---

17 Könneker, 7.

18 Pannier, foreword to *Ausgewählte Poetische Werke*.

of the Romantic era, not only recognized Sachs's vast body of work but called attention to the poet's ability to use multiple forms and structures. Although he described Sachs's poetry as *läppisch* (petty or trivial), the fact that Heine recognized Sachs's literary prolificacy is important.[19]

In the musical realm of the mid-nineteenth century, Richard Wagner took up the subject of Sachs as a tribute to Germanic literary talent. Wagner's opera *Der Meistersinger von Nürnberg* called to mind the literary genre of the *Meistergesang*, identifying verse such as that written by Sachs as a uniquely Germanic art form. Through the text of the opera, Wagner praised Sachs as having been instrumental in introducing the name of Luther to the city of Nürnberg and making Reformation ideals known.[20]

Over the last two centuries, editors of collections have noted the importance of Sachs's work to the canon of German literature.[21] Modern, current anthologies of German literature also recognize the verse of the *Meistersinger* as a unique Germanic literary genre, and most such anthologies include an example from Hans Sachs. Rarely, however, do these anthologies include Sachs's verse as an example of his expert, distinctive usage of rhythm and rhyme, but instead they include a sample of his *Schwänke* (folk stories). Little, if anything at all, is noted about his Reformation writings, except perhaps a brief mention of *The Wittenberg Nightingale*.

The plethora of work left by Sachs is often categorized by collectors as *Fastnachtspiele* or *Schwänke*, written for the entertainment of the average man. Nevertheless, Sachs's Reformation literature (the five texts translated in this volume, plus some songs written for worship services) provides a context for understanding his work through the end of his

---

19 Heinrich Heine, *Zur Geschichte der Religion und Philosophie in Deutschland*, 1835, Projekt Gutenberg, https://www.projekt-gutenberg.org/heine/religion/religion.html.

20 Könneker, *Hans Sachs*, 9.

21 Bernhard Arnold, *Hans Sachs Werke Erster Teil* (Berlin: Verlag von W. Spemann, 1881), xxxi; K. Goedeke, *Dichtungen von Hans Sachs* (Leipzig: F. A. Brockhaus, 1871), xiii; Richard Zoozmann, *Hans Sachs und die Reformation: In Gedichten und Prosastücke* (Hamburg, Germany: SEVERUS Verlag, 2017), 21.

career. *The Wittenberg Nightingale* and the four dialogues point out just how important the Reform movement was to Sachs and to the Reformation message that Sachs wanted others to see[22]—namely, his disdain toward the old practices in comparison to the new teachings and his disdain toward those fanatics who would turn the new Reformed practices into "traditions" like those practiced in the old church. Sachs focused heavily on publishing verse with scriptural and moral themes during the last half of his career,[23] and his earnestness in presenting his message was viewed at one point by the Nürnberg city fathers as being too harsh (for which Sachs was briefly banned from publishing).[24] It is his later, morality-infused pieces that are most often forgotten: histories, mythologies, and Bible stories. Although he continued to write *Fastnachtspiele* and *Schwänke*, which had a reputation of containing ribald subject matter, his later work maintained a modicum of decorum in keeping with his faith.[25] The retelling of histories, mythologies, and stories from Scripture brought all of these narratives into the homes of even those who could not read. They added to Sachs's reputation of making antiquity, the latest news, and the Scriptures accessible to the common folk, allowing them the opportunity to hear and learn through the most popular entertainment format of the time.

Many of these pieces were written for the express purpose of being performed for an audience. Some pieces contain multiple acts. Many end with his assertion of authorship, "so spricht Hans Sachs, wünscht Hans Sachs."[26] His sense of drama was timely; he was able to convey a point or a moral in a straightforward manner. Bernhard Arnold, who published a collection of Sachs's work, asked how it could be possible

---

22 Könneker, *Hans Sachs*, 33.

23 William Leighton, *Merry Tales and Three Shrovetide Plays by Hans Sachs* (London: David Nutt, 1910), xiii.

24 Könneker, *Deutsche Literatur*, 149.

25 Pannier, foreword to *Ausgewählte Poetische Werke*; Leighton, *Merry Tales*, xii.

26 So says Hans Sachs, so wishes Hans Sachs.

that in the mind of this one man was reflected a whole epoch.[27] The four Reformation dialogues were precursors to the genre of drama, which was slowly emerging in the realm of literature.[28] Through his varied interests, and because of his ability to put important topics into the popular literary form of the era, Sachs helped educate and inform the illiterate. Most of Sachs's works are written in verse, designed to be sung. When he counted his works in 1567, he had collected 16 books with 4,275 works in 275 *Meistertönen*,[29] 13 of which he had created himself. Seventeen additional books contained fun comedies, sad tragedies, and comical plays, most of which had played on stages far and wide around Nürnberg.[30] After adding in dialogues, allegories, fables, psalms, spiritual songs, war songs, and love songs, the number of pieces listing him as author totals approximately 6,100. No other author of that era or any era since has left such a legacy and vast body of work.[31]

Sachs's Reformation Writings and the German Language

Gordon A. Craig asserts that there was no German language, nor German literature, until Martin Luther translated the Bible and disseminated his theological pamphlets. Until that time, there were many varying dialects that were similar in sound and structure, but it was the popularity and widespread distribution of the Bible that set a standard for further use of the written language. Luther's language was lucid, rich, vigorous, and flexible, suitable for exposition, argumentation, satire, and humor.[32] If Luther was the father of the German language, then Sachs ran a close second. His writing contained many Nürnberg-isms that spread as his works spread. The lilt of his verse and the sarcasm of his tone when

---

27 Arnold, *Hans Sachs*, xxvi.

28 Pannier, foreword to *Ausgewählte Poetische Werke*.

29 Musical melodies.

30 Adelbert von Keller, *Hans Sachs Werke* (Hildesheim: Georg Olms Verlagsbuchhandlung: Zeittafel, 1964).

31 Arnold, *Hans Sachs*, xxi–xxiv.

32 Gordon A. Craig, *The Germans* (New York: B. P. Putnam's Sons, 1982), 311.

pointing out political and social wrongs are evident even in contempo-
rary *Fastnacht* speeches. Sachs's language has been described as fresh and
natural, happy and vivid, from the heart, original, and ingratiating. Karl
Pannier further described his language and writing style: "A childlike,
charming mind, a great peace and sedateness, which allows him to speak
about the most burning questions in an unbiased manner, an inner piety
and true religiosity, which is expressed in innumerable spiritual pieces, a
competent moral, from which he cannot in small part thank his study
of the antiquities, a homemade prudence, which sticks admirably by
him, the folk poet—these are the characteristics, which allow him as human
and poet to appear to us so valuable."[33]

Sachs's vast body of work, particularly the uniqueness and genius of
his poetry, helped the German language gain the ability to modify itself,
despite its numerous inflections (still evident in today's German), to
fit any occasion. Whether adding or subtracting morphemes or rear-
ranging word order, the German language, because of the influence of
Luther and Sachs, morphed into a language able to convey meaning in
a far wider set of contexts. Today's *Fastnacht Gedichte*[34] in particular, with
their rhythm, rhyme, sarcasm, innuendos, and double entendres, still
show the influence of the *Meistersinger* of Nürnberg.

Sachs's Reformation Writings and Reformation Literature

When considering Sachs's Reformation writings and their relevance
to the Reform movement spearheaded by Luther and Melanchthon,
it is important to consider the purpose and reception of these works.
Luther's battle was with the pope, his control of the church, and the
practices and writings that were promoted as necessary and required
of all parishioners. Most of the population of the Holy Roman Empire
in the sixteenth century considered itself Christian and subject to the
pope as ruler in partnership with the emperor. Most of the population

---

33 Pannier, foreword to *Ausgewählte Poetische Werke*; translated by author.

34 It is still common practice to write poems for the *Fasching* season, the time before
Lent, that parody current politics and culture.

was only minimally educated or not at all. Schooling was reserved for the noble class and for the church (the monastic orders). Humanistic ideas were becoming prevalent, but not for the lower classes of society.

Sachs was already a well-known *Meistersinger*. His *Fastnachtspiele* were popular, sought after, and readily available. The prevalence of printing presses allowed for wide dissemination not only among the noble classes but among the growing middle class. Traders arriving in Nürnberg could easily obtain a printed copy of a Sachs poem or dialogue and disseminate the message along the trade routes they traveled. Sachs's talent for rhyme made his works doubly popular. It can be surmised that dissatisfaction with the church was widespread, although not necessarily made public. When this popular author published *The Wittenberg Nightingale* in 1523, it was received as a bestseller. The poem, an allegory that tells of Luther's victory over the enemies of Christ, grabbed the attention of those who heard and read it.[35] To see the truth about the church and the underlying political realities described in *The Wittenberg Nightingale* in the same style as Sachs's often cynical and sarcastic *Fastnachtspiele* would have been scandalous but at the same time admired.

There is no record that Sachs ever met Luther or Melanchthon. He certainly would have had contact with church officials as churches in Nürnberg began to affiliate with the emerging evangelical church.[36] Nevertheless, it is clear that he studied the teachings of the Reformation closely. His command of Scripture is astounding (despite a few inaccuracies in verse references) considering Luther's translation of the New Testament had only been published in 1522, with Sachs's poem and dialogues appearing in 1523 and 1524. Sachs clearly agreed with the doctrine and teachings of the Reformers, putting those ideas into language that the common man could understand. He was particularly able to support these ideas with Scripture and to show how certain practices and teachings

---

35 Könneker, *Hans Sachs*, 46.

36 Guenther Vogler, *Nuremberg 1524/25 Studien zur Geschichte der reformatorischen und sozialen Bewegung in der Reichsstadt* (Berlin: VEB Deutscher Verlag der Wissenschaften, 1982), 46–64.

commanded by the church were not scriptural. Nevertheless, he never overstepped his own abilities. He did not presume to be a theologian and wrote instead in support of theologians, not to supplement their ideas. He interpreted Luther through a societal point of view.[37] Sachs's poem and dialogues put Scripture into a clear format that the average new reader or even nonreader could understand. His style was catchy, witty, and easy to remember. Luther's five solas, sometimes considered to be the crux of the break with the Catholic Church, are clearly presented in Sachs's dialogues.[38]

Despite his obvious agreement with the idea of the Reformation movement, when we look closer at the works contained in this volume, we can see that Sachs's focus reached further than the needed reforms in church practice. He addressed current, local, actual misuses that were recognizable in everyday society, his own environment.[39] He addressed these issues through the eyes of the craftsman, his own social group. Berndt Hamm notes that Sachs's focus was not on a new doctrine or following a new figurehead (Luther) but rather on the message of the gospel, *Liebe, Liebe, Liebe.*[40] Infused in Sachs's Reformation writings is the idea that *Nächstenliebe* (brotherly love) is the ideal goal for the Christian, the evangelical. As Philip Broadhead claims, "Sachs believed that the effect of the gospel would be to make people behave in a Christian way."[41] The love of one's neighbor should always outweigh the desire to develop different doctrine or church traditions.

---

37 Vogler, *Nuremberg 1524/25*, 315.

38 *Sola Gratia*, by grace alone; *Sola Fide*, by faith alone; *Solus Christus*, in Christ alone; *Sola Scriptura*, by Scripture alone; *Soli Deo Gloria*, for God's Glory alone.

39 Vogler, *Nuremberg 1524/25*, 171.

40 Love, Love, Love. Found in the third dialogue in this volume, *A Dialogue on the Content of an Argument between a Roman Catholic and a Christian Friend concerning Greed and Other Common Vices.*

41 Philip Broadhead, "The Biblical Verse of Hans Sachs: The Popularization of Scripture in the Lutheran Reformation," in *The Church and Literature*, ed. Peter Clarke and Charlotte Methuen (Suffolk: Boydell Press, 2012), 129.

In *The Wittenberg Nightingale*, Sachs used his unique *Bar*, his style of rhythm and rhyme to describe the pope and his clerics as wild animals whose sole purpose was to confuse and deceive the laity, regular Christian parishioners who did not have the ability to read the Scripture for themselves. Readers of the poem are confronted with the pope's deception, with their own culpability and naïveté, but also with the message from Luther that one could indeed read and learn the Scripture for oneself. He further clarified that many—dare we consider most—papal decrees were not aligned with Scripture but rather written for the purpose of adding to the wealth of the clergy. Recognizing that there is hope alone in Christ provided incentive for the laity to take on the task of learning to read and evaluate the Scripture. *The Wittenberg Nightingale* contains Sachs's explanation of evangelism:

> Such faith spreads widely
> To the neighbor with true love,
> That he disturbs no one, [but]
> Rather practices at all times
> In works of compassion,
> Gives to everyone from the heart as alms
> Freely given love, looking for no gain,
> With advice, help, giving, loaning,
> With teaching, punishment, guilt forgiven,
> Does to others as he himself wants,
> As that which should happen to him[self].

In *A Disputation . . .* , Sachs demonstrated that even a shoemaker could read the Scripture, learn from it, and be ready to dispute with the clergy, the parson, on matters heretofore out of the purview of the laity. In this dialogue, the shoemaker debated well the near-impossible requirements the church had placed on the laity, such as the worship practices of fasting and eating no meat on Fridays and adhering to unscriptural man-made laws while the clergy were clearly not adhering to these same requirements. He made clear that the true commandments from God were to feed the hungry, clothe the naked, and shelter the homeless, explaining the works of a Christian:

> A true Christian faith doesn't celebrate but brings forth good fruit, as Christ said in Matthew 7: "A good tree cannot bring forth bad fruit." But such good works occur not to serve heaven, which Christ earned for us; also not from fear of hell, for Christ has redeemed us; [and] also not for honor, for honor should go only to God, as it is written in Matthew 4; but rather in godly love as a thanksgiving to God and to the help and profit of your neighbor. So, dear sir, what do you think of Luther's fruit?

He additionally stated that Christ is our only salvation; we must put our faith, hope, and trust in him alone. He identifies Scripture as a sword, ready for defense. He demonstrated his comprehension that the Holy Spirit was to be a comfort and help to all Christians, not just to the clergy.

A Discussion . . . opened the debate of the scriptural validity of monastic orders. The characters Hans and Peter discussed with a monk whether monks were truly practicing their vows of poverty, chastity, and obedience. The discussion turned to Sachs's theme of *Nächstenliebe* when he questioned whether the order was feeding the hungry and caring for those in need. They questioned whether the monks who begged for cheese and candles were truly funneling the proceeds of their collections to the poor. He noted that outward appearances of holiness were nothing more than "whitewashed tombs," which do not equate to true belief. He closed with the admonition for the monk to read the Scripture and not canonical documents, reiterated when Hans referenced 1 John 3, saying, "Who of this world has goods, sees his brother in need, and closes his heart to him, how does the love of God remain in him?"

In *A Dialogue* . . . Sachs pinpointed the sin of greed and a variety of monetary practices that might have been driven by greed. (Perhaps this dialogue added to the later decision of the Nürnberg city fathers to censor Sachs and forbid publication of his writings for three years.)

The evangelical "rich citizen" was called to task by a Catholic cleric. Greed was not a fault of the church alone. Greed was a driver of commerce, even the transactions of evangelical businessmen. The debate was long and arduous as both men jousted with Scripture. In this dialogue, Sachs made it clear that the Scripture is full of warnings about greed and associated monetary practices. Sachs even included his theme of *Nächstenliebe* when he stated, "The work of love toward your neighbor is just simple in manner and without all the splendor." While the conversants did not part on friendly terms, they parted with the evangelical recognizing the need to be wary. Sin can affect both Catholic and evangelical alike.

In the fourth dialogue, Sachs again took up the possibility that even evangelicals misinterpret Scripture. In *A Conversation . . .* , Sachs (the character Hans) admonished Peter (perhaps his companion from the second dialogue) to be wary of insulting non-Lutherans so as not to drive them away from considering the teachings of Luther and the supremacy of Scripture. The evangelical Peter had been flaunting his newfound freedom to the point of insulting his Catholic father-in-law, so much so that Master Ulrich was ready to dismiss all evangelicals and their beliefs. Hans explained to Peter that "calls to action are compelled by a Christlike love for the good of the unknowing and deceived people"; he reminded him that conversations with unbelievers are to be gentle and meek, not quarrelsome but filled with love for one's neighbor. Master Ulrich confirmed that those outside evangelical belief judge evangelicals by the words that come out of their mouths and noted that more would be receptive to the message if it were given without rancor or disdain. Sachs used *A Conversation . . .* to remind us about showing love for others: "If your brother is grieved by what you eat, you are no longer walking in love"; "Love is the true test of a Christian, not eating meat, because even dogs and cats can do that well"; and finally, as the character Hans reminded Peter, "You don't have love for your neighbor, and even out of necessity, no one would know you as a disciple of Christ" because he was interested more in flouting his newfound religious freedom than sharing the evangelical message.

It is widely recognized that *The Wittenberg Nightingale* and the four dialogues are Sachs's connection to the Reformation. Less widely known are his church songs and Bible stories. While Luther's hymns are well known for having changed the way worship was conducted, it should be noted that Sachs followed suit and wrote songs that were included in Protestant hymnals well into the seventeenth century.[42] His reworking of some psalms and stories from the Old and New Testaments by putting them into verse provided greater access to the Scriptures for people of all ages and literary abilities. This practice continued throughout the rest of his life.[43]

As we further examine Sachs's body of work, it is interesting to note that after writing the four dialogues, he set aside the politics, events, and structures of the Reformation movement and set himself to the task of the spirit of the Reformation: making Scripture and faith personal and impactful in daily life. In one poem where Sachs included biographical information,[44] he mentioned having written seven Reformation dialogues,[45] but more than the four presented in this text have never been found. Two additional pieces tangentially address the Reformation message: *Wünderlicher Dialogus und neue zeitung* (1546) and *Pasquillus von dem schlos zu Blassenburg* (not published).[46] Despite this small number of documents with explicit ties to his beliefs, we see in his writings the

---

42 Könneker, *Hans Sachs*, 37–38.

43 Könneker, *Deutsche Literatur*, 157.

44 *Summa all meiner gedicht vom 1514. jar an biß ins 1567. Jar.*

45 This biographical reference in verse notes that Sachs counted seven prose dialogues among his works.

"*Auch fand ich in mein buchern gschriben*	I also found written in my books
Artlicher Dialogos siben [seven]	These sorts of dialogues seven
Doch ungereimet in der pros,	Of course unrhymed in prose,
Ganz deutlich, frei on alle glos . . ."	Clearly, free without clarification.

46 "Wonderful Dialogue and New News[paper]" (1546) and "Pasquillus on the Way from the Castle to the Blassburg" (not published); Könneker, *Deutsche Literatur*, 157.

contents of his faith. Sachs was censored between 1527 and 1530 for writing, together with Andreas Osiander, pieces that were insulting to the pope. This may be the reason he moved away from dialogues in the manner of those included in this volume and instead focused on histories, fables, and Bible stories.[47]

Sachs's Reformation Writings and Current Reformation Studies

We hope through these translations to add to the current study of the Reformation. There are several perspectives of the movement: doctrinal, political, and literary. Sachs's writings certainly made a unique contribution to Germanic literature. From a political perspective, Sachs, like Luther, did not call for changes in social class structure or a separation of church and state. Sachs's writings supported Luther's doctrine, but through the perspective of encouraging the average man to know Scripture for himself. Because of the clarity of Sachs's poem and dialogues, tradesmen and farmers alike were finally able to know and comprehend how they had been deceived for the past five hundred years. Because of the scriptural details included in his pieces, the parishioners in the churches in Nürnberg and other cities were able to satisfy their desire to worship their God without having to follow tasks prescribed to them that purported to allow them into heaven or keep them from glory if they were not properly administered.

Sachs named the practices of the medieval, pre-Reformation church in *The Wittenberg Nightingale* and the four Reformation dialogues and refuted them as nonscriptural. Sachs used allegory (sometimes vague, sometimes explicit) in the poem to detail the misapplication of papal and clerical authority. He is more direct and to the point in the four dialogues. Church abuses at that time were many. Parishioners were required to participate in "human schemes" such as burning candles, fasting, participating in required church festivals, purchasing indulgences, and paying for new church buildings and expensive accoutrements. All of

---

47 Hamm, "'Ist das gut Evangelisch?'," 138.

these were required of the parishioners by the clergy, and those who did not meet these obligations were threatened with excommunication from the church, which included the possibility of exclusion of one's soul from eternal life in heaven. Sachs reiterates often that these commandments did not come from Scripture and therefore were not God's commandments. Rituals of life such as baptism, confirmation, wedding ceremonies, and burials were all required to take place in the church. At the same time, there was a hefty fee for each of these rituals. There were procedures to ward off evil as well as practices to guarantee health or to cure maladies, both common and rare. Each of these had to be accompanied by the proper monetary contribution. Even widows and orphans, those least able to pay for assistance, were plagued with fees. Every aspect of the peasant's life fell under a tithe requirement: crops, livestock, candles, clothing. Not only was money required to support the local clerics, but additional monies were required to be sent to Rome to support the pope and his administration. Sachs elucidates the overall message of the papal hierarchy in *The Wittenberg Nightingale*:

> The Roman church cannot make a mistake;
> Do good works, keep the papal commands,
> Give alms and sacrifice, it pleases God;

Having read Luther's translation of the Bible himself, Sachs set an example for others. Because the Scripture had previously only been available in Latin for the church hierarchy, the average person could not be sure what the Scripture said and therefore whether the church officials were following scriptural authority. They could not be sure that papal encyclicals adhered to the teachings of the Scripture. Thus, they could not be sure whether the purchase of indulgences was outlined in the Scripture. They could not be sure that prayer to saints in addition to prayer to God was necessary. They could not be certain that Christ, not priests, should be recognized as the only mediator between man and God. They could not be certain that salvation comes only through God's grace, not through man's merit. They could not be certain that faith alone leads to man's salvation, not works, not baptism. They could not be certain that Scripture alone reveals truth, that no other writings provide divine revelation. Because they couldn't read the Scripture, they couldn't know what it meant to truly live as a follower of Christ. With access to the Scripture, they were able to comprehend that living a Christian life involved more than "checking the boxes" on church requirements. Sachs himself served as an example that the average man—*der gemeine Mann*—could indeed read and comprehend the salvific message of the Scripture because that message was available in his own tongue thanks to Luther's translation.

In addition to setting an example of reading the Scripture, Sachs identified the false teachings and requirements of the medieval church in a succinct manner. Sachs's writings call the common man, the laity, to practice true Christianity. The debates that take place in the four dialogues point out specific grievances against church practice and provide copious scriptural evidence that the identified practices had not been prescribed by Scripture. By infusing each of his Reformation writings with the message of *Nächstenliebe*, his readers received a clear call to combine faith and practice. It was a call to the individual to live and govern oneself apart from the demands of the church. The "works" of the Christian were not to be checked off a list created by clerics but rather to be learned and lived directly according to the Scripture.

Conclusion

The Reformation made it clear that the practices of the Catholic Church to this point were not practices mandated or supported in Scripture. They elucidated through multiple publications that Scripture alone, not the "traditions"—that is, the regular mandates and decrees given by the pope and the cardinals—carried sole authority over the Christian and the Christian's practice of religion. Luther wanted all Christians to be able to read the Bible for themselves in their own language and thereby make their own decisions regarding worship and practices of faith. The Reformers provided ample and thorough support for this argument. At the same time, the argument to reform the church was heavily couched in doctrinal, theological, academic language and was often written in

Latin. Their argument was with papal authority and the ecclesiastical structures of the day.

Hans Sachs, for all intents and purposes, was an average man, an educated businessman, but average nonetheless. He took up Luther's challenge and read. He read Luther's treatises and arguments for reform. He read the Scripture for himself and in his own language. He recognized that God's message to mankind has been revealed through Scripture alone. He recognized the truth of Luther's argument and took it upon himself to further the cause of the Reformers. As a well-known *Meistersinger*, he used his poetic skill to put Luther's arguments into the language and the genre that the general public recognized and comprehended. He moved the message from academic, theological jargon into poetry in *The Wittenberg Nightingale* and into the conversational style of the average person in the four dialogues. Through his own reading of the Scripture, he learned that next to loving God, loving one's neighbor was the highest calling of a Christian. He infused this message into his Reformation dialogues, calling on others to make loving one's neighbor the ultimate act of worship. No longer was it necessary to follow the legalistic teachings of the clergy that mandated practices that were impossible to keep. Living life with a focus on loving one's neighbor would be a much higher form of worship far more focused on Christ.

Selected Bibliography

Arnold, Bernhard. *Hans Sachs Werke Erster Teil.* Berlin: Verlag von W. Spemann, 1881.

Bergmann, Rosemarie. "Hans Sachs Illustrated: Pamphlets and Broadsheets in the Service of the Reformation." *RACAR: Revue d'art canadienne / Canadian Art Review* 17, no. 1 (1990): 9–16.

Bihl, Michael. "Order of Friars Minor." In *The Catholic Encyclopedia.* New York: Robert Appleton Company, 1909. https://www.newadvent.org/cathen/06281a.htm.

Broadhead, Philip. "The Biblical Verse of Hans Sachs: The Popularization of Scripture in the Lutheran Reformation." In *The Church and Literature,* edited by Peter Clarke and Charlotte Methuen, 24–133, Suffolk: Boydell Press, 2012.

Clark, N. Walling. "Hans Sachs, the Poet of the Reformation." *Methodist Review (1885–1931)* 11, no. 5 (1895): 698–711.

Craig, Gordon A. *The Germans.* New York: B. P. Putnam's Sons, 1982.

Deutsches Wörterbuch von Jacob Grimm und Wilhelm Grimm. Trier Center for Digital Humanities: Wörterbuchnetz. Continually updated at https://www.woerterbuchnetz.de/DWB.

Donovan, Stephen. "Discalced." In *The Catholic Encyclopedia.* New York: Robert Appleton Company, 1909. https://www.newadvent.org/cathen/05028a.htm.

Genung, Charles Harvey. "The Nightingale of Wittenberg." In *The Library of the World's Best Literature: An Anthology in Thirty Volumes,* edited by C. D. Warner et al. New York: Warner Library, 1917.

Goedeke, K. *Dichtungen von Hans Sachs.* Leipzig: F. A. Brockhaus, 1871.

Grimm, Harold John. *Lazarus Spengler: A Lay Leader of the Reformation.* Columbus: Ohio State University Press, 1978.

Hamm, Berndt. "'Ist das gut Evangelisch?' Hans Sachs als Wortführer und Kritiker der Reformation." *Luther* 66, no. 3 (1995): 125–140.

Heine, Heinrich. *Zur Geschichte der Religion und Philosophie in Deutschland.* 1835. Projekt Gutenberg. https://www.projekt-gutenberg.org/heine/religion/religion.html.

Hendrickson, Clara G. "The Translation Process in Interaction between Purpose and Context." *Linguistics Senior Research Projects* 22 (May 2019). https://digitalcommons.cedarville.edu/linguistics_senior_projects/22.

Hervey, Sándor, Michael Loughridge, and Ian Higgins. *Thinking German Translation.* 2nd ed. London: Routledge, 2006.

Hübner, Ralf. "Ohr abgeschnitten und an die Tür genagelt." Sächsische. de (Dresden), November 30, 2018.

Johnson, Ben. "The Legend of St. Ursula and the 11,000 British Virgins." Historic UK, November 15, 2016. https://www.historic-uk.com/HistoryUK/HistoryofEngland/Saint-Ursula-the-11000-British-Virgins/.

Könneker, Barbara. *Die deutsche Literatur der Reformationszeit.* München: Winkler Verlag, 1975.

———. *Hans Sachs.* Stuttgart: J. B. Metzlersche Verlagsbuchhandlung, 1971.

Leighton, William. *Merry Tales and Three Shrovetide Plays by Hans Sachs.* London: David Nutt, 1910.

LEO German-English Dictionary. Sauerlach, Germany: LEO GmbH. Continually updated at https://dict.leo.org/german-english/.

Listerman, Randall W. *Nine Carnival Plays by Hans Sachs.* Ottawa: Dovehouse Editions, 1990.

Local Life: Wroclaw. "Breslau." Continually updated at https://www.local-life.com/wroclaw/articles/breslau#.

Paltridge, Brian, and Wei Wang. "Researching Discourse." In *Continuum Companion to Research Methods in Applied Linguistics*, edited by Brian Paltridge and Aek Phakiti, 256–273. New York: Continuum International, 2010.

Pannier, Karl. *Hans Sachs' Ausgewählte Poetische Werke.* Leipzig: Verlag von Philipp Reclam, 1879. Projekt Gutenberg. https://www.projekt-gutenberg.org/sachs/poetwerk/poetwerk.html.

Pinsky, Robert. *The Inferno of Dante: A New Verse Translation*. Bilingual ed. New York: Farrar, Straus and Giroux, 1994.

Pym, Anthony. *Exploring Translation Theories*. New York: Routledge, 2010.

Quinn, J. Francis. "Saint Bonaventure." In *Encyclopedia Britannica*. Online ed., 2021. https://www.britannica.com/biography/Saint-Bonaventure.

Schaeffer, C. W. *The Wittenberg Nightingale*. Allentown: Brobst, Diehl, 1883.

Strauss, Gerald. *Luther's House of Learning*. Baltimore: Johns Hopkins University Press, 1978.

Suo, Xuxiang. "A New Perspective on Literary Translation Strategies Based on Skopos Theory." *Theory and Practice in Language Studies* 5 (2015): 176–183.

Tauber, Walter. *Der Wortschatz des Hans Sachs. Band 1, Untersuchungen*. Berlin: Walter de Gruyter, 1983.

———. *Der Wortschatz des Hans Sachs. Band 2, Wörterbuch*. Berlin: Walter de Gruyter, 1983.

Vogler, Guenther. "Imperial City Nuremberg, 1524–1525: The Reform Movement in Transition." In *The German People and the Reformation*, edited and translated by R. Po-chia Hsia, 33–49. Ithaca: Cornell University Press, 1988.

———. *Nuremberg 1524/25 Studien zur Geschichte der reformatorischen und sozialen Bewegung in der Reichsstadt*. Berlin: VEB Deutscher Verlag der Wissenschaften, 1982.

von Keller, Adelbert. *Hans Sachs Werke*. Hildesheim, Germany: Georg Olms Verlagsbuchhandlung, 1964.

Wolter, A. Bernard. "Blessed John Duns Scotus." In *Encyclopedia Britannica*. Online ed., 2021. https://www.britannica.com/biography/Blessed-John-Duns-Scotus.

Zoozmann, Richard. *Hans Sachs und die Reformation: In Gedichten und Prosastücke*. Hamburg, Germany: SEVERUS Verlag, 2017.